M000266573

America for Sale

America for Sale

How the Foreign Pack
Circled and Devoured Esmark

Craig T. Bouchard and
James V. Koch

PRAEGER

An Imprint of ABC-CLIO, LLC

A B C ⬢ C L I O

Santa Barbara, California • Denver, Colorado • Oxford, England

Copyright 2009 by Craig T. Bouchard and James V. Koch

All rights reserved. No part of this publication may be reproduced,
stored in a retrieval system, or transmitted, in any form or by any means,
electronic, mechanical, photocopying, recording, or otherwise, except for
the inclusion of brief quotations in a review, without prior permission
in writing from the publisher.

Library of Congress Cataloging-in-Publication Data

Bouchard, Craig T.
   America for sale : how the foreign pack circled and devoured Esmark / Craig T. Bouchard and
James V. Koch.
        p. cm.
   Includes bibliographical references and index.
   ISBN 978-0-313-37678-8 (hard copy: alk. paper)—ISBN 978-0-313-37679-5 (ebook)
   1. Esmark—History. 2. Steel industry and trade—United States. 3. Investments, Foreign—
United States. 4. Consolidation and merger of corporations—United States. I. Koch, James V.,
1942– II. Title.
   HD9519.E86B68 2009
   338.7'66910973—dc22   2009028583

13 12 11 10 09   1 2 3 4 5

This book is also available on the World Wide Web as an eBook.
Visit www.abc-clio.com for details.

ABC-CLIO, LLC
130 Cremona Drive, P.O. Box 1911
Santa Barbara, California 93116-1911

This book is printed on acid-free paper ∞

Manufactured in the United States of America

*Craig dedicates this book to
Melissa, his treasure; and his six gorgeous kids:
Kai, Justin, Patrick, Shale, Cambelle, and Braidy.*

His family makes him rich every day.

*To his Mom and Dad, who started
Craig and Jim in both sports and steel.*

*And to his brother, Jim, the industry's most brilliant strategist
and the greatest entrepreneur that he has ever met.*

*Jim dedicates this book to the ever-patient and understanding Donna,
his wife of 42 years; his daughter, Beth, and son, Mark;
and literally dozens of faculty colleagues spread around the world,
but especially those at Old Dominion University.*

Contents

Preface

Esmark, Inc., one of the half dozen largest steel companies in the United States, was sold to Severstal, a Russian firm, in August 2008. At that time, Craig T. Bouchard was president of Esmark and James V. Koch was a member of its Board of Directors. Hence, both of us had (and still have) vested interests in the captivating stories we recount in this book.

As a result, some readers might be tempted to take cum grano salis the views we offer here. This would be a mistake, because the remarkable story of Esmark—within the larger, evolving saga of the U.S. steel industry—really is important to the future of the United States. More than 50 percent of the U.S. steel industry is now owned by foreigners; approximately one-quarter is owned by Russian firms. These developments do not bode well, either for the future of the U.S. economy or for the security of the United States.

We, the authors, are, by instinct, free traders and free marketers, who believe that 95 percent of all foreign acquisitions of U.S. firms and assets are no problem. Such transactions provide vital capital and usually introduce vigorous, new competition. Ordinarily, we distrust the motives of those individuals (management, labor, elected officials) who seek to prohibit such sales and purchases or who advocate significant trade restrictions, even for the steel industry. The interests of those individuals nearly always diverge from those of U.S. consumers.

We draw the line, however, when more than half of a core industry that is vital to national defense—steel—has fallen into the ownership of foreigners. The Committee on Foreign Investment in the United States (CFIUS) must become more active, extend its reach, and challenge more acquisitions than it has in the past. In some cases, the CFIUS should withhold approval of transactions unless the parties agree that the CFIUS might require divestiture by the foreign owner at some future time, should it deem this wise.

Our unease about this topic has been stimulated by the secular decline of the U.S. dollar, the activities of foreign sovereign wealth funds, and the overwhelmingly large monetary stimulus now being injected into the economy by the U.S. government. We predict that "America for Sale" conditions will reoccur in 2010, after economic recovery has begun worldwide. Key to this reappearance will be a dramatic fall in the value of the U.S. dollar. A fire-sale atmosphere will reign once again, and more industries will go the way of the U.S. steel industry.

We offer here, then, both very entertaining tales of the rise and fall of Esmark, as well as some sobering thoughts about this country's economic future.

Craig T. Bouchard
James V. Koch
April 2009

Acknowledgments

We wish to acknowledge a few of the people who, along the way, made us successful:

Sheff, Dino, and friends, L and Y, and the Stahlschmidt team

Chad Buttel

Roger, Billy, Brian, and Sheri

The nimble management team at Esmark, who worked to exhaustion while constantly watching our backs

Ron, Dave, and Leo

Scott

Jeff Gendell

Jaime Rome

Dan, Dieter, Ann, and the UBS Investment Bank

Jeff Immelt, Tom Quindlen, Paul Feehan, Tom Sullivan, Rich Rogers, Matt McAlpine, Dustin Weinberger, and team. Through the difficult times, G.E. Finance never left our side. Our shareholders owe G.E. $19.25 times 40 million shares.

Jim and Shawn Tumulty, and Mike Embler

Raj Maheshwari

Madhu Vuppuluri

The great entrepreneurs whom we met and learned from: Benjamin, Keith, Victor, Sergey, Vladimir, Lakshmi, Alexei, Ravi, Shashi, and Prashant

The Esmark board of directors, who always did the right thing

Generations of industrious steel workers

Chapter 1

America for Sale?

Do we want the Communists to own the bank, or the terrorists?
Jim Cramer of CNBC, 2008

America is being sold off to foreigners at a discount.
Herman Cain in *American Chronicle*, July 21, 2008

James and Craig Bouchard, the founders of Esmark, Inc., a large steel-services firm, ignored the advice of CNBC's Jim Cramer and convinced their board of directors to sell the firm to "the Communists" in August 2008. Well, perhaps they didn't really sell Esmark to the Communists, but they did sell it to the Russian steel giant Severstal, led by oligarch Alexei Mordashov.

The tale of Esmark's sale has twists and turns worthy of *The Bourne Identity*. Esmark, Inc., was founded by the Bouchards in 2003. The company was launched with a cash investment of $750,000, a loan of $1.9 million, and a healthy dose of faith. The Bouchard brothers paid $0.25 per share for their original investment. They knew what they were doing, were quite successful, and received the equivalent of a $7.50 per share dividend in an Esmark recapitalization two years later—a rather attractive 30:1 return.

Five years later, Esmark was sold to the Russian steel firm Severstal, but only after the following had taken place:

- A roller coaster ride involving 10 acquisitions of small steel-service center firms by Esmark
- A war between Esmark and its largest investor, Franklin Mutual Advisors

- A battle between Esmark and the United Steelworkers (USW) union
- A bidding battle for Esmark by foreign steel firms that involved intrigue on three continents
- A cleverly designed poison financial pill, intended to discourage unwelcome suitors for Esmark
- A $260 million West Virginia court judgment in Esmark's favor
- A $525 million legal suit against Esmark by Arcelor Mittal, the largest steelmaker in the world
- Intense global press coverage

Nevertheless, Esmark was indeed sold to the Russian steelmaker Severstal in August 2008 for $19.25 per share. This reflected an enterprise value for Esmark of $1.31 billion, enabling the Bouchard brothers, who owned about five percent of the firm, and founding investors of Esmark, to earn roughly 60 times their original investment in five years. This is all the more remarkable because no more than 60 days later, Esmark could not have been sold for more than $10 per share. By the end of 2008, it would have sold for far less than that. Timing is everything.

Along the way, tiny Esmark successfully completed the first "hostile reverse tender merger" in Wall Street history, defeating the existing board of directors and management of its publicly traded target (Wheeling Pittsburgh Steel), as well as the Brazilian firm CSN, one of the largest steel companies in the world, in a high-stakes vote by Wheeling Pitt shareholders. This involved throwing out the existing Wheeling Pitt board, forcing Wheeling Pitt to merge Esmark into it, and then changing the name of Wheeling Pitt back to Esmark. Are you a bit confused? More than a few people were at the time.

But that's not all. Simultaneously, Esmark fought its major coal provider, Massey Energy, in courts in West Virginia and won a shocking $260 million monetary award from a jury; the award was reaffirmed by the West Virginia Supreme Court and eventually paid to Severstal. This is the same state court that had gained national notoriety for appearing to some to provide a real-world example of justice for sale, in the fashion of John Grisham's fictional *The Verdict*.[1] Esmark found ways to benefit from the adverse publicity that was showered on the West Virginia Supreme Court.

During this saga, Esmark was sued by Arcelor Mittal Steel for $525 million, a suit related to Esmark's proposed acquisition of the historic Sparrows Point steel facilities, once owned by Bethlehem Steel. Arcelor Mittal was a disappointed prospective partner with Esmark in this deal, but also had some bad blood with Severstal, which—with the help of the U.S. Department of Justice—eventually emerged victorious, for both Esmark and Sparrows Point. Regardless, Esmark's participation in the Sparrows Point sale never reached closure, but the legal suit is still pending and is now the property of Severstal.

Meanwhile, Esmark's majority shareholder, Franklin Mutual Advisors, demanded that the company's board of directors accept a buyout offer from Severstal that was $80 million less than the one that Esmark already had in hand from the well-regarded Indian steel company, Essar. Despite owning tens of millions of dollars of Esmark stock, the USW union backed the same demand in support of the Russians. When Esmark's board declined this inferior offer, the USW sued Esmark. Remarkably, this suit was filed less than one year after the USW had provided absolutely crucial support to Esmark's reverse hostile merger takeover of Wheeling Pittsburgh Steel.

Literally, one had to have a program to know which players actually were on the field and which team's uniform those players were wearing on any particular day. The confusion required the Bouchard brothers constantly to explain their strategies to their board of directors, Esmark's stockholders, and the financial institutions that owned Esmark's considerable debts. All parties on the multiple sides of these issues were under great pressure and often had to make decisions quickly and with limited information. Retrospectively, it was a wild, even breathtaking ride for everyone involved, but especially for investors. Not everyone was thrilled with the results. It is fair to say, however, that most of the former Wheeling Pitt's investors now view the Bouchards and Esmark's board of directors as heroes because the investors were able to sell their shares at prices well above previous market values.

Did the Bouchard brothers and Esmark do all of this in order to gain control of a corporate beauty? Hardly! Wheeling Pittsburgh Steel had gone bankrupt twice before, and, after winning the proxy battle for Wheeling Pitt, Esmark proceeded to lose $180 million in 2007. Wheeling Pitt was not a land of milk and honey.

THE ESMARK TALE IS PART OF A LARGER STORY

There is much more to say about the amazing story of Esmark. This is a tale, perhaps even a parable, of classic, energetic, risk-taking U.S. entrepreneurs battling to succeed. On the face of it, it is a good story because the good guys won, and they deserve recognition and kudos. Even so, the Esmark narrative is best understood as fitting into a mosaic within a much larger context—the increasing purchase of U.S. firms and assets by foreigners.

It is not outlandish to view the foreign firms that competed and often nipped at each other's heels in their attempts to purchase Esmark as the financial equivalent of a wolf pack circling and hounding a vulnerable prey. This is, by itself, a very interesting story, but Esmark's fight for survival, or, at the very least, its struggle to obtain the best possible deal for its stockholders and employees, has been repeated hundreds of times inside the United States in recent years. Certainly an Esmark-like scenario has played out many times in the U.S. steel industry, in which foreigners now own more than 50 percent of U.S. steel production capacity.

What's going on here? Why have foreign packs of investors been hunting U.S. firms? Is it likely to continue? Will purchases of U.S. assets by foreigners accelerate after the U.S. economy revives? Is this something we should worry about? Let's begin to generate the answers to these questions by getting a feel for the breadth and depth of the situation.

AMERICA FOR SALE?

In 2008, the Abu Dhabi Sovereign Wealth Fund acquired 90 percent ownership in the iconic 77-story art deco Chrysler Building in the heart of Manhattan, while a group of purchasers that included Meraas Capital, a fund from Dubai, purchased the 50-story General Motors Building only blocks away. "When it comes to real estate, the Arabs are the new Japanese," snorted a critic who went on to decry the sale of U.S. assets to foreigners and wondered where it would all end.[2]

Such transactions as these have caused many individuals to ask this question: Is the United States really for sale (to foreigners) at dangerously low prices? If so, should Americans worry about it? The short answer to the latter question is no, although only a simpleton would offer this answer without taking into account numerous factors that could change the answer to yes.

The economic conditions that stimulated sales of such U.S. assets as the Chrysler Building in 2008 have changed, so much so that, in several cases, the foreign parties that made such high-visibility purchases now are regarded as chumps. Even those in charge of the imposingly wealthy sovereign wealth funds sponsored by Middle Eastern oil countries have been mortified to find that their purchases of prestigious U.S. assets have become financial millstones around their necks. Temasek, the sovereign wealth fund of Singapore, lost an estimated $2 billion on its investment in the Bank of America.

Anyone who reads the newspaper or watches television knows well that economic conditions change, sometimes very rapidly, as in the case of the value of the U.S. dollar, for instance. When the U.S. dollar reversed its slide in value relative to major foreign currencies in the summer of 2008, this helped throttle what had become a binge of foreign acquisitions of U.S. assets. As a consequence, provocative headlines, suggesting disaster because of foreign asset purchases, disappeared from newspapers and Internet sites, and such television commentators as Jim Cramer and Lou Dobbs, who have tended toward the incendiary on this subject, moved on to other topics.

Even so, nothing is forever, and relentless economic changes are already in the wings that will alter these circumstances and produce yet another situation in which foreigners will find it especially attractive to purchase U.S. assets. Those heading up the Federal Reserve System weren't lying when, in late 2008, they pledged to print virtually unlimited amounts of money to fight the worldwide financial crisis. Coupled with the decision to move critical interest rates to almost zero, this move does not bode well for the value of the U.S. dollar, which is expected to plunge as a result. Although many factors influence the supply and demand conditions for U.S. assets, a weak U.S. dollar is among the most important, because it acts as a powerful stimulant to foreign purchasers. Hence, we expect to see "America for Sale" replayed once again in 2010.

Nevertheless, it does not follow that all sales of U.S. assets to foreigners, or even most of them, are harmful. Such sales often provide needed capital, introduce vigorous new competition, and enrich stockholders. Nevertheless, the issues are seldom black and white. Qualifications abound.

Whether one defends or attacks foreign purchases of U.S. assets usually depends upon the weights placed on the actual outcomes that are generated by these purchases. Ultimately, this reflects individual values and what people believe is most important. For example, suppose you don't really care that the "American" Chrysler automobile that you've just purchased has been assembled with parts coming from a half-dozen different countries. What you really want is a low-priced, no-frills car that is reliable. If that's your view, the fact that the German firm Daimler-Benz owned 20 percent of Chrysler Corporation and Cerberus Capital (an international investment firm that has ownership stakes in dozens of firms around the world) owned the other 80 percent doesn't really bother you.

Nevertheless, it's quite possible that you might have a different reaction if the producer of the Chrysler weren't connected to Mercedes but were instead an arm of China's Chery Motor Company.[3] What's more, you might also have a more negative attitude if foreigners already owned nearly all U.S. automobile manufacturers. You are a "yes-but" person and, like many Americans, you don't regard all foreign firms as equal. Circumstances make a difference to you and to most Americans.

On the other hand, suppose that you are concerned that companies from Russia progressively purchased major portions of the U.S. steel industry over the past few years. If so, then you might want to halt this evolution, even if the Russians promised to preserve steelworker jobs that otherwise might have been lost. To you, it makes a difference whether you perceive the asset being acquired by the foreigners to be critical infrastructure, a "strategic" part of the U.S. economy and perhaps even related to national defense. You are one of many Americans who believe that such transactions should be prohibited unless strict controls are applied: you are a "no-but" person.

The problem is that many of the most visible transactions involving the sale or lease of U.S. assets to foreigners nearly always seem to be accompanied by qualifications. Truly, the assessment of foreign purchases of U.S. assets, even by highly knowledgeable authorities, often depends upon the particular circumstances and personal values. One individual might react to the purchase of the Chrysler Building in New York City with a yawn, whereas another might regard this as a sign of a coming apocalypse. One of the foremost aims of this book is to help readers sort out what should count when considering the purchase of U.S. assets by foreigners. We will conclude that there is not nearly as much to worry about as Jim Cramer, Lou Dobbs, and others would lead us to believe. Nevertheless, they are not always wrong, either.

GRIST FOR THE MILL: FOREIGN ASSET PURCHASES THAT MOTIVATE SOME AND INFURIATE OTHERS

A surfeit of examples exists that involve prominent sales of U.S. assets to foreigners. Consider how views have changed with respect to these sales. The truth is that only recently have major sales of U.S. assets to foreign investors stirred substantial opposition.

Only about a decade ago, in 1998, the purchase of Amoco (the "American Oil Company") by British Petroleum (BP) failed to resonate strongly with the U.S. public despite the word "American" in Amoco's name and despite Amoco's ubiquitous red-white-and-blue signs. After all, this was the red-white-and-blue American Oil Company, whose logos and signs were in plain sight in most U.S. cities. The lack of outrage was something of a surprise to the heads of BP, who worried about the morphing of Amoco's red-white-and-blue signs into the customary BP green-and-white signs on prominent U.S. street corners. In most instances, however, the BP purchase of Amoco turned out to be a non-event, and there was little heartburn over the transfer of $53 billion in assets that underpinned the deal.

Similarly, purchases of such highly visible U.S. firms as Miller Brewing by South African Breweries in 2002 and the 7-Eleven convenience chain by a Japanese company in 2005 did not set off significant alarm bells. These transactions did not appear to involve critical U.S. infrastructure or national defense considerations. No one really seemed to care, because, as a news anchor put it, "Nothing big was at stake." This perception was soon to change.

When Dubai Ports World, headquartered in the United Arab Emirates (UAE), purchased a half dozen major U.S. port operations in 2006, vociferous objections were voiced immediately. The hostility was based primarily upon alleged national security issues raised by the acquisitions. The anger and concern reduced to this indignant query: How could the United States allow a foreign country, especially an Arab country, to run its major ports? This, as many people saw it, involved critical U.S. infrastructure—and even national defense.

Congresswoman Sue Myrick (R-NC) seemed to capture the sense of the times when she sent this one-sentence, not-easy-to-misunderstand letter to President George W. Bush: "In regard to selling American ports to the United Arab Emirates, not just NO—but HELL NO!"[4] Even though many other U.S. port facilities were and still are owned by foreigners (for example, 80 percent of the terminals at the Port of Los Angeles), this purchase seemed to cross the line in the eyes of many. The UAE, after all, had been the home of two of the terrorists who had attacked the United States on September 11, 2001. Ultimately, after intense political pressure, Dubai Ports World sold these port operations to American International Group, which subsequently was bailed out and virtually acquired by the U.S. government in the fall of 2008.

In retrospect, Dubai Ports World was apparently the deal that truly penetrated public consciousness and concern with respect to the foreign purchase and ownership issue. Such commentators as Lou Dobbs of CNN went on the warpath, decried the sale of U.S. assets to foreigners, and charged, day after day, that many of these sales were contrary to U.S. national interests.

IT'S NOT EASY TO DETERMINE WINNERS AND LOSERS

The port battle was followed by a swath of additional major acquisitions of U.S. assets by foreigners. Among those that attracted the most flack were two long-term leasing arrangements whereby an Australian-Spanish partnership would control and operate such public facilities as the Indiana Toll Road and the Chicago Skyway. The lure to the selling governments was several billion dollars of quick cash that they could use to plug holes in their budgets.

The operation of Chicago's Midway Airport was leased to a U.S.-Canadian firm in 2008 by the City of Chicago for 99 years at a price of $2.52 billion. Mayor Richard Daley predicted "unprecedented benefits." This made Midway the first large U.S. airport to be run privately, although foreign ownership of transportation facilities is not unusual. Many U.S. port operations are run by foreign firms. The City of Chicago subsequently sold the rights to operate that city's parking meter system to a group led by Morgan Stanley for $1.157 billion.

Source: Susan Saulny, "In Chicago, Private Firm Is to Run Midway Airport." *New York Times Reader* (October 1, 2008), www.nytimes.com/timesreader.

Let's take a moment to analyze these assets sales. Quite apart from the matter of foreign ownership, were the sales attractive financial deals for Indiana and Chicago? The State of Indiana received $3.8 billion for the 75-year lease that it granted the Australian-Spanish consortium. Was this price too low? Alas, we can't say for certain because the answer depends critically upon the expected future revenues and costs associated with the Indiana Toll Road. If we view the Toll Road strictly as an economic enterprise, then the appropriate action for the State of Indiana is to take its expected future revenues and costs from the Toll Road into account and compute a rate of return on its invested capital. Would that rate of return be high enough, or could the Hoosier State earn a more attractive rate of return by using these funds elsewhere? That is the relevant economic question.

We don't know what rate of return the State of Indiana is expected to earn on its investment in the Toll Road, because the background arithmetic was never disclosed. This issue is complicated by the fact that many of the drivers on the Toll Road are not Hoosiers and are therefore "foreigners" as far as Indiana is concerned. Should Indiana's answer take into consideration the extent to which the tolls will be paid by Hoosiers as opposed to nonresidents? Some legislators and economists believe that this should make a difference, because it presents Indiana with the opportunity to diminish the burden on Hoosiers by in effect taxing nonresidents. This is an old and time-honored strategy for both cities and states.

In any case, the State of Indiana had to forecast future traffic volumes and costs in order to get a handle on the value of the Indiana Toll Road.

Assuming that it could do so, what was the appropriate way to value revenues and costs that wouldn't be incurred until, say, 2040? Economists routinely compute the "present discounted value" of such future financial magnitudes in order to make them comparable to current numbers. This is the appropriate path for Indiana to take as well. However, it requires that the State of Indiana choose a "discount rate," whose function is to devalue these future sums of money appropriately. The further away in time a sum of money is, the less it is worth today. It would be erroneous for Indiana to equate $1.0 million of net revenues in 2009 with $1.0 million of net revenues in 2040. Indeed, if one uses a discount rate of 6.0 percent, the value of $1.0 million in 2040 is less than $165,000 in 2009. That is, the "present value" of that $1,000,000 is less than $165,000 in 2009, and it is this $165,000 that should be considered to be today's value of that future stream of income.

Of course, that future stream of income is not guaranteed. There is some risk involved, and estimates of risk associated with the Toll Road should have played a role in Indiana's evaluation as well. Changes in gasoline prices, population changes, economic decline in the region around the Toll Road, natural calamities—these are only a few of the uncertainties that the State of Indiana might face during a 75-year lease period. However, in essence, Indiana sold such risks to the Australian-Spanish conglomerate, and perhaps that was the smart way to go. Nevertheless, in order to do so, it had to give the conglomerate the right to raise tolls substantially. Nothing is free when intelligent, well-informed, uncoerced parties negotiate.

A common way to take risk into account is to incorporate it into the discount rate just mentioned. The rate of return on a 10-year U.S. government bond (thought to be among the safest investments in the world) recently has been less than 4.0 percent. Ordinarily, one would choose a rate of discount significantly higher than this when dealing with an uncertain economic situation and verifiable risk. Discount rates as high as 30 or 40 percent might be applied to estimated future revenue streams that are quite chancy.

The Indiana Toll Road example is instructive because it underlines several important truths that relate to the purchase of U.S. assets by foreign investors. First, even the best analyses are replete with assumptions about future economic magnitudes. These assumptions usually are debatable, and the assumptions may soon prove to be wrong. Second, the real world is a risky place, as firms such as Lehman Brothers learned in the fall of 2008. Ultimately, both seller and buyer must estimate future revenues and costs and then place a value on the assets involved. In so doing, they must reduce these sums to present values and take risk into account. Circumstances can change rapidly, as the Belgian-based brewer Inbev found out after it made its bid in the summer of 2008 for the U.S. brewer Anheuser-Busch. If Inbev's purchase was a good deal in the summer, by all odds it was considerably less of a good deal by the fall of 2008 because of the rising value of the U.S. dollar and the falling price of Anheuser-Busch stock. We'll have more to say about these influences in a moment.

The relevant point is this: although there is a science connected to assessing the value of a set of assets, there also is some art and guesswork involved. Competent individuals often differ in their evaluations of the worth of the same set of assets. Ultimately, this is why deals are made—valuation discrepancies. These same valuation discrepancies, however, may cause us to conclude, a few months or years later, that the seller exploited the buyer or vice-versa.

Fraud could be involved, and there's always the possibility that a Bernard Madoff is lurking in the background, but that's not the key to what we are talking about here. Instead, our focus is on situations in which honest, hard-working, even cautious individuals emerge with different views of what an asset is worth. But this makes life more interesting, no?

Many Hoosiers did not approve of the Toll Road lease arrangement. Indiana State Representative Terri Austin exclaimed at a U.S. congressional hearing that it was wrong for short-term public officials to deal away public assets for generations. "Ultimately," she said, "the public should have some level of discomfort with elected officials who serve two-, four- and six-year terms when they propose to enter into 75- or 99-year contractual obligations." She noted that Indiana maintains a part-time legislature, which makes it very difficult for legislators to conduct due diligence on the proposal.

Source: Susan Chandler, 2008. "You Pay a Lot More." *Chicago Tribune*, 162 [September 7], 1, 25.

THE PRINCIPLE OF VOLUNTARY (KNOWLEDGEABLE) EXCHANGES

In the absence of fraud or coercion, U.S. firms and governmental units won't sell or lease their assets to foreigners unless they believe, all things considered, that the price is right. This reflects a fundamental principle of economics: voluntary trade between knowledgeable parties makes both parties better off. Otherwise, there is no coincidence of interests and the parties won't make the trade. This is a very simple but oft-ignored economic reality.

This principle is just as true for the sale and purchase of such prominent assets as the Chrysler Building or Merrill Lynch as it is for an individual buying a pizza for dinner or deciding to attend a movie. Of course, it would be great if the prices for pizzas and movie tickets were lower. Other things held equal, people always prefer to pay lower prices rather than higher prices. However, if they are well-informed and no one is holding a gun to their head, when they part with their money, that is a signal that they are better off (and so are the sellers of the pizza and the movie tickets).

In general, uncoerced trades between informed individuals make both parties to the trade better off. Nevertheless, note that the voluntary, uncoerced traders must be informed and knowledgeable to guarantee that the trade will make both better off. Suppose that someone purchases a hot dog at the ballpark that, to his or her great horror, turns out to be a rat dog. When the truth comes out, the person will probably conclude that he or she is not better off for the deal. Most people would agree. However, this "informed and knowledgeable" proviso applies to the fraudulent sale of damaged and clearly misrepresented goods in general. Suppose that Acme Realty tells someone who is purchasing a home in Buffalo in the month of January that the home is air-conditioned, but the buyer doesn't discover that this is a lie until July. It's quite possible that this buyer is not better off, even if he or she has legal recourse.

Regardless, there is a tendency for some individuals to complain that they have been ripped off by sellers. College students perpetually complain about high tuition, renters persistently carp about their monthly rental payments, and gasoline prices seem to be on everyone's mind. However, taking college students as an example, very few are ever coerced to attend a particular college or university; hundreds of alternative institutions abound, and there is no lack of information available about tuition rates. What students really are saying is, "I'd prefer to pay lower tuition." But, wouldn't everybody prefer to pay lower prices? Nevertheless, if students actually pay the price, they are demonstrating by their actions that, all things considered, they have made themselves better off, even if only by a small amount. What they have received in return for their tuition payment apparently is worth more than the tuition that they are paying. Otherwise, they wouldn't bother to attend that institution and they would not trade their money for the education.

COMPLICATIONS

The pristine scenario just painted can easily become complicated. On occasion, those who purchase or sell items are coerced to do so. Consider a residential property owner forced to sell his or her house to the government as a result of an eminent domain action. That property owner may well regard the government's payment as inadequate. In such a situation, if the government didn't force the owner to sell, he or she would not. Hence, if there is coercion involved in a trade, it doesn't follow that both parties will be better off in their own eyes.[5] This conclusion applies to the sale of U.S. assets to foreigners just as much as it does to the eminent domain transaction.

There is also the matter of seller and buyer information. It is true that rat dogs being served at the ballpark rather than hot dogs may represent an unlikely occurrence. More common is the situation in which individuals could obtain information about a potential purchase, but it would take time and effort to do so, and they therefore voluntarily choose not to become well informed. Suppose that Fannie Mae, the semigovernmental mortgage agency, purchases a mortgage from a local bank in Oklahoma City, but it does so without investigating the ability of the home owner or mortgagee to pay off that mortgage. Subsequently, it turns out that the mortgagee is unemployed and doesn't have a prayer of making the mortgage payments. The mortgage subsequently goes into default. Whose lapse is this default? Economists lay blame on the mortgagee (who signed up for a mortgage that he or she couldn't realistically handle), the mortgagor (the Oklahoma City bank that made the shaky mortgage and deceptively sold it to Fannie Mae), and Fannie Mae, which did not take appropriate precautions. Fannie Mae administrators could have investigated the mortgagee's situation but didn't perceive it to be worthwhile. Perhaps they were simply lazy, although they might have concluded that the cost of investigating the financial background of the mortgagee exceeded the expected benefits.

The salient point of this example is that good, reliable information is not free. Acquiring trustworthy, dependable information often costs time and money, whether one is selling or buying, and even when one has access to the Internet. When a U.S. firm sells its assets to a foreigner, the price negotiated depends substantially upon the quality of information that each party has. Therefore, when some U.S. firms are criticized for selling out to foreigners for prices that are too low, a possible reason for this is inadequate or even faulty information on their part. It's easy to obtain equity stock prices from the New York Stock Exchange or NASDAQ, and these price quotes can help inform the eventual selling price, if one is talking about a publicly traded firm. It's usually much more difficult to determine what a non-publicly traded asset is worth. By way of illustration, what is the financial value of an electric arc steel furnace, or a piece of PC software, or the European financial operations of a U.S. firm such as Lehman Brothers? (The value of the Lehman Brothers operation is almost

a trick question. In September 2008, the Japanese firm Nomura reportedly
purchased Lehman Brothers' European operations for the magnificent
sum of $2 because of the difficulty in assessing the value of Lehman
Brothers' apparently toxic, subprime mortgage portfolio.)

There are other complicating factors to take into account. First, consider the reality that economists term the "separation of ownership and
management." Frequently, the individuals who own a firm (the stockholders) are not the people who manage and run a firm. This is nearly always
true when large firms are the focus. Yes, the "boss" (the chief executive officer [CEO]) may own shares of stock, but he or she nearly always is a
minority stockholder who owns no more than a few percentage points of
the firm's stock. Even Bill Gates, one of the founders of Microsoft, only
owns about 10 percent of that firm, and, in any case, he has moved out of
Microsoft's active management.

Will managers (CEOs) who own only a small slice of a firm make decisions that are in the best interests of the stockholders? When a foreign firm
seeks to purchase their firm, will the CEOs of the target firms evaluate
what is best for stockholders, or might they be influenced by already existing "golden parachute" compensation agreements that pay them hand-
some rewards if a "change of control" occurs and they lose their jobs? These
are not easy questions to answer, and the evidence is mixed, but there is
little doubt that some critics of foreign asset purchases believe that the
interests of CEOs and their boards of directors frequently diverge from
those of stockholders and other company constituencies.

Second, what about the rank-and-file employees? Most mergers are
premised on the basis of reducing costs by eliminating duplicative
processes and employees. The 2005 merger of AT&T into SBC Communi-
cations resulted in a reduction of 13,000 employees; Verizon's 2006 acquisition of MCI generated a workforce reduction of 7,000. Inbev quickly
moved to reduce the ranks of Anheuser-Busch employees by more than
2,000 after it assumed control of the large U.S. brewer in the fall of 2008.
Still, the question remains: Does a sale remain a good one if 20 percent of
the firm's employees are terminated, even if the end product is a more efficient, profitable firm? Even though an asset sale increases economic efficiency and eliminates administrative and employee bloat, the employees
who actually lose their jobs can be forgiven if they think that the sale stinks.

Third, what if the new owners "don't live nearby" but, in fact, reside in
a foreign country? Will these remote individuals be responsive to local
employee needs? Will they join local organizations, contribute to the
United Way, and support the Little League? The experience of U.S. cities
with banking mergers over the past two decades has been discouraging in
this regard.

The experience of Wilmington, Ohio, with the German package-delivery firm DHL has become a metaphor for those who believe that foreign owners simply do not care as much about U.S. employees. DHL, which is owned by Deutsche Post, made a decision to attempt to establish itself in North American package delivery markets as a major competitor to UPS and Federal Express. In 2003, DHL purchased Airborne Express and turned Wilmington, a city of 12,500 citizens, into a hub employing 7,000 individuals, primarily at an abandoned nearby U.S. Air Force base.

DHL subsequently found UPS and Federal Express to be very tough competitors and, in the fall of 2008, gave up on most of its Wilmington activities. This pushed all 7,000 DHL employees in Wilmington into unemployment lines. Many Wilmington residents felt that DHL's management of the formerly profitable Airborne Express left much to be desired and, furthermore, that a U.S.-owned firm would have had greater regard for U.S. employees.

The Wilmington episode underlines the frictions that often are attached to foreign ownership of U.S. assets. It's true that foreign firms compensate their workers better than the typical U.S. firms do and that they have created hundreds of thousands of jobs in the United States in the past decade. Also, DHL committed to paying $260 million in severance benefits to its Wilmington employees. It's also the case that DHL was losing $6 million per day on its U.S. operations. Nevertheless, the City of Wilmington was and is economically devastated. It cannot be a surprise, therefore, that many attribute this catastrophe to the DHL purchase of Airborne Express.

A fourth major concern with foreign ownership of U.S. assets is easily understood. Will foreign owners have the best national security interests of the United States at heart? Can they be trusted to act in the best interests of the United States? Would it make any difference if foreign-owned firms produced the steel that is used to construct our nuclear submarines, or even if the foreign-owned firms produce the nuclear submarines themselves? Clearly, some Americans are suspicious of foreign ownership of U.S. assets and worry that the interests of the United States could be a secondary consideration to foreign owners of U.S. assets. They would look askance if Exxon Mobil were to sell itself to Venezuela, which is led by Hugo Chávez, an explosive, anti-free market, and persistently anti-U.S. leader.

Inbev, the Belgian beer conglomerate mentioned earlier, is hardly to be compared to Hugo Chávez. Nevertheless, after Inbev paid $52 billion for Anheuser-Busch in 2008, this caused a disappointed critic to assert that "The Anheuser-Busch brand has a lot to do with American culture and American life."[6] His views were replicated by numerous editorial writers around the nation, most of whom were more focused on the sale of an emblematic U.S. firm to foreigners than they were about any critical infrastructure or national security considerations. Often, the major concern was whether "Bud" would continue to use comfortable patriotic themes in its advertising and whether it would still be considered to be a U.S. beer.

Lar "America First" Daly was an oddball fringe political candidate who campaigned for the U.S. presidency, governor of Illinois, and mayor of the city of Chicago, always wearing an Uncle Sam suit. "Lar" Daly's Uncle Sam suit told his story—he was suspicious of things not made in and controlled by the Untied States. Most voters regarded "America First" as a little bit nutty, but more than a few resonated to his anti-foreign trade, anti-foreign aid and entanglements message. There is a bit of Lar Daly in the misgivings of individuals who oppose virtually every visible sale of U.S. assets to foreigners.

THE CASE IN SUPPORT OF FOREIGN INVESTMENT: A QUICK LOOK

In contrast to the previous criticisms, those who support some or all purchases of U.S. assets by foreigners point out that foreign firms: (1) frequently add jobs rather than subtracting them; (2) pay higher wages on average than the typical U.S.-owned firm; (3) often introduce new technologies; (4) provide vigorous competition that results in lower prices for consumers; (5) often generate additional tax revenues; (6) may save jobs that otherwise would disappear; (7) provide new sources of capital; and (8) would never find anyone willing to sell U.S. assets unless they pay attractive prices to the U.S. asset owners.

For the purposes of this book, these eight arguments are essentially empirical in nature—although they typically have a basis in economic theory, their relevance to this discussion depends upon what the data indicate. Is it really true, for example, that foreign firms pay higher wages to U.S. workers than "native" firms owned by Americans? The answer is yes.

In general, the reliable empirical evidence supports all eight of the propositions just noted, although not to the same extent for all of them. This evidence is provided in Chapters 6 and 7, which evaluate who wins and loses when foreigners purchase U.S. assets and considers what intelligent public policy should be in this arena. In anticipation of this discussion, however, note that the benefits associated with the sale of U.S. assets to foreigners appear to have exceeded the costs over the past decade.

The major problem associated with the preceding eight arguments is less their empirical validity and more their lack of emotional impact. Everyone is appreciative when they pay lower prices for new automobiles because foreign firms such as Toyota have opened production facilities in the United States, or when they encounter low prices at Wal-Mart or Costco because of increased foreign competition transplanted to the United States. Most Americans, however, tend to take such benefits for granted and don't take the time to analyze where these lower prices came from. To put it bluntly, there isn't much passion attached to a consumer saving $10 on an electric hedge clipper because Stihl, a German firm, chose to establish a manufacturing facility in Virginia. Similarly, if Inbev's acquisition of Anheuser-Busch reduces the price of a typical six-pack of beer by as much as a dime, this won't garner much attention, even though the total benefit to U.S. consumers from this might exceed $60 million annually, taking into account the more than 100 million beer drinkers in the United States.[7]

At the end of the day, very few Americans are going to carry signs praising a foreign-owned firm for introducing competition that reduces prices or, for that matter, for paying higher wage rates than U.S. firms. Such bounty is part and parcel of the benefits that are churned out by a competitive market system and that most U.S. consumers take for granted. They want and expect Adam Smith's "Invisible Hand" to generate a stream of such benefits, whether or not they've ever heard of Smith, the Invisible Hand, or *The Wealth of Nations.*

However, as already discussed, the same absence of emotion certainly did not apply to the purchase of U.S. port operations by Dubai Ports World. It mattered little that many of the largest U.S. ports already were being operated by foreign-owned firms. This was different! Therein resides the problem: dispassionate analysis of the purchase of U.S. assets by foreigners sometime is elusive and, in any case, is always subject to the political process.

MEDIA AS OBSTACLES TO ASSESSING THE TRUTH

Alas, it is often difficult to separate the proverbial sheep from the goats when U.S. assets are sold to foreigners. Not only is there often a general lack of interest in exploring any benefits involved, but also politics and notions of national defense intrude almost immediately. Rare is the politician who is willing to endorse the sale of U.S. assets to foreigners, even when those sales appear to make most Americans better off. That's not usually a winning strategy. Flag waving nearly always works better for elected officials than thoughtful dissertations that carefully weigh benefits and costs. Lar "America First" Daly (see box) was a shrewd evaluator of U.S. political sentiment in this regard. Candor requires us to observe that this situation still exists.

Unfortunately, the troubles in attempting to tie a knot around these issues don't halt there. It's not easy to develop an intelligent score card that evaluates foreign acquisitions of U.S. assets because of the nature of mass media coverage in the United States. When the representatives of U.S. mass media choose to cover such episodes, they frequently tend to sensationalize the issues and the personalities. No doubt, such video pundits as Lou Dobbs of CNN and Jim Cramer of CNBC's "Mad Money" firmly believe what they say about the adverse effects of purchases of U.S. assets by foreigners and the negative impact of international trade on the United States. Nevertheless, their strident comments often provoke viewers, listeners, and readers to such an extent that rational discourse becomes difficult. When Mr. Cramer asks "Do we want the Communists to own the bank?" the very way that he poses the question inflames his audience (and simultaneously himself), even as it also pumps up his ratings. The more raucous Mr. Cramer's voice becomes and the more frequently he waves his arms, the greater is his identification with the ubiquitous, powerless man in the proverbial street. This may explain why Mr. Cramer is now presented by the morning NBC *Today Show* as a credible economic analyst, even though his tendency to throw lighted matches into gasoline may tax even NBC's patience.

Even so, there is another side to this coin. Ironically, in many instances, the media can legitimately plead not guilty to inciting their audiences when foreign purchases of U.S. assets are concerned. Why? Because they give these events minimal or zero coverage and then refuse to allot so much as a five-second sound bite to the "boring," deeper economic policy considerations that ultimately have a profound influence on U.S. living standards. Such coverage does not drive favorable ratings.

Barron's Magazine versus Jim Cramer

Barron's has kept close track of Jim Cramer's stock picks and, in a series of articles, has panned his predictive ability. "Cramer's recommendations underperform the market by most measures," according to *Barron's* Bill Alpert. Bombast apparently is not synonymous with accuracy.

Source: Bill Alpert, http://online.barrons.com/article/SB123397107399659271 .html.

In the media's defense, it's fair to observe that all but the most fervent economists would confess that the connection between budget deficits and the value of the U.S. dollar has limited sex appeal. It's not a topic that competes well with the likes of Monica Lewinsky or the Olympics in terms of its ability to capture interest. The aforementioned regional television news anchor (who must remain anonymous lest he be typed as an empty suit) put it best about discussions of the economics of international trade and asset purchases: "That kind of stuff can compete with Sominex." He then affected a loud snore.

Hence, we find that most major media either tend to sensationalize coverage of foreign purchase of U.S. assets or give them no coverage at all. The major exceptions to this dictum are the Public Broadcasting Service (PBS) and National Public Radio (NPR), both of which sponsor thoughtful discussions of related issues, albeit to their limited and stylized audiences. Even so, Newton Minow may not have been far off-target in 1961 when he characterized network broadcast television as a "vast wasteland."[8] It appears that his arrow still strikes a vulnerable target when international economic issues are concerned.

IS THERE AN ANGEL OR DESPERATION EXCEPTION?

Both public perceptions and media coverage of purchases of U.S. assets by foreigners are influenced profoundly by the extent to which a U.S. firm or organization appears to be in need of rescue. Bluntly put, if a U.S. firm or organization is up against the wall financially, the foreign purchaser may be viewed as a beneficent angel who is performing a good deed. When the choice is between foreign ownership and bankruptcy, foreign ownership usually triumphs.

Consequently, there was limited controversy when Temasek, the sovereign wealth investment fund of the government of Singapore, put $5 billion into Merrill Lynch in December 2007 and another $0.9 billion in July 2008. Singapore was not the only foreign country that sought to help Merrill Lynch avoid insolvency. The investment arm of the government of South Korea plugged in an additional $2 billion, and Mizuho Financial Group of Japan similarly injected $1.2 billion into Merrill Lynch. Retrospectively, even $13 billion in new foreign investments in Merrill Lynch were insufficient to save it, and it was purchased by Bank of America in the financial meltdown of September 2008.

Why so little controversy? First, critics of foreign purchases of U.S. assets frequently assert that there is a difference between foreign investments in which the purchaser simply acquires a portion of a firm's stock and situations in which the purchaser decides to assume control and operation of the firm. They dislike the latter when a major financial firm is involved. Second, Temasek, South Korea, and Mizuho were viewed as beneficial angels attempting to help the United States avert a wrenching financial collapse brought about by the housing price implosion and subprime mortgage crisis in 2008. This looming catastrophe ultimately resulted in the U.S. government providing a rescue package approximating $1 trillion for a wide variety of financial organizations (including AIG, the American International Group) that were afflicted by the subprime mortgage crisis.

Other faltering U.S. financial giants also were supplicants. Citigroup ingested $7.5 billion, from the Abu Dhabi Sovereign Wealth Fund, and $22 billion overall, from a variety of foreign government investment funds. The China Investment Corporation bought into the Blackstone Group to the tune of $3 billion and into Morgan Stanley for $5.6 billion. During the U.S. financial crunch in the fall of 2008, Morgan Stanley received $9 billion from Mitsubishi UFJ Financial Group, an amount that increased as Morgan Stanley's stock price tanked. Morgan Stanley agreed to pay Mitsubishi a generous 10 percent dividend on its entire investment, which gave Mitsubishi 21 percent ownership in Morgan Stanley. This is the same Morgan Stanley that leased the City of Chicago's parking garages.[9] Hence, this latter transaction effectively made Abu Dhabi and Mitsubishi behind-the-scenes lessees for the City of Chicago's parking garages, with no limitations upon their pricing behavior other than Windy City drivers' willingness to pay the prices the new owners and their minions charge.

Parenthetically, this surprising Chicago relationship underscores the reality that modern U.S. markets, even those thought to be entirely local in character, are often remarkably international in character. Of course, it is possible to overemphasize international financial dependence. Events in New Delhi or Caracas don't always have a significant influence upon the lives of Americans in Philadelphia, Peoria, Illinois, or Seattle. Even so, the examples provided thus far underscore how decisions in London financial markets, in sovereign wealth funds in the Middle East, or in Beijing now resonate loudly on Main Street America.

Foreign purchasers of U.S. financial assets did not stop at taking equity positions in Merrill Lynch and Morgan Stanley. Three Chinese banks invested $350 million in Lehman Brothers, which filed for bankruptcy in September 2008. Lehman Brothers subsequently sold its North American operations to Barclays Capital of Great Britain and its Asian, Middle Eastern, and European operations to Nomura of Japan—the European sale for a reported $2.00!

Americans who buy a home or a new automobile often congratulate themselves on the wisdom of their purchases. "What a great purchase!" they often exclaim. Our advice is that you should not wait up all night to hear the same superlatives uttered by the foreigners who have recently purchased U.S. financial assets. Unless U.S. financial markets recover substantially, all of the organizations previously mentioned—Temasek, South Korea, Mizuho, the China Investment Corporation, Abu Dhabi, Barclays, and Nomura—will experience painful losses on the money they have invested in U.S. assets. Indeed, nearly all of them have already lost billions of dollars on their investments.

Their investments carried with them very high levels of risk, but also the prospect of great rewards. The great rewards may yet come. Nevertheless, it is appropriate for us to observe that, over the past few years, the United States has thirstily imported the capital of foreigners and, all things considered, has subsequently treated many of these investors rather roughly. Retrospectively, one suspects these foreign entities feel exploited by the United States rather than vice-versa. This has not gone unnoticed in these countries, and no doubt will inspire more cautious investment behavior on their part in the future.

DEFINITIONS AND DATA

Let's now install a bit of what we term "plumbing and heating." It's time to be more precise about what we mean when we talk about foreign investment. The foreign investment we are concerned about has four major parts: (1) foreign direct investment (FDI) in U.S. firms; (2) foreign purchase of U.S. Treasury debt securities and U.S. government agency debt; (3) foreign purchase of U.S. real estate; and, (4) foreign purchase of U.S. intellectual property.

FDI in U.S. Firms

Foreigners purchased at least $414 billion of equity stock in all U.S. companies in 2007, up 90 percent from the previous year. Indeed, the level in 2007 was double the approximate $200 billion annual average over the previous decade and was 20 times the average in the 1980s. In June 2007, foreigners held $3.13 trillion in equity in U.S. companies, up 124 percent from $1.40 trillion in June 2002. Table 1-1 records these and related data.

> **Foreign Direct Investment** (FDI) occurs when a foreign government or foreign firm acquires ownership or control of 10 percent or more of the voting securities of a U.S. busi-

To put these magnitudes into context, consider that the gross domestic product (GDP) of the United States was about $14.3 trillion in mid-2008. Hence, foreign equity stock holdings were equivalent to 22 percent of the

U.S. GDP. Such numbers as $3.13 trillion and 22 percent are hardly to be scoffed at. Even so, they are not yet an alarming amount when viewed from the standpoint of the economy as a whole. The $3.13 trillion equity holdings of foreigners constituted only about 11 percent of the total value of outstanding stock in public companies in the United States.

The largest foreign country holder of equity in U.S. firms and mutual funds is the United Kingdom, followed by Canada. Only recently has China become a player in this area, and Russia has largely stayed away from such investments. Middle Eastern oil-exporting nations recently have augmented their holdings of U.S. equities and mutual funds; however, even when their holdings are aggregated, they fall far short of those of the United Kingdom and Canada.

Of more concern than the $3.13 trillion at this point is the rapid rate of increase in foreign ownership of stock in U.S. corporations and mutual funds—124 percent between June 2002 and June 2007. Were this trend to continue for another decade, not only would foreigners own almost one-half of the New York Stock Exchange and NASDAQ, but they would also have obvious potential economic leverage over U.S. firms and U.S. economic policy.

As we argue in the next chapter, the upsurge in foreign direct investment in the United States over the past few years has been the result of four factors: (1) the sharp decline in the value of the dollar relative to most other major currencies in the world; (2) the stagnant share price performance for many equities on the New York Stock Exchange and NASDAQ; (3) a low interest rate regime in the United States and much of the rest of the world that enabled such foreign firms as Inbev to borrow the funds they needed to

Table 1-1   Foreign Ownership of Various Types of U.S. Financial Assets

	June 2002	June 2007	Percent Change
Long-Term Securities			
and Debt	$3.93 trillion	$9.14 trillion	133%
Equities (stock and			
mutual fund shares)	$1.40 trillion	$3.13 trillion	124%
U.S. Treasury debt	$0.91 trillion	$1.97 trillion	116%
U.S. govt. agency debt	$0.49 trillion	$1.30 trillion	165%
Corporate debt	$1.13 trillion	$2.74 trillion	142%
Short-Term Debt	$0.41 trillion	$0.64 trillion	56%
U.S. Treasury	$0.23 trillion	$0.23 trillion	0%
U.S. govt. agency	$0.09 trillion	$0.11 trillion	12%
Corporate	$0.09 trillion	$0.30 trillion	233%

Source: Adapted from "Report on Foreign Portfolio Holdings of U.S. Securities," Department of the Treasury (2008).

purchase such U.S. firms as Anheuser-Busch; and (4) the bulging wealth of foreign sovereign wealth funds—a subject we treat in a following section. To some extent, in 2009, all of these influences on foreign direct investment in the United States have diminished in impact. For example, the U.S. dollar has begun to recover from its parlous low values and, by October 2008, was up 10 percent relative to the Euro. That's equivalent to a price increase of 10 percent for Euro-area investors who wish to purchase U.S. firms or assets.

Foreign Purchase of U.S. Treasury and Government Agency Debt Securities

In addition, in 2007, foreigners purchased almost $2.06 trillion of U.S. Treasury bonds and securities, and, after taking into account debt instruments that matured, this brought their total holdings to approximately $2.4 trillion. As Figure 1-1 reveals, foreigners now hold about 26 percent of the total federal debt (but more than 50 percent of federal debt not held by the federal government itself),[10] a magnitude that inspires some to question who will actually own the United States if this trend continues. Representative Paul Kanjorski (D-Pennsylvania), the chair of the House Subcommittee on Capital Markets, Insurance, and Government-Sponsored Enterprises, captured the zeitgeist on this issue when he asked, "At what point will we lose control?"[11]

Figure 1-1 Ownership of U.S. Government Debt, December 2007

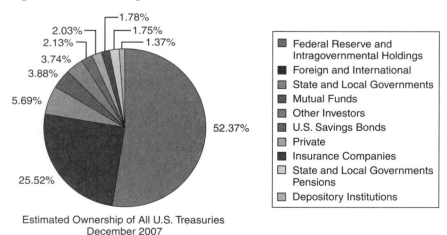

Estimated Ownership of All U.S. Treasuries
December 2007

Source: http://en.wikipedia.org/wiki/Image:Estimated_ownership_of_US_Treasury_securities_by _category.gif.

Which foreign countries own the long-term federal government debt (which includes both Treasury debt and the debt of U.S. government agencies)? China (the People's Republic of China [PRC]) was the leading creditor in June 2007, with $0.84 trillion in holdings, followed by Japan with $0.78 trillion. No other country approaches the holdings of PRC or Japan in magnitude. All Middle Eastern oil-exporting countries together own $11 billion of the U.S. government's long-term debt, and Russia is a very minor player in this arena. However, note that the U.S. government and its agencies own more than one-half of the all federal debts. In effect, one arm of the government owes another arm via its holdings of the federal debt.

Once again, it is not the absolute level of debt held by foreign countries that is so much a concern as the observable trends in that regard. Between June 2002 and June 2007, foreigners increased their holdings of U.S. Treasury debt by 116 percent and their holdings of U.S. government agency debt by 165 percent. Table 1-2 records what has happened to U.S. government debt since 1940. Note that these values are stated in constant-year 2000 dollars in order to make them comparable.

As Table 1-2 discloses, U.S. government debt has increased dramatically since 1980. If there is any comfort in this situation, it is that this debt, as a percent of U.S. GDP, has increased more modestly, although it now is about two-thirds of GDP.

Foreign purchases of U.S. Treasury and U.S. government agency debt have become quantitatively more important than foreign purchases of U.S. equities and mutual fund stock. Indeed, foreign ownership of U.S. government debt (all sources) grew by $1.89 trillion between June 2002 and 2007, whereas foreign equity holdings increased by only $1.73 trillion. The preference of foreigners for U.S. government debt over U.S. equities is unlikely to

Table 1-2   All U.S. Government Debt, 1940–2007

Year	U.S. Government Debt	% of GDP
1940	$43 billion	52.4%
1950	$257 billion	94.1%
1960	$290 billion	56.1%
1970	$389 billion	37.6%
1980	$930 billion	33.3%
1990	$3,233 billion	55.9%
2000	$5,674 billion	58.0%
2005	$7,933 billion	64.6%
2007	$9,008 billion	65.5%
2008 (October)	$9,950 billion	67.5%

Source: U.S. Treasury and wikipedia.org.

diminish in the next few years, because U.S. government debt is viewed as a safe harbor in a world full of unpredictable developments. Ironically, this tends to be true even when the source of the unpredictable developments is the United States! Furthering the irony, if the United States succeeds in revitalizing its economy and stabilizes its financial markets, economist Eduardo Porter's sage observation about the dollar will come into play: "It seems vulnerable to tranquility."[12] When financial seas are calm, many investors decide they do not need to hold assets denominated in U.S. dollars.

Sovereign wealth funds recently have plowed almost $60 billion into U.S. banks and financial institutions, and, as we note in the following, they have very little to show for it other than capital losses in the range of 50 percent as of February 2009. The general reluctance of foreigners to risk funds in U.S. equity markets bodes well to increase the already existing gap between U.S. government debt purchases and the ill-fated equity purchases. U.S. government debt still is the asset of choice when foreigners are worried about the future.

What might happen if foreigners decided to liquidate large portions of their holdings of U.S. government debt? As we argue in our discussion of sovereign wealth funds, foreigners who do so may well shoot themselves in the foot. James K. Jackson,[13] writing for the Congressional Research Service, examined this possibility and concluded that a foreign sell-off of U.S. government debt would, in fact, inflict considerable injury on the United States in the form of higher interest rates, reduced productivity growth, and dampened U.S. economic growth. But, simultaneously, the sell-off would injure the foreign parties doing the selling by driving down the prices of their U.S. government debt. They would "experience a severe loss in the value of those assets."[14] It also would reduce their ability to export goods and services to U.S. consumers.

The bottom line is that the largest foreign owners of U.S. government debt (China and Japan) would inflict significant damage on themselves if they initiated or encouraged the dumping of U.S. government debt. A more likely scenario, were either country to conclude that it needed to diminish its holdings of U.S. government debt, would be for this to occur slowly, in order to avoid disrupting U.S. government debt markets. The gradual appreciation of the PRC's yuan currency relative to the dollar that the Chinese have promoted and the PRC's slow movement into non-dollar currencies provide salient examples of how this might occur.

Foreign Purchases of U.S. Real Estate

Until mid-2008, U.S. real estate was viewed as a great bargain by foreigners. They could not purchase similar properties, or similar streams of income from rental properties, in their home countries without paying a much higher price. Two major factors were at work: (1) the declining value of the U.S. dollar reduced the price foreigners had to pay in their own currencies for U.S. properties; (2) comparatively low U.S. mortgage rates made it possible for foreigners to finance purchases easily, if they desired to do so.

Falling U.S. real estate prices (in U.S. dollars) have conflicting influences on foreign investors. On the one hand, lower U.S. real estate prices make it easier for foreigners to purchase U.S. real estate. On the other hand, few investors are anxious to acquire properties for which the prices are quite likely to decline even more in the near future.

In any case, the recovery in the value of the U.S. dollar relative to most major currencies (approximately 20 percent with respect to the euro in the last two quarters of 2008 alone) and tightening U.S. credit markets have removed some of the shine from U.S. real estate from the standpoint of foreign investors. In 2006, foreigners invested more than $43 billion in U.S. real estate (less than one-fifth of what they invested in U.S. equities in the same year and less than the record $50 billion invested in 2000). The major foreign investors in U.S. real estate emanate from Germany, Australia, Japan, and Latin America.

Historically, Japan has supplied the major foreign investors in U.S. real estate, notably on Waikiki Beach in Honolulu. This was stimulated by the healthy savings rate of Japanese citizens and Japan's extremely low interest rates. However, more recently, Japanese investors have begun to look elsewhere, and Germany and Australian investors have taken their place, at least where real estate has been concerned. Russian, Chinese, and Middle Eastern petroleum-exporting countries have not been major players.

The bottom line in the area of foreign purchases of U.S. real estate is this: highly visible foreign purchases of such iconic properties as the Chrysler Building in New York City attract lots of attention, but they hardly represent a major threat to the U.S. economy. Real estate is seldom vital to national security, and, in any case, the rising value of the U.S. dollar has dampened foreign demand for U.S. real estate.

Foreign Purchase of U.S. Intellectual Property

Intellectual property (IP) is an imprecise term, but it usually refers to products that are eligible for protection under laws that regulate copyrights, patents, trademarks, product designs, and trade secrets. U.S. firms typically earn revenues from this IP by selling licenses, and those revenues approximated $120 billion in 2007. On occasion, U.S. firms make an outright sale of IP, such as patents to foreigners, rather than selling licenses that generate royalties. These instances are not common, however.

Even though IP is becoming increasingly important in economic activity, it's unclear how much of the $120 billion relates to non-U.S. parties. After all, if I purchase a license for Microsoft Windows XP in the United States, I can use that license in Canada, Indonesia, or Morocco if I carry my PC there. But that is hardly the only reason foreign participation in IP is difficult to track. The nature of most IP is that it can be digitized, that is, encoded into a succession of 0's and 1's. Each 0 or 1 is a "bit" and a succession of 0's and 1's are "bytes." In general, nearly all music, pictures, movies, radio, television, and written documents can be digitized and turned into bits and bytes. Once digitized, IP can be copied and subsequently sent anywhere on earth—sometimes in milliseconds. This is the critical difference between IP and other classes of assets.

The bottom line is that often it is extremely difficult for owners of IP to defend the property rights associated with their IP. Perhaps 90 percent of all music CDs acquired in the PRC in recent years has been stolen. DVDs are notoriously copied and distributed without the owner of the DVD's IP receiving any payment. Veritable legions of individuals and techniques exist that are capable of breaking the digital rights management devices that many owners of IP futilely use to discourage copying.

Too Expensive to Litigate?

A 2005 report from the American Intellectual Property Law Association estimated that it would cost $2 million to litigate a patent case through a trial in a U.S. court. This deters enforcement of IP property rights even before international complications are introduced.

Source: Joseph S. Estabrook, Jennifer K. Vanderhart, and Abby J. Weinstock, "Crossing the Border: International Issues That Affect IP Litigation," *Intellectual Property Litigation*, 19 (Fall 2007), 1-2.

At the end of the day, if there is a significant problem associated with foreign acquisition of U.S. IP, it is not that foreigners are purchasing too much IP, but instead that they aren't purchasing enough. In the non-IP world, if Arcelor Mittal, the world's largest steel company, were able to use the facilities and resources of the U.S. Steel Corporation without paying for them, this would constitute a life-threatening problem for U.S. Steel. Analogously, the same reality confronts many owners of IP in the United States. The major problem facing music producers and movie theaters in the United States is not rapacious purchases of their assets by foreigners, but rather the fact that these assets are being stolen rather than purchased, leased, rented, licensed, or accessed via a legitimate reciprocal distribution agreement or joint venture. To a lesser extent, the same problem exists for U.S. owners of copyrights and patents.

Our conclusion is that foreign purchases of U.S. IP do not currently constitute a significant problem. Here, the realistic problem is the inability of the United States to convince or force foreigners to purchase or license U.S. IP.

THE ROLE OF SOVEREIGN WEALTH FUNDS

Sovereign wealth funds are governmentally controlled agencies that purchase assets in foreign countries. Sovereign wealth funds have existed for more than 50 years; Kuwait opened its Reserve Fund in 1953. The investment dollars of sovereign wealth funds usually are derived either from oil and natural gas sales, or from the sales of other natural resources such as copper, uranium, and other extractable minerals.

Table 1-3 discloses the dollar value of the assets held by the 10 largest sovereign wealth funds in the world at the end of 2008. Sovereign wealth funds held more than $4.6 trillion in assets at the end of 2007, and they purchased $21.5 billion of assets in the United States in 2007. McKinsey predicts these assets will grow to $7.7 trillion by 2013.[15] "This is a new phenomenon that could be called the growth of state capitalism as opposed to market capitalism," observed Jeffrey E. Garten, a former undersecretary in

Table 1-3   Ten Largest Estimated Sovereign Wealth Fund Assets, December 2008

Abu Dhabi Investment Council	$875 billion
Government Pension Fund of Norway	$380 billion
Government of Singapore Investment Corporation	$330 billion
Saudi Arabia (various)	$300 billion
Kuwait Investment Authority	$250 billion
China Investment Corporation	$200 billion
Hong Kong Monetary Authority	$163 billion
Temasek Holdings (Singapore)	$159 billion
Stabilization Fund (Russia)	$157 billion
Australian Future Fund	$61 billion

Sources: Economist (January 17, 2008, and September 20, 2008); "Sovereign Wealth Fund," Wikipedia, http://en.wikipedia.org/wiki/Sovereign_wealth_fund; Bank for International Settlements; Research Recap, http://www.researchrecap.com/index.php/2008/03/31/ sovereign-wealth-funds-assets-up-18-in-2007/.

the Department of Commerce and former dean of Yale's School of Management.

Ownership of U.S. assets by foreign governments is seen by many as far more problematic than ownership of the same assets by private individuals who are foreign citizens. This concern presumably reflects the greater ability of foreign governments to exercise pressure on U.S. decisions and foreign policy.

The largest sovereign wealth fund appears to be the Abu Dhabi Investment Authority, whose assets were estimated to be $875 billion at the end of 2008. Norway was second with $357 billion. "Appears" and "estimated" are the appropriate word choices here, because at least one-half of the sovereign wealth funds in the world, including that of Abu Dhabi, are unaudited and often secretive in their activities. It's not clear precisely how large the sovereign wealth holdings of countries such as the UAE and Singapore ($100 to $300 billion) actually are, what their asset mix is, or how they have been using those assets.

The need to estimate the holdings of many sovereign wealth funds underscores the uncertainty that is attached to their motives and conduct. These funds have immense potential to do good or bad, and it is not yet clear which will predominate. The paragon in the area is the sovereign wealth fund of Norway, which employs highly professional managers, is transparent in its activities, and has no visible political agenda. At the other end of the spectrum, there is suspicion over the motives and activities of Russia's Stabilization Fund and Libya's Arab Foreign Investment Company.

The Committee on Foreign Investments in the United States (CFIUS) is an interagency body of the U.S. government that was established by presidential executive order in 1975. It exists to assess the national security implications of foreign investments in U.S. companies and operations. The 1988 Exon-Florio amendment to the Defense Production Act explicitly gave the president of the United States authority to investigate the impact of proposed mergers, acquisitions, and takeovers of U.S. firms and operations by foreigners. If CFIUS decides to proceed with a full investigation of a proposed purchase, it must conclude its initial review in 45 days, after which it submits a recommendation to the president, who has 15 days from the date of referral to clear, prohibit, or suspend a transaction. Since the passage of Exon-Florio, CFIUS has launched 45-day reviews in only about two dozen cases.

The notion that individuals such as Iran's President Mahmoud Ahmadinejad and Russia's Prime Minister Vladimir Putin might control key U.S. industries via sovereign wealth funds has been sufficient to cause even otherwise imperturbable individuals to sweat. Mr. Putin has volleyed thinly veiled threats of nuclear destruction against a variety of Western countries, has turned off natural gas supplies to countries he wishes to discipline, and has invaded Georgia. Meanwhile, Mr. Ahmadinejad has threatened to wipe Israel off the map and has promised to oppose U.S. foreign policy with all his power. Their actions do not inspire investor confidence. With respect to the sovereign wealth funds of countries that aggravate the United States, the issue quickly reduces to this: Is there a danger that such individuals (or any foreign sovereign wealth fund) will decide to use their asset holdings in the United States as a club to influence U.S. foreign policy, military behavior, and economic actions?

Many individuals, including a healthy number of legislators, don't want to wait to find out. They want to stimulate and strengthen the Committee on Foreign Investment in the United States (CFIUS) that reviews the national security implications of foreign investments in the United States. CFIUS ordinarily makes recommendations to the president on proposed foreign acquisitions within 45 days of their announcement. However, since CFIUS was established by presidential executive order in 1975, it has questioned less than 2 percent of all foreign acquisitions and recommended rejection in only a handful of cases.

Pending more rigorous action by CFIUS, eight U.S. legislators urged President Bush to block the proposed purchase of the Massachusetts-based 3Com Corporation, a high-technology company that specializes in computer and Internet networking and security. The legislators argued that the $2.2 billion transaction threatened U.S. national security. Similarly, the proposed purchase of a 20 percent stake in NASDAQ by the Dubai International Financial Exchange, in exchange for a one-third stake for NASDAQ in the Dubai Exchange, excited a variety of individuals.

Such astute observers as Laura Tyson, one-time chair of the President's Council of Economic Advisors, former dean of the London Business School, and a member of a variety of corporate boards, assign passing marks thus far to the behavior of sovereign wealth funds. Professor Tyson is not one who appears to be greatly worried about most foreign purchases of U.S. assets. She predicts that state ownership of foreign companies is likely to become more common but asks, "So what? The simple dichotomy between private and state-owned does not tell us very much at this point."[16]

In the same vein, when allegations of adverse foreign behavior are concerned, Gilson and Milhaupt argue that "no one can point to a reported incidence of such behaviors."[17] But they also acknowledge that "the fear is that SWFs will use their influence on portfolio companies to secure technology (a concern raised explicitly in the discussion of the Abu Dhabi fund's investment in AMD), gain access to natural resources, improve competitive positions for domestic companies, or [do so] in a fashion that has national security concerns for the portfolio company's country of incorporation."[18]

Professor Tyson (who now teaches economics at the University of California, Berkeley) notes that conflicts of interest can clearly emerge if the interests of a foreign country diverge from those of a U.S. firm that they own. This is a manifestation of the classic "principle-agent" problem of economics, whereby those who own a firm may have interests that diverge from those who manage it. But the principle-agent problem is not limited to foreign firms. Separation of ownership and management, which we outlined in a preceding section, is an illustration of this phenomenon, which may find owners unable to get managers to do what the owners want. With respect to foreign firms, the explicit worry is that the owners of the firm (foreign sovereign wealth funds) will force their U.S. managers to take actions that are not in the best interests either of that firm or of the United States.

It remains to be seen how sovereign wealth funds will behave as their economic clout grows. That clout is heavily dependent upon high prices for oil, natural gas, and natural resources. But these are unpredictable, and, as the prophet Job observed, "what the Lord giveth, the Lord also taketh away."[19] Energy and natural resource prices frequently reverse course, and, in 2008, the price of oil per barrel increased by 75 percent, to $147 per barrel, only to decline later by more than 70 percent, to less than $40 per barrel. Hence, it is not inevitable that the assets held by sovereign wealth funds will increase at their recent rates. Their portfolios were battered dreadfully by the worldwide financial crisis that unfolded in the fall of 2008.

Nevertheless, if the managers of these funds behave intelligently, they will be a force to reckon with for many years to come. This will require intelligent, quality management and a certain degree of good fortune. To some extent, the value of these funds is tied to the value of the U.S. dollar. Because many of the funds (and the countries they represent) have invested heavily in dollar-denominated assets (most especially U.S. government debt), they are particularly vulnerable to declines in U.S. asset values and the depreciation of the U.S. dollar. Table 1-4 reports recent sovereign fund investments in major U.S. financial institutions. Although this is a relatively recent phenomenon in the United States, foreign ownership of banks has traditionally been much more common in other countries. About two-thirds of the banks in South Korea are foreign-owned, and approximately 80 percent of the financial system of Mexico is foreign-owned. Of course, much (perhaps everything) depends upon who the foreign owners are.

The substantial recent investments of foreigners in U.S. financial institutions (for example, more than $10 billion has been invested in Citibank by petrodollar sovereign funds) underline how things have changed. In a formal sense, the U.S. financial system is no longer independent of the rest of the world, if it ever was. Yet, the reverse also is true. Foreign sovereign wealth funds now have substantial exposure to both U.S. financial distress and the value of the U.S. dollar. When the U.S. financial system sneezes, they get a cold.

Consider the plight of the Chinese in this regard. The PRC owns approximately $1.0 trillion in U.S. government debt, and the value of these assets has declined dramatically because the value of the U.S. dollar declined 37 percent relative to most major currencies between the end of 2001 and mid-2008. Many investors, when facing such declining asset values, would pitch them overboard and sell them. No doubt the Chinese have harbored similar thoughts. Unfortunately for them, as previously noted, if they begin to dump their U.S. government debt holdings or if they refuse to purchase new U.S. government debt issues, this will only drive down U.S. government bond prices and therefore reduce the value of their holdings even more.

Do foreign-owned firms in the United States underperform U.S. firms that invest overseas?

If the measure of productivity is a firm's rate of return on its invested capital, the answer may well be yes. Over the past 25 years, the rate of return on foreign capital invested in the United States has been 4.3 percent, whereas the rate of return on U.S. investments abroad has been 12.1 percent according to Mihir Desai.

Source: Mihir Desai, "America the Difficult," *The American* (May 29, 2008), http://www.american.com/archive/2008/may-june-magazine-contents/america -the-difficult/?searchterm=mihir%20desai.

The bottom line is that U.S. government debt has evolved into a form of narcotic financial poison for the PRC. U.S. financial problems and the

Table 1-4   Estimated Sovereign Wealth Fund Investments in U.S. Financial
Institutions, March 2007–June 2008

Citigroup	$6.6 billion Asian Sovereign Funds $10.5 billion Petrodollar Sovereign Funds
Merrill Lynch	$6.2 billion Asian Sovereign Funds $2.0 billion Petrodollar Sovereign Funds
Morgan Stanley	$4.7 billion Asian Sovereign Funds $0 Petrodollar Sovereign Funds
Blackstone	$2.8 billion Asian Sovereign Funds $0 Petrodollar Sovereign Funds
Carlyle	$1.3 billion Asian Sovereign Funds $0 Petrodollar Sovereign Funds

declining value of the dollar reduce the value of the huge portfolio of U.S. government debt that the Chinese already hold. Alas, if they attempt to get rid of that debt or begin to boycott U.S. government debt sales, then they will depress the value of their holdings even more. The PRC is damned if it does and damned if it doesn't.

Interestingly, one of the best potential outcomes for the PRC, economically speaking, is to have the U.S. economy recover and expand robustly and to have the U.S. dollar increase in value. An expanding U.S. economy in 2009–2010 would generate increased Chinese exports to the United States. At the same time, a strengthened U.S. dollar also would help China, because it would make Chinese exports to the U.S. more price-competitive. A strengthened dollar would also increase the value of the substantial portfolio of U.S. government debt that the Chinese own.

Improved economic conditions might also help the Chinese recover from their abysmal 2008 U.S. investment performance. The market value of Chinese investments in the United States fell by an estimated 73 percent in the first three quarters of 2008, from $3.4 billion to about $900 million. Most of these losses were generated by the crisis in the U.S. financial system. Ironically, even though China may be very reluctant to invest additional funds in the United States, given the financial pounding that it has taken recently, prudent additional investments in the United States may help preserve the value of its existing U.S. investments. At the end of the day, the United States is China's largest international customer and one of its largest creditors. Nearly anything that improves the economic condition of the United States at this juncture is likely to benefit the PRC.

IS THERE NOW A JAPANESE EXCEPTION?

There was a time in the 1980s and early 1990s when some agitated individuals would invoke, *sotto voce,* the time-worn notion of the "yellow peril" when discussing the wave of purchases of U.S. assets by Japanese. High-profile acquisitions of prominent tourist hotels on Waikiki Beach in Honolulu by Japanese were sometimes greeted with hostility by Americans. For example, all four Sheraton properties on Waikiki were owned by Japanese, and this was the subject of some hand-wringing. Over time, however, the suspicion associated with Japanese ownership dissipated, not the least because it was difficult for U.S. tourists to make meaningful differentiations between hotels that were owned by Japanese and those that were not.

The wave of Japanese acquisitions of U.S. and other foreign assets crested in the early 1990s, revived about the turn of the twentieth century, and then spiked dramatically upward in 2006. Figure 1-2 provides visual evidence of this. Representative was the acquisition of American Millennium Pharmaceuticals, a Massachusetts biopharmaceutical firm with anti-cancer drugs for $8.8 billion, by Japan's Takeda Pharmaceutical.

Even as the acquisitions of U.S. assets by foreign sovereign wealth funds began to sputter and decline, the Japanese took their place in robust fashion. Why? In contrast to most foreign currencies, the Japanese yen actually appreciated by about 10 percent relative to the U.S. dollar during the financial crisis in the fall of 2008. As a result, each yen could purchase more U.S. assets than before. In addition, falling U.S. asset prices (especially equity prices for publicly traded firms) made U.S. asset purchases more attractive as well, if the Japanese purchasers were willing to take a long-run view, which they were. Finally, Japan had accumulated a huge reserve of foreign currencies, especially U.S. dollars, and Japanese savings rates continued to be among the highest in the developed world, even though real interest rates in Japan were close to zero or even negative. Hence, despite its problems, the United States was (and is) perceived as a good place for the Japanese to invest their funds. Mitsubishi UFJ Financial Group's purchase of a 21 percent share of Morgan Stanley in the fall of 2008 exemplified this attitude.

Japan has gradually migrated in public perception from being seen as an avaricious real estate speculator, doing unsolicited knocking on doors, to a highly regarded financial angel, with deep pockets and a highly regarded stable, long-term point of view. This evolution should inspire caution among those who ritually condemn foreign purchases of U.S. assets. Yesterday's perceived vultures can easily become today's best friends. Furthermore, national circumstances and objectives change over

Figure 1-2 Japanese Foreign Acquisitions 1985–2008

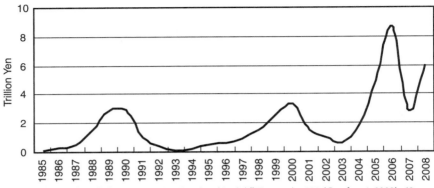

Source: Adapted from "The Japanese Are Coming (Again)," *Economist,* 389 (October 4, 2008), 69.

time, both for sellers and buyers. Hard and fast rules that discourage or even prohibit foreign purchases of U.S. assets can easily become counterproductive when economic situations change.

SUMMING IT UP

Foreign purchases of U.S. assets have increased dramatically in recent years, but they now appear to be tailing off for two reasons. First, the value of the U.S. dollar is recovering from the very low levels that encouraged many to suggest that U.S. assets were on sale, much like a post-Christmas sale of leftovers at Macy's. For example, the value of the U.S. dollar increased about 20 percent relative to the euro at the end of 2008. Effectively, this raised the price of U.S. assets by 20 percent insofar as euro-based foreign purchasers were concerned.

Second, falling U.S. equity prices have made the acquisition of U.S. companies more attractive. However, what foreign purchasers want to do is to buy at the bottom of the price cycle. Unfortunately for them, their timing has been less than precise, and the prices of the equity they have purchased usually have declined significantly after the purchase. Notably, several sovereign wealth funds have lost billions of dollars in U.S. financial institutions within a few weeks of their purchasing positions. It remains to be seen whether Asian sovereign funds will lose most or all of the $6.2 billion they invested in Merrill Lynch.

As we have noted, the policy actions taken by the Federal Reserve System and the U.S. government to counteract the financial crisis in the fall of 2008 may produce conditions in 2010 or later that will revive the interest of for-eigners in purchasing nongovernmental U.S. assets. Specifically, it seems quite likely that the value of the U.S. dollar, relative to major currencies, will be driven down to levels that once again will put "America on Sale."

Regardless of the future, past foreign purchases of equity in U.S. firms and even larger purchases of the debt of the U.S. Treasury and U.S. gov-ernment agencies have evoked great concern. The $52 billion purchase of U.S. icon Anheuser-Busch by Inbev does not involve critical infrastructure or national defense considerations, but it does suggest to many U.S. observers that something is wrong. The ownership by foreigners of 26 per-cent of the debt of the U.S. government and its agencies (and almost one-half of the federal debt not owned by the federal government itself or its agencies) sends the message to many individuals that things have gone astray, economically speaking.

Legitimately, these critics want to know why. Why is this happening? What are its causes? Can this be reversed if the United States pursues a different set of economic policies? These are among the questions we address in the next chapter.

Russian Prime Minister Vladimir Putin (a former KGB executive) sent shivers down the sides of many investors in July 2008 when he vocally criticized Mechel, the giant Russ-ian coal and steel company, for alleged price gouging. He also appeared to threaten Mechel's CEO. Almost immedi-ately, Mechel's stock share price plunged by a third. Shortly thereafter, Russia invaded neighboring Georgia. The inter-national financial community regarded these actions as highly arbitrary and indicators of an absence of the rule of law that is conducive to productive investments. These events, plus global financial instability, ripped 72 percent of the value from the Russian MICEX stock exchange by mid-October 2008, well above the average international stock market decline of about 30 percent. Panic ensued, and the Russian government was forced to close MICEX and inject more than $190 billion in funds to stabilize matters. Never-theless, foreign investors pulled $57 billion out of Russia during this time, and Russian citizens themselves followed suit by sending almost $17 billion abroad. U.S. critics of for-eign sovereign wealth funds argue that Putin's behavior demonstrates the increased risk the United States incurs when such funds purchase U.S. assets.

Chapter 2

I Want Euros—You Can Keep Your Dollars

I don't want this. This is nothing.

The reaction of a street beggar in Marrakesh to a U.S. tourist
who gave her a one-dollar bill, 2007

Russian Oligarchs Lose Big in Financial Meltdown.

International Herald Tribune, October 9, 2008

Here is the trillion-dollar question: Why have foreigners purchased so many U.S. assets in recent years? Why have the Russian oligarchs (yes, "oligarch" is hardly a neutral term, but it is one used repeatedly) purchased so many U.S. steel companies? Why do foreigners now own one-quarter of the entire U.S. government debt and one-half of all the U.S. government "public" debt that the U.S. government itself doesn't own? Is the weather the only reason that so many Germans have purchased condominiums in Florida?

It would be lovely if we could point to a single cause for the surge in the purchase of U.S. assets by foreigners during this decade. Alas, life is not that simple. What motivates a German condominium purchaser in search of smooth, white Gulf Coast beaches is not necessarily what pushes the managers of Middle East petroleum-based sovereign wealth funds into action. Furthermore, on occasion, there is a gap between what investors of all stripes say and what they actually do. It would be impolitic for a sovereign wealth fund to confess that it wanted to obtain economic and political leverage over the United States by means of its purchase of a key U.S. asset.

Instead, foreign investors talk about buying assets in order to achieve synergies, enjoy additional economies of scale, and reduce transportation costs. Innocent phrases are the flavor of the month. Sage observers don't ignore such rhetoric, but they appropriately focus their attention on what investors actually do rather than on what they say.

The motives of foreign purchasers of U.S. assets therefore are mixed and sometimes almost inscrutable. Nevertheless, we are prepared to state that the four major influences (positive and negative) upon foreign purchases of U.S. assets of all kinds in recent years have been the following: (1) the fluctuating, mostly declining value of the U.S. dollar; (2) the perception that U.S. equities could be purchased at bargain, discount prices that wouldn't be seen again for many years; (3) the feeling of many foreigners that U.S. government debt still constitutes the safest, most secure harbor in a stormy world full of economic upheaval and uncertainty; and (4) higher corporate tax rates in the United States than those of many other countries. Let's examine each of these sometimes competing influences in turn.

I. THE INFLUENCE OF THE FLUCTUATING VALUE OF THE U.S. DOLLAR

Anyone who pays attention to international finance knows well that the values of foreign currencies ebb and flow over time. These fluctuations affect both rich and poor. If you are fortunate enough to vacation in the south of France each year, then you soon learn that the price of the dinner you just purchased at that wonderful, small brasserie in Rives on the Mediterranean coast depends critically upon the foreign exchange rate between your dollars and the euros you need to acquire to pay for the dinner. The mathematics are simple. Because of fluctuations in exchange rates, a 200-euro dinner that you could have purchased for about $240 in January 2006 rose in price to almost $300 in January 2008.

Of course, expensive French dinners are not the prism through which most of us see the world. We may want to purchase, at the nearby Wal-Mart, a television set that was made in China or a pair of slacks, at a Macy's department store, that were sewn in Malaysia, or a computer disk drive, at Radio Shack, that was manufactured in Taiwan. That's how most of us experience firsthand the fluctuations that continuously occur in the values of foreign currencies versus the U.S. dollar.

The reality is that we Americans purchase lots of foreign-made goods— $2,345 billion in 2007, including $322 billion from the PRC. But, pragmatically, what does a dollar mean in these situations? That is, how much is a dollar worth to a Chinese, or a Malaysian, or a Taiwanese?

Therein lies the rub. Fluctuating currency values affect every purchase, whether the object being purchased is an inexpensive pair of athletic socks made in Thailand or an expensive S-class Mercedes manufactured in Germany. Eventually, people have to exchange their domestic currency for a foreign currency when they purchase imported goods. If I want to purchase a pair of athletic socks made in Thailand, then at some point, either I or my financial agents must convert our dollars into Thailand's currency, which is the estimable baht. What results, via the interaction of supply and demand, is a price for bahts in terms of U.S. dollars or, looking at it the other way around, the price of U.S. dollars in terms of bahts. This price is the exchange rate. In late May 2009, this exchange rate approximated 34 bahts per U.S. dollar.

Of course, the same thing is true for our foreign customers. Changing international currency values influence the price they pay for what they purchase from us. If Russians take a vacation in the United States, purchase a (legal) copy of Microsoft Windows, or even acquire an entire steel-making firm, such as Esmark Company, then they must turn their currency (the ruble) into dollars at the established rate of exchange. Those infamous Russian oligarchs are no exception. When they actually acquired Esmark in 2008 for $1.25 billion, the oligarchs had to supply their Russian rubles in order to obtain the necessary U.S. dollars. Yet the number of required rubles can be a moving target. In 1997, in the middle of a currency crisis, it took 5,785 rubles to obtain a single U.S. dollar. In July 2008, when the transaction was being completed and after a major Russian currency reform, the exchange rate was only 23.1 rubles per U.S. dollar. By late July 2009, the value of the ruble had retreated to approximately 32.5 per dollar. Quite a difference!

The salient lesson is that currency values change over time. In the fall of 2001, someone who wanted a single euro could make that trade for only 0.82 U.S. dollars ($0.82). However, by early 2008, it took $1.60 to obtain one euro. Thus, the value of the U.S. dollar (stated in euros) fell almost in half in the seven-year period, 2001–2008.

Semiautomatic Adjustments

Movements in the value of a particular currency seldom occur only in one direction for long periods, because noticeable changes in value automatically set into motion forces that eventually tend to moderate or even reverse the situation. In this respect, the value of foreign currencies does not differ from that of most other goods and services. When the price of gasoline per gallon rose above $4.00 in the United States in September

Figure 2-1 Canada/U.S. Foreign Exchange Rate

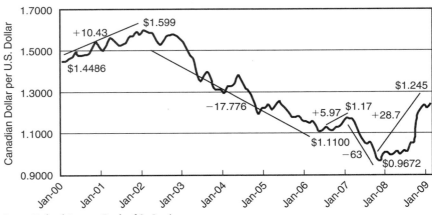

Source: Federal Reserve Bank of St. Louis.

2008, this inspired consumers to drive 6 percent fewer miles, purchase more fuel-efficient automobiles, increase their use of public transportation, and even ride their bikes more often. It also stimulated the development of alternative fuel sources, which became comparatively more attractive.

Hence, when the value of the U.S. dollar falls to low levels, this makes what Americans sell to other nations less expensive in the eyes of those foreigners. Consider this illustration. In 2001, a Canadian who wanted to purchase U.S. goods worth $1.00 had to fork over 1.61 Canadian dollars. However, by January 2008, the price of a single U.S. dollar had fallen to only 0.91 Canadian dollars (see Figure 2-1). This was the equivalent to a decline of 43 percent in U.S. prices insofar as Canadians were concerned. Holding other factors constant, this meant that a Canadian who vacationed in the United States in 2001 and spent $1,000 would only have to pay about $570 to obtain the same vacation in January 2008. Alas (for Canadians anyway), those bargains did not last, and the prices they had to pay had gone up by about 25 percent by November 2008. As Heraclitus the Greek once observed, the only thing that is constant is change.

Not surprisingly, more attractive exchange rates caused Canadians to purchase more goods and services from the United States. This trend was quite visible in U.S. cities and resorts near the Canadian-U.S. border, as Canadians flocked to take advantage of what most perceived to be bargain-basement prices. Such consumer goods as ski tickets, clothing, and lattes appeared to be much less expensive in the United States than in Canada if you were a Canadian. But this relationship extended far beyond vacations.

U.S.-made machine tools and Caterpillar earth movers also appeared to be on sale to Canadians.

The falling value of the U.S. dollar was the major reason that the volume and value of U.S. exports to foreign countries surged in the first half of 2008. This provided a welcome stimulus to a decelerating U.S. economy. U.S. exports totaled $123.2 billion in August 2006 but increased to $164.7 billion by August 2008.

Even so, the adjustment process relating to foreign exchange rates was not yet finished. When the U.S. exports more to foreigners, this stimulates their demand for U.S. dollars, because these foreigners eventually must turn their currency into U.S. dollars in order to obtain the U.S. goods and services they want. Sometimes foreign consumers do this directly and in person by going to a foreign exchange booth at an airport or bank, where American Express or a similar firm helps them turn in their currency for dollars. In other cases, the necessary currency trade is accomplished for them by their credit card company (such as Visa or MasterCard), a bank, or the firm from which they purchase U.S. goods. Regardless, the effect is to buoy upward the value of the U.S. dollar, a phenomenon one can observe in Figure 2-1 during 2008.[1]

For most of this decade, except for a few ups and down, the value of the U.S. dollar has gradually declined versus that of most other major world currencies. Still, a glance at Figure 2-2 reveals a nuanced picture. The value of the U.S. dollar in terms of Japanese yen has imitated a roller coaster since 2000. Between 2000 and 2002, the value of the U.S. dollar in terms of yen increased by more than 32 percent but then declined by 24 percent

Figure 2-2 Japan/U.S. Foreign Exchange Rate

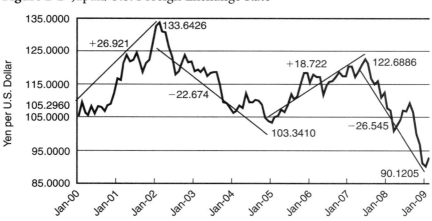

Source: Federal Reserve Bank of St. Louis.

through the beginning of 2005, only to recover by more than 21 percent by the middle of 2007. This was followed by yet another decline of almost 22 percent, which culminated in March 2008. Yet this recent trend also reversed itself as the financial crisis in the United States began to spread abroad. The value of the U.S. dollar versus the yen hit its lowest levels in this decade (only 90 yen per dollar) in the summer of 2008.

The Curious Case of the PRC's Yuan

There is one major foreign currency against which the value of the dollar has declined gradually since 2000: the yuan of the PRC. Figure 2-3 shows that the value of the U.S. dollar declined by more than 18 percent relative to the PRC yuan between the end of 2005 and the middle of 2008. Note that the PRC government rigidly held the exchange value of the yuan at about 8.3 per U.S. dollar for many years. At the end of 2005, it gradually began to loosen the strings and allowed the value of the yuan to increase (meaning the value of the U.S. dollar relative to the yuan was decreasing). Rather than $1.00 U.S. converting to 8.3 yuan, by late May 2009, the conversion ratio had changed to only 6.83 yuan.

The change in the value (the rising value) of the yuan relative to the U.S. dollar had two effects. First, it made U.S. goods and services less expensive to Chinese customers. A Chinese customer purchasing, say, $100 worth of U.S. goods and services now only had to present 683 yuan rather than the 830 yuan the same items would have cost years previous. Second, the alteration in the exchange rate also made Chinese goods appear to U.S.

Figure 2-3 China/U.S. Foreign Exchange Rate

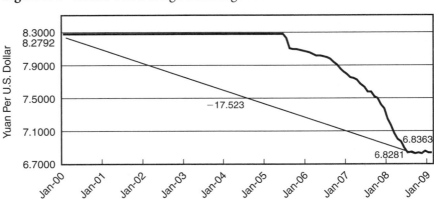

Source: Federal Reserve Bank of St. Louis.

consumers to be more expensive. A computer monitor that cost 1,500 yuan previously (this was $180.72 in U.S. dollars) now cost quite a bit more—$219.62.

Although the government of the PRC is notoriously opaque about the rationale behind its financial decisions, it appeared to have several goals in mind. One was pragmatic and probably related to U.S. political pressure. Many Americans argue that the PRC yuan has long been seriously under-valued. Indeed, even at 6.83 per U.S. dollar, many observers believe the yuan still is undervalued and should be trading as low as a 5:1 ratio.

So what? Why might the PRC intentionally undervalue its yuan cur-rency? Why should we care? The PRC presumably did so because this directly stimulated Chinese exports. When the yuan is undervalued, PRC exports are less expensive to U.S. customers. Simply put, U.S. consumers don't have to put up as many of their dollars when they want to purchase Chinese goods. This stimulates the expansion of Chinese export industries and enables the PRC to accumulate U.S. dollar currency reserves.

International economic life can be complicated, however. When the PRC artificially reduced the value of its yuan currency, it actually subsi-dized U.S. consumption and lowered the standard of living of Chinese citizens. How so? The low value of the yuan causes Americans who walk the aisles of such outlets as Best Buy, Wal-Mart, and Nordstrom's (all of which sell many goods imported from the PRC) to find attractive, low prices that give them the urge to buy. Suppose the yuan is undervalued by 25 percent. Then, if nothing else changes, this means that the price tags on Chinese goods at the local Wal-Mart are 25 percent lower than they would be if the yuan were being valued in freely operating foreign exchange markets.

The end result of the PRC currency controls is that the Chinese sell more goods to U.S. customers, but at lower prices. This quite likely trans-lates into lower wage rates for the workers who produce these goods, unless they can also somehow increase their productivity by the same 25 percent that the yuan is undervalued. In the jargon of economics, the eco-nomic value of what Chinese workers produce (their "marginal revenue products") is reduced because these items are being sold for 25 percent less in the United States.

This underlines that the Chinese government faces a tradeoff—it can increase employment in export-oriented industries with an artificially cheap yuan, but this will come at the cost of lower worker wages. The PRC government has made its choice—it has decided to expand production and employment in its export-oriented industries, albeit at the cost of lower wages being paid to its workers.

Almost needless to say, Americans like low prices because low prices increase our standard of living. The reality is that, for years, we have been

> **"In the past decade, China arguably enabled an American boom.** Low-cost Chinese goods helped keep a lid on inflation, while the flood of Chinese investment helped the U.S. government finance mortgages and a public debt of close to $11 trillion" (Landler, 2008). Hence, a portion of the boom in foreign purchases of U.S. assets was facilitated by a symbiotic financial relationship between China and the United States.
>
> Source: Mark Landler, "Dollar Shift: Chinese Pockets Filled as Americans' Emptied," *New York Times* (December 26, 2008).

buying billions of dollars of Chinese goods. In the second quarter of 2008, the United States imported $97.16 billion of goods and services from the PRC, while exporting only $24.93 billion to the PRC.

Okay, the Chinese have been subsidizing our consumption by offering us artificially low prices. Nevertheless, they aren't dumb. They must be receiving benefits from this arrangement. What are they? Well, for one, employment has risen in China's export-related industries. This may enable the Chinese to realize economies of scale in production and reduce their costs even further.

Furthermore, every time the PRC cash register rings and it sells items to foreign countries, it accumulates dollars, euros, pounds, and other foreign currencies. The *Wall Street Journal* estimated that, in early 2009, China had accumulated $1.9 trillion dollars in foreign currency reserves (see Table 2-1). That's quite a stash, and it gives the PRC a great deal of freedom. The Chinese government can use these reserves to purchase U.S.

Table 2-1   Largest Foreign Exchange Holdings by Country, 2008–2009

Country	Reserves (in billions of U.S. dollars)
China (PRC)	$1,900
Japan	$740
Russia	$433
Taiwan	$175
Kuwait	$175
India	$152
Brazil	$123
Algeria	$108

Source: "Who Has the Money?" *Economist*, 389 (October 13, 2008), 26 and *Wall Street Journal*, 253 (February 20, 2009), A8.

government debt (and it has done so in large amounts). It could also purchase other U.S. assets (equities ownership in U.S. firms or entire firms, such as GSP, an auto parts manufacturer in South Carolina), purchase technology and selected military hardware from foreign countries, or parcel out foreign aid to developing countries (especially in Africa) that it wishes to influence. The bottom line is that this huge bank account of foreign exchange reserves makes China a powerful international player. Any future international monetary or financial conference that doesn't include the PRC would be equivalent to an attempt to ignore the proverbial 10-ton gorilla lurking in the corner of the room. It's no longer possible to have an intelligent international financial discussion without including the Chinese.

China has become a creditor country because of its policies. Creditor countries wield vastly increased clout in international circles. A country such as the United States cannot now contemplate any major action involving international trade without taking the Chinese into account. What's more, the PRC influence may go beyond international trade. Domestic U.S. policy decisions (for example, whether the United States should run a higher federal deficit in order to straighten out its financial system) must now take the Chinese into account. Will the PRC purchase additional U.S. government debt or not?

In any case, the decision of the PRC to undervalue its currency as a means to build its export-oriented industries and currency reserves has an impact on its own citizens. The irony is delicious to some. The "People's" Republic has coldly chosen to exploit many of its own citizens—its workers—and to subsidize U.S. consumption in order to achieve a set of economic growth-oriented national goals. In the long run, this may well redound to the benefit of most Chinese citizens. In the interim, however, the typical Chinese worker probably unknowingly subsidizes U.S. consumers by working for a lower wage rate, although this worker and many others may occupy international trade-oriented jobs that otherwise might not exist.

How China chooses to use its foreign exchange bounty is a concern to many. Senator James Webb of Virginia has warned, "While foreign governments may invest money in a country to make a profit, they may also do so in order to further their foreign policy ambitions, to acquire national security assets, or to purchase a stake in strategic industries."[2] Even so, as we noted in the previous chapter, the actual behavior of foreign governments and sovereign wealth funds that have invested in the United States has been more benign. Indeed, rather than being a bad actor after accumulating U.S. dollars, the reverse may be true. China has invested large slices of its foreign exchange reserves in U.S. firms and U.S. government

Would an appreciation of the yuan really make Americans better off?

The Congressional Research Service estimated in early 2008 that the PRC yuan is undervalued by 15 to 40 percent. In February 2009, the yuan traded at 6.83 per U.S. dollar. If the Congressional Research Service was on target, this suggests it would be trading between 5.81 and 4.10 per U.S. dollar if its price were not controlled by the PRC government. Many elected officials and leaders of business firms have demanded that such an adjustment take place immediately ("let the yuan float freely"), believing that this will reduce Chinese exports to the United States and stimulate U.S. exports to China. Events might play out this way, but it is more likely that the shelf space of the Chinese in U.S. stores would quickly be taken by other low-priced competitors (think Taiwan, Malaysia, Thailand, etc.). The current problems with the U.S. account balance of payments go far beyond the question of the PRC.

debt; however, most of these investments have turned out badly for the PRC because of the lethal combination of a weakening U.S. dollar and falling U.S. equity prices. The PRC might legitimately view itself as a semi-helpless victim of unwise U.S. banking and financial policies that eventually precipitated the financial crisis of the fall of 2008. If America has been

The PRC was badly burned by the falling value of the U.S. dollar over most of this decade

Firms in other countries, observing this, decided to bet against the dollar, assuming it would continue to fall. Alas, nothing is entirely predictable in the realm of foreign exchange rates. When the U.S. dollar reversed course and began to increase in value beginning in mid-2008, CITIC Pacific of Hong Kong lost $1.89 trillion as a result of its currency trading. Comercial Mexicana lost $1.4 trillion, and Grupo Votorantim of Brazil forfeited $1.04 trillion. If nothing else, this demonstrates that nothing is forever where foreign exchange rates are concerned. This, in turn, underlines that the "America for Sale" phenomenon was not destined to become a permanent feature of U.S. economic life.

on sale to the Chinese and other foreigners, many foreigners now wish that they had turned a deaf ear to these seductive possibilities and even put their money in a mattress. Had they done so, they would now be better off.

The U.S. Dollar as the Global Reserve Currency

Notwithstanding its recovery during the first months of the global financial crisis, the value of the U.S. dollar at the end of 2008 was generally lower with respect to major currencies than it was five years previously. Table 2-2 summarizes the evidence for six major currencies: the yen, the euro, the pound, the Australian dollar, the Canadian dollar, and the yuan.

Despite the sometimes atrocious performance of the U.S. dollar in the area of value maintenance, it remains the world's major reserve currency. Figure 2-4 reveals that 62.5 percent of the world's currency reserves were held in U.S. dollars in the second quarter of 2008. The euro accounted for a respectable 27.0 percent of global currency reserves, and no other national currency exceeded a 5-percent share.

Those who have held dollars have typically realized significant negative rates of return for their efforts. The combination of the falling value of the dollar, relative to most major currencies, and price inflation have eaten away at the real value of any returns they might have realized. Nevertheless, in 2007, foreigners invested approximately $2 trillion in U.S. assets of all kinds, including U.S. government debt. Parenthetically, we note that this helped the United States finance its huge current account deficit of $730 billion in 2007. The U.S. continues to import far more than it exports.

Table 2-2   Value of the U.S. Dollar versus Six Major Currencies, January 1, 2004, and February 16, 2009

	One U.S. Dollar Trades for	
Currency	Currency Units, 1/1/04	Currency Units, 1/16/09
Yen	117	91.73
Euro	1.00	0.7825
Pound	0.64	0.7006
Australian dollar	1.78	1.5406
Canadian dollar	1.56	1.2441
Yuan	8.3	6.8254

Source: Exchange Rates, Federal Reserve Bank of St. Louis, Economic Data—FRED®, January 2009, http://research.stlouisfed.org/fred2/categories/15/downloaddata.

Figure 2-4 Global Allocated Reserves by Currency, Q2 2008, % of Total

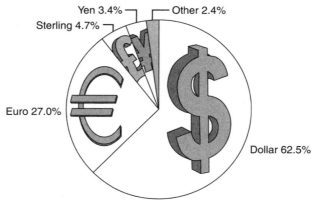

Yen 3.4% ⌐   ⌐ Other 2.4%

Sterling 4.7% ⌐

Euro 27.0%

Dollar 62.5%

Total Reserves = $4.4 Trillion

Source: Adapted from "Buck Up," *Economist,* 389 (October 4, 2008), 84.

Why do foreigners continue to invest heavily in U.S. assets, even though they have been burned consistently by such investments during this decade? The answer is this behavior represents a flight to safety and security. In an uncertain world wracked by financial disruption and upheaval, U.S. assets, after all, may still constitute the safest bet. Iceland may teeter on bankruptcy, but not the United States, or so goes this argument. International investors believe that the U.S. government, unlike that of Argentina, is not going to default on its debt and that the U.S. economy remains the largest and, by some measures, the most productive in the world. No other country can match the United States in this regard. True, the PRC and India are growing much faster, but, during the financial crisis of the fall of 2008, equity prices in those countries fell substantially more than in the United States. By default, the United States has been the best place to put one's money and to attempt to preserve capital. U.S. safety has been on sale, and there have been many international buyers.

There are those who dispute this interpretation for a variety of reasons, although it is frequently cited in the popular press and among many economists. At least as important as the perceived safety associated with foreign investments in the United States is what the *Economist* has labeled "the size, liquidity, efficiency and transparency" of U.S. financial markets.[3] U.S. financial markets, including especially U.S. government debt markets, are huge and generally "thick," in the sense that many transactions occur daily. They tend not to be dominated by small numbers of sellers and buyers, and they tend not to be dogged by corruption. Furthermore, large proportions of most classes of U.S. assets (and, once again, especially U.S. government debt) are highly liquid and can be converted into cash at a moment's notice.

Pricing and sales information about U.S. government debt instruments is easily available, and one can purchase a wide variety of such debt over the Internet. This means that transaction costs in U.S. financial markets are generally minimal compared to what one encounters in the financial markets of many other countries. Finally, relatively speaking, political authorities tend to keep their hands off U.S. financial markets, except for emergencies and conspicuous displays of malfeasance or dishonesty. There is no equivalent to Vladimir Putin or Hugo Chávez in the United States. All in all, markets for U.S. government debt are "efficient," as economists use the term. They are paragons compared to many other financial markets worldwide.

To the surprise of some, the worldwide financial calamities of the fall of 2008 therefore actually redounded sometimes to the benefit of the United States. All things considered, large numbers of investors, including foreign governments, still considered the United States to be the safest and most secure place to invest their funds. U.S. government bond prices rose because there was a surge of buying. This was a welcome turn of events for such countries as China and Japan, because those countries hold large amounts of U.S. government debt. This counteracted (but only partially) the diminution of value in the U.S. government debt holdings that they have suffered over the past few years because of the decline in the value of the U.S. dollar.

Nothing is forever, however, and a variety of factors could change this picture. In particular, if the United States fails to deal successfully with its financial market challenges, foreign investors will progressively desert the country and invest their funds elsewhere. Furthermore, even successful actions by the United States to combat the financial crisis will result in large increases in U.S. government debt. In the long run, this will depress the value of the U.S. dollar, as markets are flooded with federal debt issued in order to pay for sundry financial bailouts. As the Moroccan street urchin quoted at the beginning of this chapter says, this will tempt individuals worldwide to reject the U.S. dollar in favor of other currencies. Clearly, the euro is the major alternative, although recently the Japanese yen has increased in value because it has been viewed by some as another safe harbor in the middle of a worldwide financial storm. Some even believe that the Chinese yuan will become an international reserve currency.

Even if the United States deals with its financial challenges successfully, this could result in declining value for the U.S. dollar. During the financial crisis of the fall of 2008, many international investors fled to the U.S. dollar and to U.S. government securities because they perceived that they were safe. To the extent financial markets stabilize, the needs of investors for safety and security decline. Other things held constant, this would cause them to reduce their holdings of U.S. dollars.

Secretary of State Hillary Clinton as Bond Salesperson

On Secretary Clinton's first trip abroad, she urged the People's Republic of China "to continue buying U.S. Treasuries." Said Mrs. Clinton, "We have to incur more debt. It would not be in China's interest if we were unable to get our economy moving again." Press reports indicated that the Chinese were noncommittal.

Source: "Clinton Wraps Asia Trip by Asking China to Buy U.S. Debt." http://www.breitbart.com/article.php?id=CNG.42a44b0f5d9cf5c9762e80574e79a3d5.831&show_article=1.

Ultimately, it is the interaction of demand and supply that determines the value of the U.S. dollar with respect to other currencies. The Federal Reserve System pumped enormous additional liquidity into financial markets as a part of its financial recovery plan in the fall of 2008. As one wag put it at the time, "The Fed is basically dropping dollars from helicopters."[4] This increase in the supply of dollars, coupled with rock-bottom interest rates in the United States that discourage investment in assets denominated in U.S. dollars, will ultimately have predictable effects. It will push down the value of the dollar with respect to that of most other currencies.

This dollar-diminishing phenomenon was already in evidence in December 2008, as Figure 2-5 illustrates. In the second half of 2008, the Federal Reserve doubled the size of the monetary base (which is roughly composed of bank reserves plus currency).

If the time-worn but durable equation of $MV = PQ$ continues to obtain, then a virtual doubling of the money supply (M) will generate considerable price inflation (P), unless V (the velocity of money) decreases dramatically or Q (output) increases by leaps and bounds. The most likely outcome—unless the Fed is very clever, has exquisite timing, and can deal effectively with the political obstacles associated with tight money—is price inflation reminiscent of the early 1980s (annual rates of 10 percent or more). This will feed a sharp decline in the value of the U.S. dollar, which will respond to conventional supply and demand influences.

No one really knows how low the value of the U.S. dollar will have to go before large holders of dollars, such as the PRC and Japan, jump overboard and either sell their dollar reserves actively or seriously reduce their intake of the currency. A tipping point may exist, but no one really knows where

Figure 2-5 The Monetary Base Increases, Fall 2008

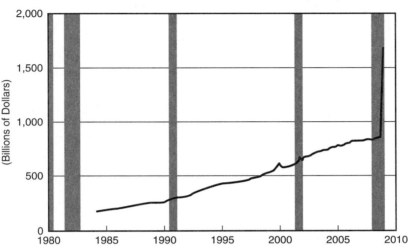

Shaded areas indicate US recessions as determined by the National Bureau of Economic Research.
Source: 2008 Federal Reserve Bank of St. Louis: research.stlouisfed.org

that point is. Given a sufficient decline in the value of the U.S. dollar, China and Japan (and other international holders of dollars) could decide to take decisive action. Nonetheless, in light of the potential of China and Japan to shoot themselves in their own feet if they reduce their dollar holdings actively, the most likely scenario is a more gradual reduction in their dollar holdings, accompanied by an augmentation of their holdings of other currencies, such as the euro.

The "Yen Carry Trade" also has been responsible for some of the increased value of the Japanese yen. For many years, interest rates in Japan have been below those in most other countries. This encouraged international investors to borrow funds there and then invest those funds in other countries, such as the United States, where rates of return have been higher. This had the dual effect of pumping up the value of the yen and increasing the demand for U.S. government debt, which offered safety and, often, higher rates of return.

If economic disaster for the United States means "failing to deal successfully with the financial market challenges caused by the 2008 financial crisis" and this results in a refusal of the Chinese to buy our debt and in a major, sustained run against the dollar, what other effects will we see?

Suppose owners of U.S. government debt (but especially the PRC) dump their holdings of that debt. Higher interest rates will result almost immediately, as the U.S. government finds it impossible to sell its debt instruments without raising its rates of return. Interest rates inside the United States will rise on everything from home mortgages to college loans and credit cards. The Federal Reserve System might well attempt to ameliorate this effect by increasing the money supply, loosening credit, and actively supporting U.S. government bond market sales. Indeed, in order to finance the U.S. government deficits associated with the recovery plan, the Fed might be forced to make significant increases in the money supply. If so, then price inflation almost surely will result. This might in turn cause the Congress to conclude that it is necessary to raise taxes in order to pay for expenditures that would previously have been paid for by issuing debt. At the end of the day, a scenario in which foreign countries shed U.S. government debt would not be a happy one and likely would result in a contraction in U.S. economic activity, price inflation, or both.

All things considered, the "dump U.S. government debt" scenario we have just painted seems unlikely because of the harm it would impose on such countries as China and Japan if they began to reduce their holdings of U.S. government debt. Figuratively, they would be spitting into the wind and would pay a high price for their actions. The value of all dollar-denominated assets they held would likely decline substantially, including their remaining holdings of U.S. government debt.

Even so, we should bear in mind that the PRC government has demonstrated many times over the decade that it is willing to incur huge financial and human costs in order to obtain an objective that might be political or symbolic. Only a fool would discount the PRC's ability to bear pain should it decide that the U.S. dollar's ride on the proverbial merry-go-round is going to come to an end. The same assessment does not apply to the Japanese.

In any case, in early 2009, the value of the U.S. dollar recovered with respect to nearly all currencies except the Japanese yen. A "we're getting out and heading for the door" scenario with respect to U.S. government debt does not appear to be imminent. Whatever problems that U.S. economy and financial system were perceived to have had in the fall of 2008, the United States was still perceived as the best place to park funds until the economic storm abated. Insofar as the Chinese and Japanese are concerned, U.S. government debt remains on sale.

Nevertheless, we would be well advised to take the same long-term view that the Chinese and Japanese have taken. If the United States wishes to avoid a "we're getting out and heading for the door" situation, then it must increase its relatively low savings rate and shore up the dollar. Few dispute the judgment that the United States saves less than most industrial countries and substantially less than it should if it wishes to expand its capital stock. The U.S. Department of Commerce reported that the nation's personal savings rate was −1.0 percent in 2006, the lowest in 73 years.[5] Contrast this to savings rates between 12 and 15 percent in countries such as Japan, Germany, and France and to the U.S. rate of approximately 12 percent in 1976. True, arguments exist about the appropriate way to measure national savings rates, for example, whether capital gains and losses should be factored in when savings rates are computed. Nevertheless, virtually no one disputes the judgment that the U.S. savings rate is among the lowest in the developed world.

The intrusion of the U.S. government in the fall of 2008 into U.S. financial markets represented a departure by the U.S. government from its historical stance of only moderate involvement in such markets. In this case, however, it was taken by most observers as positive because it was seen as restoring order and transparency to financial markets that were bedeviled by lack of information about the scale and risk associated with subprime mortgages, financial derivatives, and credit default swaps. This intervention only increased the attractiveness of U.S. government debt and supported the *Economist*'s observation concerning the liquidity, efficiency, and transparency of U.S. financial asset markets.

Rising house and equity prices in the United States are among the reasons why the country's measured personal savings rates have been so low. Many home owners found it irresistible not to extract funds from their houses and spend the proceeds. Between 2002 and 2006, U.S. home owners used second mortgages and other techniques to reduce the value of their home equity by an average of 7 percent of their disposable incomes. Home owners treated the increasing value of their homes as the conceptual equivalent of an ATM from which they could make withdrawals. Not surprisingly, nationally declining housing prices in 2007 put a serious crimp in this behavior, and, by 2008, equity withdrawals had declined to approximately 2 percent of household disposable incomes.

The uncomfortable and almost unavoidable verdict is that the United States has consistently been spending more than it has earned for many decades. U.S. government debt (including agencies) has tripled in the past two decades and now exceeds 70 percent of U.S. GDP. This percentage will climb rapidly as the U.S. government's financial rescue plan ($1 trillion plus) of 2008 is implemented and the U.S. economy stagnates in the middle of a recession.

Still, as we have seen, it is not simply government that has exceeded its means. Household debt has doubled in less than a decade and now approximates the value of GDP. The proportion of household income spent on debt service payments rose from 15.90 percent in the first quarter of 1980 to 18.83 percent in the second quarter of 2008 (see Table 2-3). Thus, U.S. households not only are incurring more total debt, but also obligating a greater proportion of their incomes to servicing their debts.

Although there are many ways to rationalize these circumstances, it is difficult to avoid the conclusion that, collectively, Americans have been living beyond their means. The brutal truth is that foreigners have been subsidizing excessive U.S. consumption for many years. One means by which they have been doing so is by purchasing U.S. assets.

Does Dollar Depreciation Spur Foreign Direct Investment?

The first choice of most firms is to produce their product in their home country and subsequently export that product abroad. However, if transport costs are high, trade barriers exist, or there are political and perceptual advantages to producing abroad, then firms may decide it is less expensive to develop production facilities in foreign locations. This has been a major impetus for Japanese firms to open foreign automobile production facilities inside the United States.

A "cheap" dollar can have a similar effect. When the dollar falls in value relative to a currency such as the Japanese yen, it becomes increasingly expensive for the Japanese to export goods to the United States. Simply put, if Americans are accustomed to supplying only $75 in order to purchase a Japanese camera priced at 10,000 yen but a deteriorating exchange rate raises that price to $100, then this will discourage Americans from purchasing that camera. In such a situation, falling camera sales could convince the Japanese that it makes more sense to open a camera production

Table 2-3   Proportion of Household Income Devoted to Servicing Debts

Year	Percentage
1980, 1Q	15.90%
1990, 1Q	17.29%
2000, 1Q	17.62%
2008, 2Q	18.83%

Source: The Federal Reserve Board, Household Debt Service and Financial Obligations Ratios, September 22, 2008, http://www.federalreserve.gov/releases/housedebt.

facility inside the United States so that they no longer have to deal with the adverse exchange rate problem.

Foreign direct investment (FDI) inside the United States appears to be sensitive to broad swings in exchange rates. This enables the foreign investors to avoid many of the problems associated with a long-term decline in the value of the U.S. dollar.

II. FALLING U.S. ASSET VALUES

An important part of the "America for Sale" story is the falling value of many U.S. assets, independent of foreign exchange rates. In a period of approximately 18 months that began in early 2007, the NASDAQ stock index lost more than 40 percent of its value. The Standard and Poor's 500 Stock Index matched that decline. Even if the value of the U.S. dollar had not been deteriorating, these reduced equity values made the United States increasingly attractive to foreign investors.

Falling equity prices in the United States stimulated foreign interest in a wide variety of U.S. assets, not just the banks and financial institutions we already have noted. In the eyes of many foreign investors, they could acquire productive capacity less expensively in the United States than they could in their home countries. As an Indian financial group interested in purchasing U.S. coal producers put it, "It's a buyer's market."[6]

A Special Case of Declining U.S. Asset Prices: The U.S. Housing Market Imbroglio

Declining residential housing and commercial property prices have made U.S. real estate increasingly attractive to foreign investors. Some foreigners (especially Canadians, Britons, and Germans) have acquired residential properties, often for vacation purposes. The National Association of Realtors reported that 7.3 percent of all home sales in Florida in the spring of 2007 were made to foreigners.

Other foreign real estate buyers (especially those from the Middle East) have focused upon commercial properties. Intertwined in these activities has been the crisis in the U.S. residential housing market. This predicament has had profound effects on both U.S. asset values and world financial health. It is worthy of discussion because of its impact upon the "America for Sale" phenomenon.

The housing portion of the financial crisis in the United States is appropriately viewed as a single, but very significant, chapter in a longer book whose overarching theme is overconsumption. Lenders (some predatory, but not the majority) sold home mortgages to some individuals who had no realistic chance of servicing their mortgage over time because their scheduled mortgage payments clearly exceeded their ability to pay. However, if housing prices continued to climb, they could flip these properties and sell them for a profit. Or, they could extract some of that increased housing value and spend it while continuing to live in the home.

Using hindsight, it is easy now to conclude that many new U.S. mortgage recipients simply did not have the income necessary to support their mortgage payments. More than a few were "Ninja" borrowers: no income, no job, no assets. They were among those home buyers who caused the proportion of subprime mortgages among all new mortgages to skyrocket from approximately 2 percent to 30 percent in a single decade.

During the early part of this decade, the only way many subprime mortgage borrowers could purchase a home was via a subprime mortgage that usually involved extremely low down payments and an adjustable mortgage rate. Low down payments and "interest only, option ARM" mortgage payments guaranteed that most subprime borrowers had little actual equity in the homes they purchased. When the housing bubble began to deflate in the United States, many of these individuals found themselves "under water," financially speaking. Their homes were worth less than the amount of their mortgage. In the first quarter of 2009, fully 21.9 percent of all mortgage holders were "underwater." This perilous situation was aggravated when these home owners' mortgage rates began to adjust, that is, to increase above the attractive "teaser" rates that they paid when they purchased the home. It was not uncommon for subprime mortgage recipients to find that their mortgage rate had doubled.

What we are describing are instances of "America for Sale," yet these are ones that are clearly differentiated. The overwhelming majority of subprime home buyers were Americans, not foreigners. But, like foreigners purchasing U.S. firms at what they perceived to be bargain-basement prices, many subprime mortgage recipients were sucked in by "little or no money down, low teaser mortgage rate" offers. The proportion of Americans owning their own home (or, at least, having a mortgage on a home) rose by approximately 10 percent in less than a decade. Viewed retrospectively, we can say this was an unwise and overly generous development. It contributed to the financial crisis that burst upon the United States and the world in October 2008.

Dancing in the background of this tragedy were elected political figures who strongly encouraged the lowering of mortgage standards in order to stimulate home ownership. Two of their primary tools in this regard were Fannie Mae (the Federal National Mortgage Association) and Freddie Mac (the Federal Home Loan Mortgage Corporation), both of which are stock-holder-owned corporations.

The fact that Fannie and Freddie have stockholders makes it sound as if they are ordinary, private corporations. However, Fannie Mae and Freddie Mac are hardly commonplace private firms, because they also are "government-sponsored" enterprises. Until recently, the precise meaning of government sponsorship had never been tested, although it was interpreted by most to mean that the U.S. government would stand behind Fannie Mae and Freddie Mac and prevent their default in times of crisis. In fact, no such U.S. government guarantee existed, but even those who knew the truth believed the two organizations were too big to be allowed to fail and therefore were effectively backed by the U.S. government. Nobel Prize-winning economist Vernon Smith termed this an "implicit government guarantee."[7]

In 1999, Fannie Mae in particular came under strong financial pressure from President Clinton and a variety of members of Congress to reduce the standards that it had set for purchasing mortgages from lenders. The laudable aim, and one that was supported by many, was to encourage more lending to moderate- and low-income U.S. households that wished to purchase their own home. There also was pressure from stockholders who wanted Fannie Mae to maintain its profitability. Fannie Mae grew receptive because it believed that its higher standards were simply pushing mortgage business in the direction of private firms that had already adopted less demanding standards. Unfortunately, the lower standards created a slippery slope that would lead to disastrous consequences in housing markets.

The lower standards enabled Fannie Mae and Freddie Mac to become highly leveraged and, by mid-2008, together they guaranteed approximately one-half of the $12 trillion mortgage market in the United States. The usual Federal Deposit Insurance Corporation (FDIC) requirement is that each one of its banks should hold capital equal to at least 3 percent of its outstanding obligations. This implies a maximum 33:1 leverage ratio. Fannie Mae and Freddie Mac, however, were not subject to this restriction and sported leverage ratios of 50:1 and 60:1. Furthermore, Fannie Mae and Freddie Mac were exempt from Securities and Exchange filing requirements, and so the actual extent of their leverage was not immediately apparent to many.

Even so, a variety of economists and political figures waved red flags above Fannie Mae and Freddie Mac and did so well before they crashed in financial flames in the summer of 2008. Nassim Taleb, who has achieved fame for his notion of "Black Swans" and how we deal with events that we believe to be highly unlikely, bluntly observed, "The government-sponsored institution Fannie Mae, when I look at its risks, seems to be sitting on a barrel of dynamite, vulnerable to the slightest hiccup. But not to worry: their large staff of scientists deem these events 'unlikely.'"[8]

In fact, on September 7, 2008, Fannie Mae and Freddie Mac were placed "under the conservatorship" of the Federal Housing Finance Agency (FHFA) and their major executives and boards of directors were dismissed, because both organizations were approaching bankruptcy. Falling housing prices and an increasing number of mortgage foreclosures had reduced the capital of Fannie Mae and Freddie Mac to alarmingly low levels. The U.S. government, via the FHFA, took ownership of 79.9 percent of both Fannie Mae and Freddie Mac by means of both preferred and common stock holdings.

Nevertheless, Fannie Mae and Freddie Mac were not the only villains in this picture. There were several other participants that we would label unindicted co-conspirators if we were in a courtroom. A variety of large financial institutions developed new and complex financial instruments to sell investors large mortgage packages containing various proportions of subprime mortgages. Investors who purchased these new asset combinations not only included other large financial institutions, but also public pension funds, business firms, and even some universities. All participated eagerly in order to gain some "alpha," or return above market averages. The new financial instruments, usually financial derivatives whose value was based upon the value of other securities or magnitudes, were often remarkably opaque in terms of failing to reveal the mixture of mortgages and assets contained within them. In July 2008, $530 trillion of these financial derivatives existed.

Because no regulatory financial reporting was required, little was known about the new financial derivative packages. What resulted was a world of very low transparency, truly a dark corner understood by remarkably few individuals. Nevertheless, considerable risk was attached to these tranches, but the record now demonstrates that this risk was consistently underpriced (underestimated).

It is fair to say that many of the large, institutional purchasers of these new financial mixtures, despite having in their employ hundreds of smart MBAs from elite institutions, did not fully comprehend what they were purchasing or the risks involved. Nor did the firms selling them these new financial assets always engage in full disclosure and call their attention to the contents of the potentially poisonous packages they were selling. These are among the reasons why risk was not identified accurately and the actual risk was underpriced.

Parenthetically, we should observe that, after the financial implosion of October 2008, the reverse occurred. Badly burned investors drew in their horns and seemingly overemphasized the actual risks attached to many assets. Because many investors and financial institutions either could not identify the risks involved or did not fully understand the risks that they knew existed, they decided to withdraw their funds in favor of very low risk, easily understood assets such as U.S. government inflation-protected bonds (TIPS).

Retrospectively, we can say regulators largely did not react to the new ways of packaging financial risk. Whether or not "sleeping at the switch" is the appropriate metaphor to apply to this situation, most regulators did relatively little to probe what was going on and even less to inform investors. No *caveat emptor* advisories were issued, and, even in mid-2009, some of the institutions that purchased opaque asset tranches were attempting to figure out the value of what they actually own. For example, what is a package of 100 defaulted residential housing mortgages worth? Is it 25 percent of the value of the mortgages? Or is it 75 percent? Or is it somewhere in between? The lack of information (and sometimes even basic documentation) about these mortgages makes them difficult to evaluate.

It is easy to skewer regulators who did not pay sufficient attention. One reason that regulators are such an inviting target is that the current structure of financial regulation in the United States is a veritable alphabet soup of agencies that appear to overlap and, even at times, compete with each other. Relevant financial regulators include the Federal Reserve, the Securities and Exchange Commission, the FDIC, the Comptroller of the Currency, the Office of Thrift Supervision, the Commodities Future Trading Commission, the Financial Industry Regulatory Authority, plus agencies in the 50 states (although New York provides an example in which state regulation is hardly *pro forma*).

Who is (or should have been) responsible for the rapidly developing market in financial derivatives? Should one of these agencies have assumed responsibility for regulating the risk levels assumed by Fannie Mae and Freddie Mac? Did the Federal Reserve System really have the authority in the fall of 2008 to insist that nine large banks grant stock in their banks to the Fed in return for an injection of capital? Most economists agree that it was a good idea for the Fed to take this action, but it is difficult to point to any statute that gives the Fed that specific authority.

Regulatory reform is obviously needed, although less in the sense of prohibiting financial institutions from ever undertaking certain activities and more in terms of providing badly needed transparency to their actions. Everyone, including foreign investors, would benefit immensely from more and better information. In addition, the confusing authorities and relationships among the financial regulatory bodies previously noted must be clarified. It is plausible that a smaller number of regulatory agencies with broader but clearly defined authorities would serve the public better.

If America has been for sale, then those buying and selling have been proceeding in a state of relative ignorance on occasion. In particular, the absence of transparency relating to newer financial instruments has made it difficult for buyers and sellers to negotiate intelligently. Were some U.S. financial assets purchased because the buyers were fundamentally ignorant about what they were buying? Almost certainly.

Did foreigners understand that virtually no documentation existed to back up as many as one-quarter of the subprime mortgages that were granted in recent years? Almost surely they did not. The fact that foreign purchasers were not aware of what they were buying reflects both their own failures to undertake due diligence and the often deliberate obfuscation of the situation by U.S. asset sellers.

Retrospectively, the substantial investments foreigners made in some U.S. financial institutions (several of which went bankrupt) made sense only if the purchasers did not understand what they were buying. Foreigners thought they were purchasing stakes in some of the world's most prestigious financial institutions, but in fact they were acquiring a memorable pig in the poke.

The relative ignorance of those who purchased financial packages (tranches) containing potentially toxic mortgages existed because many relied upon the ratings assigned these packages by ratings agencies such as Standard and Poor's and Moody's. Both agencies assigned unrealistically high ratings to many bonds and financial packages. Many believe that Standard and Poor's and Moody's failed to undertake full due diligence in assessing the risk attached to the tranches of new financial assets they were now seeing in large numbers.

Regardless, in most asset markets, it is possible to hedge one's risks by means of futures markets contracts, or by means of insurance. The primary insurer of the new financial instruments—containing potentially lethal proportions of toxic, nonperforming mortgages—was and is American International Group (AIG). The largest insurance company in the world in early 2008, AIG also was the 18th largest company in the world. The London office of AIG sold "credit default swap" insurance to many firms that had purchased tranches (often termed "collateralized debt obligations") containing subprime mortgages. When the value of the tranches went south because of falling housing prices and mortgage foreclosures, AIG found itself under siege.

A particularly stunning blow to AIG was the failure of Lehman Brothers, which the U.S. government refused to rescue. Its share price plummeted from $70.13 to $1.25 on September 16, 2008. Using hindsight, many observers argued that the failure of the Fed to rescue Lehman Brothers led directly to the unraveling of world financial markets in October 2008. The decision not to rescue Lehman Brothers was a judgment call, made primarily by Henry Paulson, the Secretary of the Treasury. It is a decision that will be bandied about for many years to come.

On the same day that Lehman Brothers was allowed to fall, the Fed took decisive action to create a credit line of $85 billion for AIG so that AIG could meet its financial obligations. However, the Fed took 79.9 percent ownership in AIG and required an interest rate on its loan of the three-month LIBOR (the London Interbank Offered Rate, which represents the rate at which banks loan to each other) plus 8.5 percent. Thus, AIG faced an interest rate of about 11 percent. Maurice Greenberg, the former CEO of AIG, complained that this constituted a nationalization of AIG, but AIG had little choice in the matter.[9]

Even the $85 billion line of credit proved insufficient for AIG, however, and, by the end of October 2008, the U.S. government had extended $123 billion in aid to AIG. However, the depth and severity of AIG's financial problems appeared to be larger than originally forecast, and, in November 2008, a new $150 billion deal was struck with the company that lengthened the term of AIG's loan but lowered the interest rates AIG would pay on that loan. As a part of this agreement, the U.S. government injected $40 billion of new capital into AIG, in return for preferred stock shares that carry annual interest (dividend) payments of 10 percent. The terms of the new deal are more favorable to AIG, but they also come much closer to the outright nationalization of AIG.

One of the U.S. government's most public responses to the grief in the fall of 2008 was to inject up to $250 billion of new capital into the nation's largest banks in return for partial government ownership. The primary intent was to stimulate the banks to make more loans, although the initial reaction of many of the recipients was to use the funds to shore up their balance sheets and, in some cases, to make bids for other struggling banks rather than to make loans. Excess bank reserves (those non-interest-bearing funds held by the Fed over and above those funds required to back banks' loans) skyrocketed, signaling banks' reluctance to make loans, even to each other. This exacerbated difficult credit conditions.

Meanwhile, the U.S. government also embarked on a campaign to deal with troubled mortgages already in existence. One part of this program involved renegotiating the terms of troubled mortgages so that individual home owners would not have to abandon their homes. In general, this activity resulted in lower mortgage interest rates being paid by home owners and stretching out repayment over a larger number of years. The other part of the program involved limited efforts to purchase toxic, defaulted mortgages from financial institutions. This forced the Fed to make an unprecedented set of discretionary financial judgments: first, about whose toxic mortgages should be purchased (if at all), and second, about the price that should be paid for these mortgages. Were they worth nothing, 25 percent of their original face value, 75 percent, or some value in between? The financial discretion exercised by the Fed in this regard was virtually unprecedented in the history of the United States, because the Fed's decisions resulted in financial life and death for banks, individuals, and foreign investors.

It is those foreign investors that immediately concern us here. The Fed's rescue activities necessarily benefited some foreign investors, either because their assets were purchased or saved or because the Fed's actions improved general market conditions and therefore made their assets more valuable. What could have been an unmitigated and total financial disaster for foreign investors (including several sovereign wealth funds) was ameliorated by the Fed's activities. This did not go unremarked, because U.S. taxpayers were footing the bill. The arguments for undertaking financial rescue actions that coincidentally helped foreign investors were several. First, financial markets today are highly international in scope. The day when only Americans owned U.S. financial assets has long passed. As noted previously, foreigners own approximately one-half of the public U.S. government debt (the debt not owned by the U.S. government to itself). Failure to recognize this would almost inevitably result in a financial meltdown. Second, discrimination against foreign investors would result in their withdrawing funds and would severely damage numerous U.S. banks and firms. Third, helping foreign investors would in fact also help U.S. investors. The best way for U.S. taxpayers to obtain the most bang for their bucks was (and is) to reestablish and maintain orderly, secure financial markets in the United States. Like it or not, foreigners constitute a vital part of that equation.

Nevertheless, there is little question but that numerous foreign investors were badly singed by the financial fires of October 2008, both in the United States and worldwide. Particularly hard-hit were foreign sovereign wealth funds that invested billions of dollars in such financial firms as Lehman Brothers and Merrill Lynch. Singapore's Temasek, for example, invested more than $6 billion in Merrill Lynch; sovereign wealth funds from Kuwait and Korea invested more than $5 billion. Merrill Lynch's shotgun marriage with Bank of America caused the value of these investments to drop like a cannon ball falling off the Empire State Building.

This was a sobering lesson for foreign investors, yet the results confirmed the findings of previous studies: over the long term, foreigners investing in the United States have generally earned lower rates of return on their investments than similarly situated U.S. firms. Speaking internationally, multinational firms tend to outperform local firms when the local political and economic situation is volatile and insecure. In such circumstances, viable local competitors may not exist, and multinational firms are able to use their greater experience and assets to access resources and take advantage of the instability. In general, these situations have not existed in the United States, and what some observers term opportunities to benefit from "low-hanging fruit" are minimal. Highly competitive U.S. firms already exist in most markets and know the territory. Hence, foreign firms in the United States possess no special advantages, but they may actually incur higher costs relating to transportation, communication, and conforming to local customs.

Whether or not these hypotheses are valid, the empirical evidence is clear, perhaps surprisingly so. The rate of return on FDI in the United States has averaged only a little more than 4 percent, whereas U.S. firms have typically earned more than twice that amount. Even more revealing is the fact that U.S. firms investing funds abroad have earned average returns exceeding 12 percent.

It's possible that these differentials in rates of return are accounting illusions brought about by clever transfer pricing by multinational firms and their abilities to move profits from high-tax to low-tax jurisdictions. We would be foolish to argue that this never occurs, because intelligent, profit-maximizing managers will attempt these strategies, if allowed. Still, as we note in a following section, U.S. corporate profits tax rates appear to be higher than the rates of its major international competitors. Other things equal, one would expect this to result in U.S. firms earning lower profit rates than multinational firms that have some ability to move their profit streams across borders. That, however, is not what we observe, and we should therefore give credence to studies that tell us that foreign investments in the United States typically have resulted in surprisingly low rates of return being earned by the foreigners investing those funds. This has been true whether we are talking about foreign investments in U.S. firms or foreign purchases of U.S. residential real estate—where the S&P/Case-Shiller Home Index declined about 18 percent from its 2006 peak but more than 25 percent in metropolitan areas such as Los Angeles.

The upshot is surprising, at least for those individuals who have been highly critical of foreign purchases of U.S. assets and real estate. The reality is that foreigners have been supplying the United States with significant amounts of capital over recent decades. However, they have either been earning low rates of return on those investments or losing their financial shirts outright. Voluble and often emotional commentators, such as Jim Cramer and Lou Dobbs, aren't always off the mark with their pointed commentaries, but on this issue, they are simply misinformed.

III. U.S. GOVERNMENT DEBT AS A SAFE HARBOR

Amid the pain that has been inflicted upon foreign investors that have purchased U.S. assets during this decade, there is one recent bright spot (at least as far as the foreigners are concerned). Although the declining value of the U.S. dollar throughout this decade seriously reduced the value of the U.S. government debt owned by foreigners, increases in the value of the dollar relative to most foreign currencies in early 2009 dulled the throbbing pain. Relative to the U.S. dollar, for example, the value of the euro increased by more than 93 percent between mid-year 2001 and early 2008. The implication for foreign owners of U.S. government debt from the euro sector was devastating: during this period, the value of their U.S. government debt holdings, expressed in euros, declined almost in half. Since that time, however, the strengthening of the U.S. dollar relative to the euro (approximately 20 percent from its low in 2008) has salved some of the foreign debt holders' wounds.

The strengthening of the U.S. dollar accelerated during the financial crisis of the fall of 2008. There was a flight to safety, as frightened investors (including foreign governments and sovereign wealth funds) concluded that U.S. government debt was the safest alternative in an unpredictable, chaotic world. In the words of Scripps News, the situation was "U.S. Treasuries: A Safe Harbor in Tumultuous Financial Times."[10]

This view was shared by many investors, domestic and foreign. When the U.S. government bond market opened on May 30, 2008, the yield on a two-year U.S. government note was 3.142 percent. By November 7, 2008, that yield had been driven down to only 1.335 percent, and it had fallen to 1.00 percent by mid-February 2009. Why? Because bond yields and bond prices exhibit an inverse relationship. When bond prices rise, bond yields fall and vice-versa. Between May 2008 and February 2009, bond prices rose significantly because of dramatically increased investor demand for them. They were, once again, the safe, protected investment harbor away from a worldwide financial storm. By contrast, the yield on Triple-C rated corporate bonds (junk bonds) rose to an amazing 29.70 percent by November 7, 2008, reflecting a tremendous decline in their prices.

Table 2-4 illustrates the flight of foreign investors to security and quality. Note first of all that Japan's holdings of U.S. government debt did not increase, because, as we noted previously, Japan and the Japanese yen have been viewed as safe harbors, along with the United States. In fact, the strength of the yen enabled Japan to be one of the few countries that was active in the international acquisitions market after the financial crisis of the fall of 2008. Japanese purchases of foreign assets almost tripled in 2008 over 2007.

However, we can see in Table 2-4 that a wide range of foreign investors, ranging from the British to oil-exporting countries, gobbled up U.S.

government debt in hopes of preserving the value of their capital. It is also significant that some of these foreign investors simply wished to park their money for short periods. Foreign holdings of U.S. Treasury bills (short-term debt) rose 35.9 percent. Even through the yield on a 30-day U.S. Treasury bill shrank to a miniscule 0.1% by the middle of November 2008, many investors judged this to be superior to the alternatives, most of which involved investing funds in more risky assets in which loss of capital was a distinct prospect.

Hence, when we talk about "America for Sale," the major way this was in evidence at the end of 2008 was no longer via the purchase of privately owned assets, but rather in the sale of U.S. government debt to foreigners. This pushed up bond prices and drove down yields on U.S. government notes and bonds. Were this trend to continue without pause for several more years and were increasingly large portions of the U.S. government debt to become owned by foreigners, we would have national security concerns. For the moment, however, this inflow of foreign capital has been quite beneficial to the United States and has made it easier for us to deal with our manifold financial challenges.

Note well, however, that nothing is forever, at least when the value of the U.S. dollar and the apparent flight to safety are concerned. The massive financial bailouts of U.S. financial institutions engineered in 2008 were paid for by expanding the money supply and issuing additional U.S. government debt. Both of these actions will likely exercise downward pressure on the value of the U.S. dollar as time passes. Indeed, a weaker U.S. dollar, rather than a stronger U.S. dollar, is a probable result of the financial crisis of 2008.

Table 2-4   Change in the Holdings of U.S. Treasury Securities by Foreign Countries, August 2007–August 2008

Country or Area	Holdings (Billions of $) August 2007	Holdings (Billions of $) August 2008	Percent Change
Japan	$595.8	$585.9	−0.2%
China (PRC)	$471.2	$541.0	14.8%
United Kingdom	$99.8	$307.4	208%
Caribbean banking centers*	$103.8	$147.7	42.3%
Oil-exporting countries**	$134.7	$149.8	33.5%
All countries	$2,217.5	$2,740.3	23.6%

* Bahamas, Bermuda, Cayman Islands, Netherlands Antilles, Panama.

** Ecuador, Venezuela, Indonesia, Bahrain, Iran, Iraq, Kuwait, Oman, Qatar, Saudi Arabia, the UAE, Algeria, Gabon, Libya, Nigeria.

IV. INTERNATIONAL CORPORATE TAX RATE DIFFERENTIALS

Do business firms and even countries pay attention to corporate tax rates when they make decisions about investing in a foreign country? Yes, they do, according to economic research.

Foreign investors do not like to see their profits taxed away by host governments. This is not an insight that qualifies as rocket science. Nevertheless, it is not so easy to give concrete substance to the implications of this insight. The major problem is that the stated, statutory corporate tax rates of countries differ from the "effective" rates that corporations actually pay after exemptions, deductions, and exclusions from corporate income are taken into consideration. The ever notorious "loopholes" in the corporate tax code are included in this ménage.

Thus, the United States, whose highest statutory corporate tax rate (35 percent) is one of the highest in the world, looks much better when its relatively liberal depreciation rules and other adjustments are taken into account. An investor can depreciate many assets more quickly and offset more income with that depreciation in the United States than in many other countries. One recent study suggested that the effective U.S. corporate tax rate was only 25.3 percent in 2005.

Even so, a Congressional Budget Office Study in 2003 found that U.S. marginal corporate tax rates on various kinds of corporate investment activities usually clustered toward the upper middle of those of Organization for Economic Cooperation and Development (OECD) countries when effective tax rates were computed, even though its effective marginal tax rate on equity-financed investments in one particular asset—industrial structures—was, at 41 percent, the highest in the world. Furthermore, there has been an international tendency in recent years to reduce corporate tax rates (a trend not imitated in the United States). If an international tax competition among countries exists, the United States appears to be losing that fight insofar as effective corporate tax rates are concerned.

Why should we care? What difference does this make to our discussion of "America for Sale"? At the margin, high-marginal corporate tax rates discourage investment, and foreign investment is no exception. Thus, the splurge of foreign investment in the United States that occurred during the first half of this decade certainly did not occur because the United States is a tax haven. Just the opposite is true, and hence the proper conclusion is that foreigners who invested in corporate assets in the United States bit their tongues and did it anyway. The falling value of the U.S. dollar and low equity prices overcame what continues to be an international U.S. corporate taxation disadvantage.

Presidential candidate John McCain campaigned on a platform that included a corporate tax rate cut. Not only did Senator McCain lose the election, but also this particular plank in his platform stimulated a degree of ridicule from populist voters and media commentators alike. That reaction, however, is an issue for another day. We must be satisfied here with noting that tax rate differentials among countries do not appear to have been the cause of the surge in foreign purchases of U.S. assets, 2001–2008. Indeed, quite the opposite was probably true. If the intent of U.S. decision makers was to discourage foreign purchases of U.S. corporate assets, then our U.S. corporate tax rate structure seems to have been well designed for that purpose. On balance, U.S. corporate tax regulations appear to discourage foreign purchases of U.S. assets. Hence, those who believe that attractive corporate tax provisions are responsible for the surge in private sector foreign investment during the first part of this decade have very little evidence in favor of their view.

SUMMING IT UP

FDI in the United States is sensitive to a variety of economic influences, among them the foreign exchange value of the U.S. dollar, the general level of U.S. asset prices relative to other countries, perceived levels of financial risk in international markets, and the corporate marginal tax rates in countries that might be targeted by investors. The declining value of the U.S. dollar during most of this decade probably stimulated foreign investment in the United States more than any other single factor. Figure 2-6 demonstrates this with respect to Canadian investors, who, between 2000 and 2006, diminished their new investments in the United States, when the Canadian dollar weakened with respect to the U.S. dollar, and then increased their new investments in the United States when the Canadian dollar waxed in value relative to the U.S. dollar.

If nothing else, Figure 2-6 and our discussion underline the extent to which financial markets have progressively globalized in recent decades. Events in the United States now visibly affect Canadians, Germans, and Egyptians, and vice-versa. If and when America is perceived to be on sale, this is the joint result of our actions and the behavior of foreign countries. Although the United States still accounts for about one-quarter of the value of all goods and services produced in the world, events elsewhere in the world now affect us, whether we like it or not. International oil prices, comparative rates of price inflation, and stability or chaos in foreign financial markets are among the many international factors that help determine whether U.S. assets are purchased by foreigners. The United States still

Figure 2-6 Canada Direct Investment in the U.S. versus CAD/USD Exchange Rate

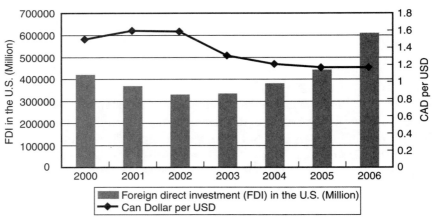

Source: Adapted from data from the Federal Reserve Bank of St. Louis.

makes huge economic waves around the globe, but only Robinson Crusoe on his desert island could now fail to notice that the actions of foreigners affect us as well.

The final lesson we should draw from our analysis is that circumstances inevitably change. *Plus ça change, plus c'est la même chose.* Whereas a veritable public panic existed in 2007 in the United States over increased purchase of U.S. assets by foreigners, in 2009, we can recognize not only that this trend has almost disappeared, but also that the United States nearly always made out handsomely on those sales. A variety of factors—fluctuating exchange rates, falling asset values, and the financial crisis in the fall of 2008—knocked the feet from underneath foreign investors and imposed huge financial losses on most of them. We took their money and ran. Yes, some long-term economic problems exist in the United States, but those problems do not typically relate to foreign purchases of U.S. assets. We would do well to remember this in future years.

Chapter 3

Can It (Will It) Happen to Me?

He is a fool who tries to match his strength with the stronger. He will lose his battle, and with the shame he will be hurt also.
The Greek poet Hesiod, *Works and Days*, 800 B.C.

The enemy came. He was beaten. I am tired. Good night.
The Vicomte de Turenne after his victory at the Battle of Dunen, 1658

The value of anything is not what you paid for it, nor what it cost to produce, but what you can get for it at an auction.
William Lyon Phelps, 20th-century American writer and educator

After months of rumors, in early June 2008, Anheuser-Busch, the largest U.S. brewer, received an unsolicited buyout offer from the Belgian-based brewer Inbev. It was a sweet deal if Anheuser-Busch's share prices were a fair indicator. Inbev offered $65 per share ($46.3 billion) even though the stock of the "King of Beers" had been trading for only about $45 per share as recently as mid-March 2008, prior to analysts suggesting that Anheuser-Busch was vulnerable to a takeover.

Anheuser-Busch, whose advertising and labels had become iconic in the United States, decided to resist Inbev's offer and called in a variety of troops for support—investors, politicians, labor leaders, foundation grant recipients, St. Louis-area citizens, and outright chauvinists (there existing some overlap among these categories). It filed a lawsuit against Inbev, seeking to stop it from soliciting support from Anheuser-Busch stockholders. Perhaps the firm's management and board legitimately believed they could resist Inbev's offer. Alternatively, in his heart of hearts, Anheuser-Busch President and CEO August A. Busch, IV, may have understood that the brewery, founded by his ancestors in 1860, was quite vulnerable to a hostile takeover and that his realistic task now was to negotiate the best deal.

This he accomplished, although perhaps it was imposed upon him by his board, presumably representing the best interests of stockholders. On July 13, 2008, Anheuser-Busch and Inbev announced a deal. Inbev pledged not to close any of Anheuser-Busch's 12 U.S. breweries, promised it would maintain brands such as Budweiser, and stipulated that the headquarters of its U.S. operations would be in St. Louis. The sweetened all-cash $52 billion buyout revolved around an attractive price of $70 per share.

Nevertheless, Inbev's acquisition did not go down as easily as one of Anheuser-Busch's Michelob beers at a St. Louis Cardinals baseball game on a hot, humid day in August. When, finally, on November 13, 2008, 96 percent of Anheuser-Busch stockholders voted in favor of the sale, there was much hand-wringing by stockholders and employees alike. CEO and Chairman Busch averred that this was "a bittersweet day,"[1] although by then his family owned less than 2 percent of Anheuser-Busch's stock.

The mixed nature of the merger day to Anheuser-Busch was immediately apparent to that firm's employees, who noted that Inbev promised to reap $1.5 billion in savings from the merger. To the typical employee, this translated to a smaller workforce. This was confirmed shortly thereafter, when Anheuser-Busch's workforce was reduced by 1,000 by means of voluntary departures sweetened with financial incentives. However, an additional 1,400 employees were terminated, underlining that mergers and acquisitions do not affect all of a firm's constituencies in the same way. This is a seemingly obvious observation, but one that often is ignored in the overall excitement generated by mergers and acquisitions.

Indeed, this had to have been a bittersweet day for many Anheuser-Busch aficionados, who feared that this most American of beers actually might disappear. Nevertheless, the firm's stockholders could hardly complain about the selling price. Furthermore, the strengthening of the U.S. dollar after the deal of July 13, 2008, made Anheuser-Busch appear to be prescient. The waxing of the U.S. dollar relative to the euro increased the price Inbev had to pay in euros by approximately 20 percent (see Figure 3-1). In the interim between July 13 and November 13, a variety of media reports speculated that Inbev might find a way to back out of the deal. However, the apparent financial penalties associated with reneging were reported to be huge.

Figure 3-1 Inbev's Problem: The Strengthening of the U.S. Dollar
Relative to the Euro, July 13, 2008, to November 13, 2008

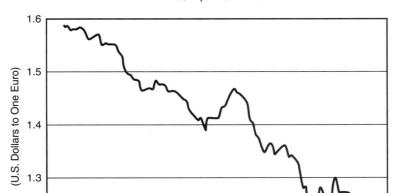

The new firm formed by Inbev's acquisition of Anheuser-Busch became known as "Anheuser-Busch Inbev." It inherited an eye-popping $55 billion in debt, the great majority of which was accumulated by Inbev to pay Anheuser-Busch's stockholders the buyout price of $70 per share. Consequently, in need of liquidity, the new company decided to raise $8.1 billion by selling new shares of stock to its existing stockholders. Equity investors did not react favorably to either the $55 billion revelation or the need of Anheuser-Busch Inbev to raise $8.1 billion in additional capital. The firm's stock (pre-merger) had traded as high as $95 per share, but it languished at only $16.50 per share in early December 2008. Not even the approximate 40 percent decline in overall equity prices in the final quarter of 2008 could account for the punishment that investors inflicted on Anheuser-Busch Inbev's stock price.

CIRCUMSTANCES CHANGE

Hindsight is 20/20, or so it is said, although historical hindsight can be astigmatic as well. The buyout of Anheuser-Busch by Inbev took place, and the famous U.S. brewer became a part of Inbev, creating the world's largest brewing company. Nevertheless, for Inbev, this turned out to be an unexpectedly painful financial experience. Of course, this is not the only situation in which such adverse subsequent developments have occurred. It's actually rather common. The tenor of economic research on post-merger performance is that the stock price of merged firms tends to lag that of the two firms prior to merger.

This general conclusion serves to remind us of Shakespeare's observation five centuries ago that all that glitters is not golden. Things don't always turn out as hoped for, or even according to a game plan defined by well-meaning promises. In the case of the Anheuser-Busch purchase, $70 per share was regarded as a good deal by Inbev, but perhaps one that stretched it to its limits, until the subsequent euro equivalent of a 20-percent increase in that price (to $84 per share) made that deal considerably less attractive.

Those who purchase assets frequently undertake such actions on the basis of current economic conditions, which they extrapolate forward. It is as though current economic trends will never change, or, at least, not for a long time. In mathematical terms, it is equivalent to assuming that a linear trend relationship exists and is not going to change. Unfortunately, such an assumption often results in extensive (and usually unforeseen) problems. The Inbev–Anheuser-Busch episode provides a prominent example, but Inbev is hardly the only victim of altered economic circumstances. We live in a constantly changing world. As Herodotus put it felicitously more than two millennia ago, "The river that flows by today is not the river that flowed by yesterday." Circumstances change.

Consider the case of passenger airlines, which must cope with fuel bills that account for up to 70 percent of their total operating costs. Not surprisingly, airline fuel costs are directly related to the price of oil. As the price of oil surged upward in 2008, toward an all-time high of $147 per barrel, numerous airlines, including especially Southwest Airlines, negotiated hedges that gave them the right to purchase oil in the future at negotiated, lower prices. Both sellers and buyers benefited from the arrangement. The oil sellers obtained a guaranteed selling price, and the oil buyers insured themselves against possible additional increases in the price of oil.

In the case of Southwest, it negotiated hedges that gave it the right to purchase oil at approximately $80 per barrel. This agreement was a lifesaver for Southwest when oil prices climbed toward $147 per barrel. On the other hand, airlines that did only minimal hedging of their fuel costs (Delta was an example) felt the full pain of per barrel increases in oil prices that translated quickly into airline fuel price escalations.

> **Hedging in futures markets** may seem complicated, but it reduces to a first party selling its risks to a second party. An airline might be worried about rising fuel prices. Alternatively, a farmer may be concerned about the falling price of wheat. In either case, the first party (either the airline or the farmer) can use futures markets to "hedge" its risks. For a price, the second party will agree to assume all price variation risks and guarantee a price. In essence, the first party purchases a price-insurance policy from a second party, who willingly accepts the risks involved—but only in return for a payment.

However, when the price of oil plummeted below $40 per barrel, these hedges no longer seemed quite so clever. In fact, what had been smart now turned out to be dumb, because these hedges now forced the airlines to pay more than the going market price for their fuel.

This situation is not limited to oil. Individuals who purchase many other assets can be burned in a similar fashion. Foreign condominium purchasers in Miami found that the value of their new investment fell precipitously in 2008, sometimes by 50 percent or more. The combination of a deteriorating housing market and a strengthening U.S. dollar was deadly for such investors. Many of the world's sovereign wealth funds had the same experience, often worse, when they purchased stakes in U.S. banks and financial institutions, 2006–2008. By 2009, for example, those who had invested in Lehman Brothers or Merrill Lynch had lost everything they had invested.

BUYER REMORSE

Granted, life is full of uncertainties. Changing circumstances soured many of the acquisitions of U.S. assets made by foreign parties. That is the primary reason that these acquisitions declined so significantly in the second half of 2008.

What are the conditions that most often lead to asset buyer remorse and which therefore brought the splurge of foreign-asset buying in 2000–2007 to a halt? Let's summarize them in general terms.

The World Usually Isn't Linear

First, as we just suggested, there often are major problems associated with the assumption that current conditions and relationships will not change. This isn't the way the world operates, and those who acquire assets assuming that current conditions will not change frequently end up being disappointed. Investors large and small would be well advised to pay attention to Herbert Stein, one-time chairman of the Council of Economic Advisors, who once famously remarked, "If something cannot go on forever, it will stop."[2] The import of this pungent observation seems to elude many investors, despite its elementary and obvious nature.

In fact, many critical economic magnitudes behave cyclically, albeit around a trend line. This has been true not only for foreign exchange rates, but also for a wide variety of other variables, including gold, copper, and real estate. Thus, observers who decried as permanent and irreversible the binge of foreign-asset purchases in the United States, 2001–2008, were shortsighted. Conditions would (and did) change, so much so that many of these purchases appeared to be positively stupid in retrospect.

To illustrate this most important point, let's use the example of the housing price bubble in the United States that began deflating already in 2006. Even in 2007, many home buyers acted as if they believed housing prices would continue to rise forever, and they disastrously purchased real estate and housing under heretofore unusual financial terms. "Ninja" mortgages ("no income, no job, no assets") were granted; many mortgages had adjustable interest rates that doubled or even tripled after short periods; some mortgages involved large balloon payments that defied borrowers' ability to satisfy them; and many borrowers with questionable job and credit histories were granted mortgages without significant investigation. This was a recipe for a financial calamity, which was close on the horizon.

Housing prices always have fluctuated over time and, taking inflation into account, have actually fallen in some metropolitan areas for periods as long as a decade. Furthermore, U.S. housing markets always have been characterized by bubble-like activity, with dramatic upsurges in prices and sales ultimately being followed by stagnant or falling prices and minimal sales activity. Moderation in U.S. housing markets has been surprisingly rare.

Historically, the median price of a home in the United States hovered around 3.0 times median household income. Thus, if median household income were $50,000, the median price of a residential home would be about $150,000. By 2006, however, this fundamental ratio (fundamental because it directly addresses the ability of buyers to pay for their housing) had increased to 4.6:1 nationally. In Los Angeles, it skyrocketed to a stratospheric 10:1.

Only the very bold, or those who paid no attention to history, assumed that the upward trend in housing prices in 2000–2006 would continue indefinitely. Of course, that which was virtually inevitable did occur. Housing prices did not continue to rise, and the bottom had fallen out of

housing prices by 2008. The oft-cited Case-Shiller home price index for
the 20 largest urban areas in the United States fell by 32.0 percent between
September 2006 and March 2008 (but 37.1 percent in Los Angeles). This
generated a raft of foreclosures and evictions, as individual home owners
discovered to their astonishment that they now owed more on their home
than it was worth. The onset of economic recession in December 2007 and
rising unemployment only accentuated the extent to which many households could not meet their mortgage payments.

Still, this was hardly the first time this had happened. In Los Angeles, for
example, housing prices fell by roughly 25 percent between July 1990 and
April 1995. Nationally, the decline during that period was much more
modest, only about 7.0 percent. Nevertheless, for almost half a decade,
absolute housing prices fell and "real" housing prices (actual prices
deflated by the rising Consumer Price Index) fell even faster. During this
period, the Consumer Price Index for Urban Consumers rose by 16.3 percent. Hence, the "real" price of housing fell by more than 23 percent
nationally and by more than 41 percent in Los Angeles.

Despite this history, hundreds of thousands of home buyers (including
many foreigners) were taken by surprise by the general decline in housing
prices and the falloff in home sales that began in 2006. Foreign investors
who believed that they could "flip" their vacation home purchase found, to
their regret, that housing markets had soured so much that sales in such
areas as Miami and southern California fell by more than 50 percent. Such
individuals should not have been surprised, because the new, economically
outlandish relationship between housing prices and income was not going
to continue indefinitely. Simply put, "Herb Stein's Law" (something that
cannot go on forever is not going to go on forever) once again came into
play. The highly cyclical nature of U.S. housing markets once again
reasserted itself. The housing price bubble was punctured. However, this
had happened before, in both the 1980s and the 1990s, and these experiences were well within the lifetimes of virtually every one of the 2000-
decade home buyers. Yet, those participating in housing markets
apparently had occluded memories, and adjustments in housing markets
were so harsh that numerous builders and developers went under.

What about those who purchased commercial real estate, for example,
the Chrysler Building in New York City? Investors who purchase commercial real estate often are thought to be more analytical and less emotional
about their purchases. After all, for them, it's supposed to be all about the
money. They are investors. Hence, the critical question for them is whether
or not they earn a profit on the commercial property.

However, the notion that commercial real estate purchases are more
rational, precise, and analytical than residential home buyers may have

some empirical validity, but the behavior of commercial real estate investors during the 2000–2006 interval does not provide strong encouragement for that view. Foreign investors, in particular, repeatedly made investments in U.S. commercial real state after the turn of the 20th century that turned out to be questionable. Indeed, many foreign investors plunged into the commercial real estate market at its peak—the very worst time.

The truth, however, is that unexpected future occurrences are not confined to asset bubbles in housing and commodities. Consider a very different kind of example, one involving the impact of television and VCRs upon movies. Both innovations led to ill-advised predictions that the moving picture industry would collapse. Of course, that did not occur. More than 1.3 billion movie tickets worth almost $10 billion were sold in 2007. Although the movie business continues to face major challenges and movie ticket sales have not come close to keeping up with population growth, this was not a shabby performance for an industry that was likened to a horse and buggy.

Or consider IBM, which originally was not in the computer business at all, but subsequently morphed itself into a punch-card accounting equipment firm; then a mainframe computer manufacturer; subsequently, a personal computer supplier; and, most recently, a service-providing information technology firm. IBM figured out (some would say guessed) which way the waves were going and then rode the surf to shore. All things considered, IBM performed well during these decades of upheaval, although we would be remiss if we did not note that it unwisely sold out its dominant interest in computer operating systems to an unknown young man named Bill Gates.

If there is a lesson here, then it is that the world is full of uncertainty. Those who acquire a firm (or sell it) cannot predict the future and may not even know the probability distribution associated with possible outcomes. As Robert Lucas, the Nobel Laureate from the University of Chicago, has observed, it is nigh upon impossible to foresee all critical events in advance. Indeed, with respect to the financial crisis of the fall of 2008, Lucas noted, "I don't know anybody involved who thought he could predict these turning points."[3]

The Cyclical Nature of Economic Activity

Quite apart from asset pricing bubbles, a surprising number of economic magnitudes behave in a cyclical fashion. Unfortunately, it's not easy to predict the duration and amplitude of those cycles. Consider the prices of gold and silver, metals that are often promoted in television advertisements as the ultimate stores of value in an unpredictable world. Table 3-1 reports the prices of one ounce of gold and one ounce of silver stated in terms of constant 2006 dollars. Since 1910, the beginning-of-decade price of gold has varied between $208.79 and $1,567.73 per ounce in constant dollars and has been up and down like a yo-yo. The constant dollar price of gold fell by 50 percent between 1940 and 1960 but then rose by an amazing 531 percent between 1970 and 1980, only to fall by a precipitous 80 percent by 2000. The price of silver has varied from $3.98 and $38.26 per ounce in constant dollars. Between 1970 and 1980, the price of silver rocketed upward by 348 percent; however, it fell precipitously (83 percent) during the next decade. Any investor who believes that gold and silver are a stable, reliable investment probably also believes in the Tooth Fairy.

By comparison to gold and silver prices, the Dow-Jones average (which everyone knows rises and falls), is a comparative model of stability. *Nota bene,* however! Although the overall Dow-Jones Index may be relatively smoother over the long term, this does not mean that its individual components are. The prices of individual stocks may have high beta (β) coefficients, reflecting the reality that their prices vary substantially more than the market as a whole.[4] A well-diversified portfolio, however, will smooth out those fluctuations.

Table 3-1   The Price of Gold and Silver in Constant 2006 U.S. Dollars

Year	Price of One Ounce of Gold	Price of One Ounce of Silver
1910	$421.84	$11.02
1920	$208.79	$5.45
1930	$249.04	$3.98
1940	$500.00	$5.07
1950	$335.42	$6.67
1960	$248.30	$6.19
1970	$195.83	$8.54
1980	$1567.73	$38.26
1990	$654.01	$6.44
2000	$318.68	$5.39
2007	$979.04	$14.29

Source: Adapted from http://en.wikipedia.org/wiki/Gold_as_an_investment.

Can we predict asset price cycles?

In general, the answer to this question is no. We may know that steel prices exhibit cyclical behavior, but this does not tell us when steel prices will head up or down. Furthermore, even if we knew the cyclical pattern of the price of an asset, that knowledge might not do us any good. For example, it's true that the Dow-Jones average usually rises in January. Since 1900, the index has risen 63 percent of the time in January, for an average increase of 1.0 percent. If there is money to be made relying upon this information, we can rest assured that this already has been acted upon by investors and probably is thoroughly discounted in current equity prices. Hence, anyone seeking to gain from this knowledge has already paid the price, in a sense, when he or she buys a stock.

The moral to these stories? Critical economic magnitudes not only change in value over time, but also often behave cyclically. The old adage, "Whatever goes around, comes around," frequently applies to asset prices. Consider Figure 3-2, which records the GFMS Metals base metal price index for primary aluminum, copper, lead, nickel, tin, and zinc. The index is an average of the six prices, with equal weighting given to each of the six metals. One can see that metals prices almost quadrupled between the end of 2005 and the beginning of 2008, but then they crashed almost back to their January 2004 level by the end of 2008.

Figure 3-2 Five-year GFMS Base Metal Index

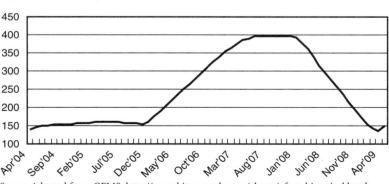

Source: Adapted from GFMS, http://www.kitcometals.com/charts/gfms_historical.html.

Do basic metals prices behave cyclically? Yes. Did the fourfold increase in metals prices between 2005 and 2007 help stoke foreign purchases of U.S. assets? Yes, again, because these tremendous price increases enhanced foreigners' desires to purchase their own sources of metals in the United States. The declining value of the U.S. dollar made this much easier for them to accomplish.

Will metals prices recover and again increase substantially? Yes, and we think we will already see evidence of this at the end of 2009 and most obviously in 2010. Will this again spike foreign purchases of U.S. assets upward? Yes, and if it once again is accompanied by a deteriorating U.S. dollar, which we predict as a direct consequence of the tremendous increase in the U.S. money supply that has been a central part of the U.S. financial bailouts, then we will again see "America for Sale."

The problem with asset prices is straightforward—even the smartest investors don't know precisely when the turning points for asset prices will occur. And, if they do know, it's likely that others know as well and that their profitable behavior will soon be imitated, thus diminishing or removing any benefit.

In any case, foreign purchasers of U.S. assets during this decade have been rudely shocked by plunges in the prices of the assets they have acquired. If they acquired the stock of a publicly traded U.S. company, they experienced a decline of 33 percent in the Dow-Jones average in 2008 and another 15 percent in early 2009. Furthermore, they may live through long periods when stock prices are disappointingly stagnant. This certainly has happened before. Between February 1966 and August 1982, the Dow-Jones average rose at the rate of only 1.5 percent per year.

It could happen again, primarily because of the worldwide economic recession that began in the fall of 2008. Profits are likely to shrink for many firms and in many industries. Although price-to-earnings ratios (P/E) are not infallible guides to equity prices, they are useful rules of thumb. Declining profits will not push equity prices upward. Thus, those foreigners who purchased significant U.S. assets in the first decade of this century may have to wait a while before they begin to realize respectable rates of return on their investments. We predict that this will not occur until 2010, and then only if economic recovery has taken hold.

Of course, the opposite also could occur, whereby foreign purchasers might benefit from rising prices for the assets they have purchased. But this seems unlikely. Regardless, as the experience of 2007–2008 has shown, even some of the smartest minds have failed to predict asset price cycles accurately enough to make them money. Asset price cycles occur, and with them both the feasibility and the profitability of foreign purchases of U.S. assets. Thus, it should come as no surprise that purchases of U.S. assets by foreigners often rise and fall like the mercury in a traditional thermometer.

Why don't investors (including foreign investors) learn? One of the enduring findings of modern behavioral finance research is that many investors, even those with imposing reputations, are susceptible to bouts of overoptimism and overpessimism. This tendency produces cyclical asset price behavior and may even lead to the formation of asset price bubbles that inevitably burst. This often has been the case with basic metals, as Figure 3-2 demonstrated. The expansionary portion of such price cycles tends to attract many investors, some of whom are foreign. They assume (frequently to their subsequent demise) that these price increases are likely to continue for some time to come. Witness the predictions of some savants (both domestic and foreign)—when oil prices hit $147 per barrel—that oil at $400 per barrel was just around the corner. Unfortunately for them, less than six months later, oil prices had fallen by more than 70 percent, to less than $40 per barrel.

All of us are creatures of our environments, and it is difficult (although not impossible) for us to escape the perceptual shackles of those environments. The immediate events of yesterday and today tend to loom quite large in our thinking. As behavioral finance researchers have shown, many individuals consistently downgrade or forget negative economic news and signals. Hence, we saw otherwise intelligent analysts project the recent past into the future and then generate predictions of oil prices at $400 per barrel. In fact, we may see oil at $400 per barrel before another decade has passed, but one would have to be quite brave to predict when that will occur. OPEC ministers now are scrambling to reduce production, just as they were exhorted to increase production in the very recent past. The old German adage, "Do not praise the day before you have seen the evening," is appropriate here. What is true in markets today may not be true tomorrow.

At the end of the day, economic cycles in production, prices, profits, and exchange rates cause foreign purchases of U.S. assets to be episodic in nature. We lived through one episode between 2001 and 2008. No doubt, we will see another episode within the next few years. Our prediction in that regard is for 2010, and we believe that readers should prepare for the eventuality.

The Critical Role of Foreign Exchange Rates

We already have sketched the central role that foreign exchange rates played in stimulating the surge of foreign purchases of U.S. assets in the first decade after the turn of the 20th century. Over a period of years, the declining value of the U.S. dollar vis-à-vis the most important foreign currencies made U.S. assets appear to be on sale to foreigners. They acted accordingly.

It should not escape us, however, that when the dollar strengthened in value in late 2008, this raised the price of U.S. assets to foreigners and was one of several reasons why the gush of foreign acquisitions and mergers was reduced to a trickle. Even so, nothing is forever, particularly in the world of foreign exchange rates. If, as we have suggested, the U.S. government rescue plans dramatically increase the U.S. money supply and, in the process, U.S. interest rates are driven down, the value of the U.S. dollar will almost surely fall relative to major foreign currencies (assuming foreign countries don't use the same actions).

In a period of only 90 days in the fall of 2008, the assets of the Federal Reserve System increased by 155 percent, from about $900 billion to about $2.3 billion. The Fed accomplished this by increasing the money supply—literally by printing Federal Reserve notes. Unless the application of the laws of supply and demand has been suspended by some higher being or the Fed is exceptionally clever, this will eventually result in substantial price inflation and also will push down the value of the U.S. dollar relative to other currencies. This flood of dollars may well have averted a deeper recession, but it will also result in substantial inflationary pressures in the future. This spells bad news for the U.S. dollar and prepares the ground for another extended bout of "America for Sale."

We will go out on a limb (but not very far, we believe) and predict that the United States will again see such inflationary pressures and the onset of new asset price bubbles—especially for physical commodities—in 2010. The cheapened U.S. dollar will help motivate these asset price bubbles and will inexorably attract foreign investors and assets purchasers. A year or two of this scenario will have editorialists wondering whether one-time Fed Chairman Paul Volcker might not be brought back to conquer yet another inflationary beast nurtured by the anti-recessionary policies of 2008 and 2009.

In the fall of 2008, one could only sympathize with U.S. government economic policymakers and specific individuals in the hot seat, such as Federal Reserve Board Chairman Benjamin Bernanke and U.S. Treasury Secretary Henry Paulson. They were confronted with what became the worst U.S. economic contraction since the Great Depression. Furthermore, they found that the application of the usual monetary policy tools (reduction in the federal funds and discount rates, expansion of the money supply) did not achieve the hoped-for reversal of economic fortunes. The Fed set its interest rates close to zero, and the Treasury embarked on a $700 billion TARP (Troubled Assets Relief Program) to prop up banks, financial institutions, and businesses, primarily by injecting capital into them.

New commodity price bubbles are likely to develop as we move into the next decade. The Fed's historically large expansion of the money supply (see Chapter 2) will exert upward pressure on prices of nearly all goods and services. The oft-cited equation $MV = PQ$ retains its simple relevance. It is quite likely that output (Q) will not expand as fast as the money supply (M). Holding velocity (V) roughly constant, this implies that P (the price level) must rise. Price increases in basic commodities markets (coal, copper, steel, aluminum, nickel, oil, lumber, natural gas, etc.) will rise even more, because productive capacity in those industries was decimated by the recession that began in December 2007 but then conflated dramatically by the financial crisis in the fall of 2008. We believe the United States will begin to see substantial commodity price bubbles in 2010. No doubt, policymakers found themselves between the proverbial rock and a hard place in 2008, as they reacted to the worst economic crisis in the United States since the Great Depression. In the process, however, they set the stage for another inflationary spiral reminiscent of the late 1970s.

Alas, none of these actions appeared to stem the tide of bad economic news, not the least because of a substantial lack of transparency in worldwide financial systems. Which financial assets were "troubled" and why? If banks held "toxic" mortgages, which ones were they? Financial markets are actually very skilled at dealing with risky situations, if there is transparency in those situations and information is reliable. For example, if individuals want to insure themselves against the financial damages that might accrue if their house burns down, ordinarily they can do so easily if the characteristics of their house, neighborhood, and city are known. Except in unusual cases, there is a price that will be sufficient to provide them with the insurance they desire. In a roughly similar fashion, individuals who wish to cushion themselves against the vagaries of price changes in oil or the ups and down of the stock market can find ways to do so—if the markets are transparent, that is, if the trading conditions are clear and characteristics of the assets and the traders are accurately known to all concerned.

A problem, perhaps *the* problem, associated with the financial crisis of 2008 was the lack of such transparency in a wide range of financial markets, but especially in those involving mortgages and packages of risky financial assets. Except for a select few, there was little general knowledge of the extent to which subprime mortgages had penetrated the portfolios of financial institutions. Nor were most investors and even financial institutions aware of the precarious nature of the credit default swaps that underpinned the portfolios of numerous institutions.

As a consequence, risk was mispriced. Quite risky assets were treated as if they were not very risky at all. Furthermore, as 2008 drew to a close, the extent to which the portfolios of the keystone financial institutions of the world were infected by mispriced, "toxic" assets was still unknown. This had two immediate effects. First, it stymied economic recovery efforts (the efforts of the Fed were once again likened to "pushing on a string"); second, it brought a virtual halt to purchases of U.S. assets by foreigners, except for a few rescue buyouts at severely reduced prices. For our purposes, however, it is the second conclusion that is salient. If buyers can't properly determine the value of an asset, then they will not purchase it. Along with a half-dozen other factors, this is a reason why the binge of foreign purchases of U.S. assets came to an end.

WILL IT HAPPEN TO ME?

Suppose you own U.S. assets, work for a U.S. firm, or live in a typical community that contains many U.S. firms and asset clusters. Whether or not you might end up better off, what are the circumstances that might lead to your firm or your employer being sold to a foreigner and/or the nature of your community being changed? Here are the 15 most important circumstances to consider.

1. Falling U.S. Dollar

Foreign exchange rates may well be the single most important determinant of foreign bids to purchase U.S. assets. Every 1 percent of decline in the value of the U.S. dollar relative to the acquiring country's currency reduces the price of the target by the same amount. A long-term decline in the value of the dollar will, by itself, stimulate U.S. asset purchases by foreigners. Simply put, a weak dollar means a strong market for asset purchases in the United States by foreigners.

2. Rising Commodity Prices

Rapidly inflating commodity prices for coal, iron ore, steel, lumber, grains, and the like encourage foreign firms to find and own their own sources of supply closer to their final markets. If a foreign firm has many customers in the United States and it has been importing inputs from outside of the country, then it has a strong incentive to acquire sources of supply in the United States. The commodity price bubble that dissipated in 2008 may reappear in the future. When it does, input suppliers will once again become targets for acquisition by foreign firms.

3. Rising Transportation Costs

In the digital world of software, music, and movies, one does not worry much about transport costs because these items can be downloaded and uploaded in a millisecond from thousands of miles across the globe. The same cannot be said for bulky, heavy inputs, such as automobiles, construction equipment, drill presses, steel, and natural gas. Transporting such items to the United States can eat up any perceived production cost advantages that foreign sellers previously possessed. Hence, they may seek to acquire U.S. production locations so that they are near their customers. This is a dynamic that U.S. producers always have pursued inside the United States, and so we should not be surprised when foreign producers do the same.

4. Accommodating Monetary Policy

U.S. monetary policy, reacting to a variety of influences, including the dot.com bust in 2001, emphasized an accommodating monetary policy that kept interest rates low, for example, on home mortgages. Low interest rates also made it easier for foreign firms to find financing for their purchases in the United States, if they needed to do so, and, at the same time, placed downward pressure on the U.S. dollar.

5. Accommodating Regulatory Policy

As we have seen, the United States seldom has used the Committee on Foreign Investments in the United States (CFIUS) to halt any proposed acquisition of a U.S. firm by a foreign firm. In general, foreign sovereign wealth funds have not been prohibited from acquiring U.S. assets. Furthermore, U.S. financial regulatory bodies have turned what some believe to be a blind eye to the complex financial transactions that have supported some acquisitions of U.S. assets by foreigners. This atmosphere could change.

6. Economic Uncertainty

High levels of economic uncertainty (and the usual lack of transparency that accompanies such uncertainty) ordinarily reduces international transactions across the board. The major exception is the "flight to safety" that periodically occurs when international investors decide that U.S. government debt is, all things considered, still the safest asset available. In the usual case, however, uncertainty snuffs out foreign investment in non-U.S. government debt.

7. Stagnant Firm Economic Performance

This is the first of a series of firm-specific or asset-specific criteria. This condition is not difficult to understand. If a firm or an asset is perceived to be underperforming relative to its potential, then it clearly becomes an attractive takeover target by investors of all stripes, including foreigners.

8. Opportunity to Gain Market Share

Foreign firms often believe they can acquire productive capacity and market share less expensively by purchasing a U.S. firm than they could by building their own plant and expanding from there. There is empirical evidence in favor of this notion. Thus, acquisitions that would enable a firm to gain entry into a market or vastly expand its market share are more likely than others.

9. Alleged Cost Savings and Synergies

Foreign firms nearly always believe they can operate a U.S. firm more efficiently, at least partially by reducing costs. In some cases, the basis for these claims is valid, but it is often dependent upon the foreign firm substituting its organization for that of the U.S. firm. Speaking generally, there is greater prospect for true cost savings if information technology infrastructure is involved and if the foreign firm can substitute its information technology for that of the U.S. firm. However, in other cases, the foreign firm may own valuable intellectual property or other assets that dovetail nicely with those of the U.S. firm.

10. Complementary Customer Markets

If a foreign firm is already competing within the market served by the U.S. firm, then an acquisition is less likely. The probability of an acquisition increases when the U.S. firm serves a different set of customers in terms of geography or product. This is a matter of "fit," and perception does not often meet reality when voracious, acquisitive managers are involved. Still, mergers that move a firm ahead, in terms of the customers it has the ability to serve, make more sense. Inbev levied this argument concerning its acquisition of Anheuser-Busch by asserting that the two firms produced different kinds of beers that were sold to quite different customers.

11. Absence of National Security Interest

The Dubai port management dispute was driven by perceptions of many Americans that national security would be endangered if major U.S. ports were operated by a firm headquartered in Dubai. To the extent that a U.S. firm is involved in national defense work or represents what someone could argue is a "vital," core industry, an acquisition is less likely to occur, usually because cold water is thrown on it before it goes too far. Even when a foreign acquisition is not prohibited, foreign investors don't want to be treated like the proverbial skunk at a picnic and therefore often exhibit sensitivity to perceived national security considerations.

12. Absence of a Trade Union Veto

In some industries, strong labor unions have acquired the ability to veto proposed acquisitions of the U.S. firm with which they bargain. This usually means the union owns a significant portion of the firm and is more likely to be in evidence in traditional manufacturing industries, such as automobiles and steel. Regardless, union leaders have been known to march to their own drummers and can easily decide to veto an acquisition by a foreign firm. However, union leaders also are very sensitive to job preservation and may actually join the team of the proposed foreign acquirer in order to increase the probability that the union's membership does not disappear.

13. Absence (Presence) of a Dominant Stockholder

When a single stockholder, or a cohesive family of stockholders, dominates a firm's ownership, this usually makes it less likely that a firm or asset will be sold to a foreign suitor. Still, there are exceptions, and they generally occur when there is generational change within a firm. A CEO retires or dies and his or her progeny do not wish to become involved actively in management. In such cases, they may "take the money and run" (the words of one who did so). In the general case, however, dominant stockholders tend to be more obstinate and less likely to sell. They may have the best interests of their long-term employees (the company's "family") at heart when they do so.

14. The Characteristics of the Management

We have just treated one critical aspect of management—the extent to which there is a dominant manager or stockholder and whether or not that person is approaching normal retirement age, or another major juncture in life. Consider now another absolutely critical characteristic of management in general—skill and acumen. Incompetent or lazy managers invite takeovers. This usually is, but need not be, evidenced by conspicuous under-performance relative to industry norms. Less capable managers inspire prospective acquirers to believe they can do better, most immediately by replacing existing management with their own. Hence, if you believe the management of your firm or the local organization is mediocre, then this increases the likelihood they will be acquired by foreigners.

15. State Characteristics

Economically speaking, the 50 states compete to attract businesses. Each offers a peculiar combination of location, climate, workforce, cost of living, proximity to inputs and customers, tax rates, incentives, regulations, and prospective worker relationships. Foreign purchasers of U.S. assets are no more immune to these factors than are domestic producers. Limited empirical evidence indicates that foreign asset purchasers disdain high tax regimes and prefer "Right to Work" states where compulsory trade unionism does not exist. Nevertheless, note that some foreign firms conclude that, when all is said and done, it is less expensive for them to build their own plant, *de novo*. In such case, they attempt to entice a series of state and local governments in the United States to bid against each other to produce financial incentives for the foreign firm to locate in their jurisdiction. Virtually every city and state maintains an economic development agency that is tasked with attracting new firms and can call on a variety of tax and development incentives to make its situation attractive. Skillful foreign firms coax even doubtful possibilities to submit competitive bids, and many fibs are told on both sides of the negotiating table. Not surprisingly, the cities and states that are the least attractive to foreign investors (for example, those that sponsor high tax regimes) may be the ones that are forced to offer the largest tax and development concessions to remain in the game. Even so, they frequently fail, because, as one foreign firm's CEO put it, "They have made themselves ugly and we behave accordingly."

SUMMING IT UP

What causes a foreigner to seek to acquire a U.S. asset? Although we have placed strong emphasis upon foreign exchange rates, we hasten to say that, in the end, it is a combination of these 15 factors (and perhaps others) that tell the tale when foreign acquisition are concerned. Transportation costs, locational advantages near inputs and customers, and the like also are important. Furthermore, rather different factors apply to the purchase of U.S. government debt instruments, in which case perceived safety often trumps nearly all other considerations, and foreign investors have been known to accept zero or even negative real rates of return if their investment is secure.

Finally, all should understand that foreign acquisitions of U.S. assets tend to occur in waves and cycles that reflect the mixture of conditions previously noted. As we write these lines (in 2009), foreign acquisitions of U.S. assets have receded, and such media commentators as Jim Cramer and Lou Dobbs are focusing upon other, more immediate concerns. Nevertheless, our prediction is that successive diminutions in the value of the U.S. dollar, relatively low U.S. asset prices, and a degree of international economic recovery will once again make U.S. assets much more inviting targets, most likely in 2010. We believe that the unprecedented expansion of the U.S. money supply renders a high degree of inevitability to this outcome.

Chapter 4

All That Is Made of Steel Is Not Unbreakable

The $800 billion global steel industry may be on the verge of a new merger wave, as large, wealthy steelmakers try to swallow smaller rivals weakened by the financial crisis.

Humeyra Pamuk in the *International Herald Tribune,* December 10, 2008

[R]estricting foreign imports cost $105,000 annually for each automobile worker's job that was saved.

Alan Blinder, Princeton University economist

The history of the steel industry in the United States is one of cyclical booms and busts. The year 2008 marked the end of an era of unprecedented product quality and financial success, and the industry is now in the throes of misery and contraction. It is during such periods of economic pain that the industry tends to undertake significant consolidation and restructuring. Typically, restructuring reduces the number of steel firms, produces healthier income statements and balance sheets, and provides stockholders with a competitive return on their invested capital. It doesn't happen easily, however.

By certain measures, the steel industry in the United States has been doing well. Steel labor productivity has more than quintupled since the early 1980s. In the 1980s, it took an average of 10.1 man-hours of labor to produce a ton of steel, but by 2006 it took an average of only 2.0 man-hours.

Nonunionized steel mini-mills currently produce a ton of steel in less than one man-hour. This is startling progress.

Since World War II, the North American steel industry has reduced its energy intensity by 60 percent. In the past 10 years alone, the industry has achieved a 90-percent reduction in the discharge of air and water emissions. Steel parts now are more dent resistant and are up to 30 percent stronger than they were a decade ago. Innovation is alive. More than one-half of all the types of steels present in today's automobiles did not even exist 10 years ago. Much the same circumstance applies to U.S. military vehicles and weapons.

Almost 69 percent of steel is recycled in North America each year—more than paper, aluminum, plastic, and glass combined. The decades-long remaking of the U.S. steel industry is, in many ways, truly a success story on all fronts—product quality, environment, finance, innovation, and national defense.

These are impressive achievements and are among the reasons why the demand for steel rose consistently in the United States (and around the world) until the final quarter of 2008. Wall Street signed on to this and essentially rediscovered the industry several years ago. The steel industry had strong access to capital until the slowdown in the latter part of 2008. This reflected the reality that steel firms here and abroad were expanding and profitable.

However, even while the U.S. steel industry was booming between 2005 and 2008, its ownership was being progressively transferred to foreigners. It is interesting to note that this occurred without much of a struggle and did not generate very much adverse publicity. Dozens of U.S. steel producers and suppliers were purchased by foreign firms in recent years. Steel firms quickly became one of the best examples of U.S. enterprises being "hunted by the pack" and gobbled up in acquisitions. Perhaps the overall prosperity of the United States deflected the gaze of those who might have questioned what one steelworker told us was "the foreignization" of the U.S. steel industry.

As we write this, the United States has already walked a good distance down a path that eventually will cause it to lose domestic control over steel industry assets located in the United States. Remarkably, few seem to notice or even care that this is happening, in spite of the fact that steel is an absolutely vital input for numerous products within the U.S. economy and that the U.S. military uses huge quantities of steel. Steel is a major component in consumer appliances, automobiles, buildings, furniture, machines of all types, railroad infrastructure, road and bridge construction, ships, surgical and medical equipment, tools, trucks, wire, and numerous other goods. Steel constitutes about two-thirds of the weight of a typical U.S. consumer appliance or automobile. The bottom line is simple—steel is not something about which we could say, "We don't really need it; we could get along without it."

The CFIUS (about which we say more in Chapter 8) possesses the legal authority to decide whether specific foreign acquisitions of U.S. assets are appropriate. Notwithstanding the CFIUS's statements, its lack of action suggests that it apparently does not currently consider a strong, viable, and U.S.-owned steel industry to be a high priority. Actions (or lack thereof) speak louder than any of its words in this arena.

Even though we have already made the case that many, probably most, purchases of U.S. firms and assets by foreigners are not harmful, we believe the steel industry constitutes an exception at this point. A U.S. steel industry owned predominantly by countries antagonistic to the United States is a recipe for future problems, perhaps even disasters.

THE STEEL INDUSTRY AS A METAPHOR FOR MANY U.S. INDUSTRIES

So, what has been going on in the steel industry that is worth our attention? Why should we care if the Russians buy up our steel industry? What are the most important issues?

The authors of this book, Craig T. Bouchard and James V. Koch, respectively, were the president and vice chairman of the board, and a senior member of the board of directors, of Esmark, Inc., one of the largest U.S. steel companies. Esmark was sold to the Russian steel conglomerate Severstal in August 2008 after a hostile international bidding process that contained more twists and turns than the TV show *24*. Having survived this, the two of us possess both experience and a few war wounds to offer in support of our views concerning steelmaking and the changing of the guard in steel industry ownership.

We believe the steel industry story we have to tell is valuable for three reasons. First, we believe that another sustained burst of "America for Sale" is just over the horizon. By 2010, we will once again begin to see large-scale purchases of U.S. industrial and financial assets by foreigners because of significant declines in the value of the U.S. dollar relative to major foreign currencies and the relatively depressed values of U.S. assets.

Second, the steel industry differs qualitatively from many other U.S. industries that also are under competitive pressure. Steel is a core industry that supports economic activity across the U.S. economy. Furthermore, as we demonstrate in the following, steel also is a vital input to U.S. military production. Plainly stated, if our steel industry contracts severely or disappears, we will face a host of potential problems. The bottom line is that we believe it is risky business to trust Russian oligarchs (among the major recent purchasers of U.S. steel companies) to do what is best for us if they own most of our steel industry.

Third, the steel industry provides a useful metaphor for future developments in the U.S. economy because it reflects so many of the economic stresses currently dogging U.S. companies:

- Steel firms have increased their productive efficiency in recent years, but they still trail many foreign producers in cost effectiveness. In this regard, the steel industry is a poster child for many other U.S. manufacturing industries that have been forced to confront cost-efficient foreign producers. "Better" performance by U.S. steel producers often times has not been good enough when international competition has been concerned.

- Steel firms and their employee unions have continually sought protection against foreign competition in the form of tariffs and import restrictions that are demonstrably costly to U.S. consumers. The cost of defending and retaining one U.S. steel worker's job via tariffs and import restrictions easily exceeds $100,000. Our firm, Esmark, benefitted from such competitive restrictions, but, in general, we must say that such protectionism is bad public policy. The *Wall Street Journal* reported in February 2009 that U.S. steelmakers intended to press for increased tariff protection on the grounds that foreign steel imports are subsidized.[1] If successful, such efforts will raise prices to U.S. consumers. A major thrust within President Obama's economic recovery package was a "Buy American" provision championed by labor unions. If pursued aggressively, "Buy American" restrictions will start a trade war that will yield the same ill effects as the infamous Smoot-Hawley tariff of the 1930s.

- More than half of all steel employees in the United States are not represented by labor unions such as the USW. Alas, the USW's labor agreements with steel firms are often monuments to inefficient work rules, and they frequently provide the USW with veto power over any significant action taken by these firms. Those steel firms that do not have collective bargaining may well represent the future if a viable U.S. steel industry is to survive.

- Foreign steel producers have found it less expensive to purchase existing U.S. steel producers than to start their own firms, *de novo*, in the United States. This is a scenario that has been played out repetitively throughout the U.S. economy over the past few decades.

A BIT OF STEEL INDUSTRY BACKGROUND

How Steel Is Made

To understand the issues, we need to provide a small glimpse of steel industry. Making steel is a complex industrial process. Anyone who visits a steel mill should be prepared for an experience that is hard to forget. A steel mill producing 2 million to 5 million tons of steel per year is equivalent to a small city; it involves a massive web connecting thousands of people and firms involved with the raw materials, massive equipment, energy consumption, and production technologies that characterize steelmaking today. The end product—steel—is a metal alloy consisting mostly of iron,

---

Lou Dobbs, on his website, in February 2009 about the U.S. Senate weakening "Buy American" provisions in the stimulus bill, says, "The Senate has caved into special interest groups and even foreign governments by softening 'Buy American' provisions in the stimulus bill. Lawmakers have, once again, failed to protect the interests of the American people" (http://loudobbs.tv.cnn.com/ [February 8, 2009]). We grant Mr. Dobbs both laudable motives and passion but conclude that his prescription would be disastrous for the United States. It would result in a retaliatory trade war and have undesirable spin-off effects with China and other countries that we expect to fund the huge U.S. government deficits required by the stimulus package.

---

but also containing carbon and other elements that promote hardening of the final product.

In a steel mill town, nearly every family and its extended groupings of relatives is touched daily by the activity of the mill or its employees. Every employee of a nearby restaurant, gas station, club, cleaners, construction firm, police or fire station, or school, plus innumerable electricians, plumbers, accountants, real estate agents, automobile dealers, and the like rely on the mill for their livelihoods. Yes, local air and water may be less than pristine because of a steel firm, and nearby residents know this, but they defend "their mill" to their last breaths. Few complain, because this is how they have chosen to make their living. The culture that grows up around a steel mill is close to the vest, often nontrusting in nature, but hardworking and very passionate. In some ways, it is a throwback to earlier frontier generations of interconnected, closely knit Americans.

There are two dominant processes used in the steelmaking process. The first involves the use of a traditional blast furnace; the second relies upon an electric arc furnace. Both processes heat iron ore, scrap metal, and carbon to temperatures that may approach 2,000 degrees Fahrenheit. The United States Steel Corporation (U.S. Steel), once the largest steel producer in the world, achieved this status with blast furnaces. In recent years, the mini-mills, which rely upon electric arc furnaces, have taken market share and now represent roughly half of the North American steel manufacturing market.

Let's look briefly at each technology. Steel mills using blast furnaces bring very large quantities of raw materials to the mill location by truck, train, or ship. Major ingredients are iron ore, limestone, and coal. Coal is converted to coke in ovens that remove impurities. The remaining pure carbon product is sent to the blast furnace, to be combined with iron ore in order to produce molten pig iron. This molten iron is transported by insulated vessels to a "basic oxygen" furnace, where it is mixed with some amount of recycled steel and other alloys to make fresh new steel.

After some refining, it is transported to a slab caster, where the molten steel is poured into a casting machine that produces steel slabs. Each slab may be 20 to 30 feet long, 8 to 12 inches thick, and weigh up to 20 tons. The slabs come out of the casting machines at very high temperatures, but they are then "reheated" to temperatures as high as 2,000 degrees Fahrenheit before entering several processes that reduce the thickness of the slab to approximately one half inch. This thin slab of steel is rolled into a coil that is sent to customers as "hot rolled" steel. Hot roll is used to make automobiles, construction material such as pipes and tubes, and many other construction and original equipment manufacturer (OEM) products.

> **In 1970, five large U.S. steel producers dominated the U.S. market:** U.S. Steel, Bethlehem Steel, LTV, National Steel, and Wheeling Pittsburgh Steel. Domestic production was roughly 120 million to 140 million tons per year, and 80 to 90 percent of this steel was produced in blast furnaces via the "basic oxygen" process. By blowing oxygen through molten pig iron, the carbon content of the alloy is lowered and changed into high quality, low-carbon steel.

Many manufacturers require further processing of the steel at the mill location. Consequently, large quantities of hot rolled steel continue to undergo additional work—to become "cold rolled" steel, various types of galvanized steel, or tin. These products typically create greater hardness, strength, or anti-corrosion properties and often must be painted before being used in such products as autos or appliances. The sequences just described constitute a massive industrial exercise, requiring large scale in real estate, buildings, energy consumption, equipment, and transportation that is expensive to create and maintain.

Nearly always, there are significant environmental issues connected to a steel mill using a blast furnace process. Because of this, there may never again be a full-scale, integrated steel mill relying upon blast furnaces built in the United States.

Nearly all of the steel mills built in recent decades are referred to as "mini-mills." They use scrap (recycled steel) that is fed into "electric arc furnaces." This scrap metal typically constitutes 75 to 100 percent of the raw material they use to make steel. Sometimes molten iron is added to the scrap iron in a furnace to increase the quality (iron content) of the steel. As steel is continually recycled via the mini-mills, it tends to lose iron content. Because this reduces the quality of this steel, mini-mills often must add additional iron to cope with this problem.

Steel moves from the arc furnace through a metallurgy station to a slab caster. The slabs produced are "rolled" in a hot strip mill, just as in the blast furnace process, and the eventual products are the same hot rolled, cold rolled, coated and galvanized steel, or tin, that comes from more traditional blast furnaces.

Mini-mill operators such as Nucor (NUE) and Steel Dynamics (STLD) have grown steadily and have become the industry's low-cost producers. Their cost advantages relate to the fact that they rely on less costly inputs, create fewer environmental problems, and employ fewer (and nonunionized) employees per ton of steel produced. Some major steelmakers use both blast furnaces and electric arc furnaces. Wheeling Pittsburgh Steel, now owned by Severstal, is one such example. Canadian Dofasco, owned by the world's largest steel firm, Arcelor Mittal, is another.

There is a third variation on steelmaking that is worthy of mention. This involves making slabs by either process and then shipping those slabs to a hot strip mill in a different location, where they are rolled into hot rolled steel or downstream, manufacturing-oriented products. Currently, the world's low-cost slab producers are located in Brazil, Russia, and Ukraine. Iron ore is plentiful in such locations; the labor these firms hire is relatively inexpensive and their steelmaking expertise is quite strong. They are tough competitors.

In recent years, tariffs on steel imports made it prohibitively expensive for steel customers to import finished steel coil into the United States. However, there have been no tariffs on steel slabs. When the price of steel slabs rose rapidly on the world markets between 2006 and 2008, this created a splendid opportunity for foreign firms to expand into North American markets if they could purchase a facility with a large hot-strip mill that could use steel slabs imported from such locations as Brazil, Russia, or Ukraine. California Steel (controlled by Brazilian CVRD) and Duferco Farrell (controlled by Russian NLMK) provide two examples. The purchase of our firm, Esmark, by Severstal occurred in part because Esmark owned a hot-strip mill with much greater capacity than its own furnaces could satisfy. It is worth noting that the typical collective bargaining agreement of firms unionized by the USW contains clauses that restrict the importation of slabs from foreign sources without USW approval.

Steelmaking History

In 1970, roughly 85 percent of the steel produced in the United States came from blast furnaces and only 15 percent from mini-mills using the electric arc process. In the 1970s, it was the fully integrated producers who controlled the steel market. Typically, they owned their own sources of supply of coal, coke, and similar items. U.S. Steel was the king of the hill, having taken that mantle from Bethlehem Steel, by then in serious decline. Foreign competition was limited.

This was soon to change. In the 1980s, foreign steel imports began to challenge U.S. steel producers. Steel prices were relatively low because of the intensified competition. Customers benefitted. However, domestic steelmakers cried foul over what they termed "subsidized" foreign steel. Whether or not this argument was valid, foreign steel was flowing into the United States in increasing amounts, and this was squeezing the profit margins of domestic steel producers. There was some validity to the complaints of U.S. steel producers. Around the world, governments seeking to build their manufacturing bases subsidized their national steel companies, allowing cheap steel to flow globally to the largest and most lucrative markets. This meant subsidized steel landed on a regular basis in the United States.

Domestic steel production fell below 100 million tons per year in the 1980s as steel imports climbed to 20 million tons per year.

Actual steel consumption in the United States throughout this period remained relatively flat, although labor costs and raw material costs began to climb. Furthermore, integrated U.S. steel producers often had aging production facilities plants that required large investments. Meanwhile, many of their foreign competitors were unconstrained by strong labor unions or environmental regulations and could produce steel less expensively. The result was falling rates of return on invested steel capital in the United States. Not surprisingly, in the 1980s and 1990s, Wall Street kept its distance from most U.S. steel producers. Except for the mini-mills, the steel industry in the United States was viewed as stagnant and inefficient.

The hard times of large, integrated U.S. steel producers continued in the 1990s. They seemingly lacked the management skills to innovate and change. The mini-mills expanded their share of the market, reaching 50 percent of domestic production by the turn of the 20th century. Companies such as Nucor, not burdened with union contracts, developed significant cost advantages over the integrated mills.

When the U.S. economy decelerated in 2000–2002, the demand for steel fell by 40 million tons, and steel prices spiraled downward. Domestic steel mills went from 95 percent capacity utilization at the beginning of the recession to 70 percent by the end of 2001. This was highly problematic, because the huge capital investments of these companies required that they operate near full capacity in order to spread these fixed costs over more units of production. During a downturn in the economy, steel inventories tend to increase. Experience demonstrates that, when the inventories held by steel distributors exceeds 3.5 months of supply, steel prices fall. What's more, the price declines are seldom gentle, profit margins are squeezed unmercifully, and competition for customers is cutthroat. Long-term relationships with satisfied, happy customers become especially valuable. Those firms that have not cultivated their customers over time are shoved to the rear of the line.

Although these principles are easy to recite and understand, steel producers have somehow continually managed to forget them over and over in the past 50 years. In 2002, selling prices for hot rolled steel plummeted from $350 per ton to $225 per ton. By the end of 2002, almost 40 steel companies in the United States, representing 40 percent of production capacity, had been forced into bankruptcy. Employment in steel production fell from more than 500,000 to a little more than 100,000. Included on the list of bankruptcies were no fewer than four of the five major producers previously listed: Bethlehem Steel, National Steel, LTV, and Wheeling Pittsburgh steel. Of these large players, only Wheeling Pittsburgh Steel was able to reorganize and come out of bankruptcy.

U.S. Steel was able to survive without filing bankruptcy, but it was helped mightily because of its ownership of the highly profitable Marathon Oil and because it purchased a bankrupt steel mill in Slovakia that it turned around. This mill, in Kosice, Slovakia, quickly became the star of the U.S. Steel operating units, generating cash that was used to keep the company off life support at home through the recession. With these two investments as a buffer, U.S. Steel survived the recession of 2000 to 2002. Steel firms in general also used the political mechanism to convince the U.S. government to erect substantial tariffs against foreign steel imports, and this also helped them through this very difficult period.

The global recession that began very late in 2007 is going to be long and deep, and the term "depression" is sometimes mentioned on the cable business channels as a possibility. Nevertheless, conditions have deteriorated dramatically and now compare to the brutal period the U.S. steel industry experienced between 2000 and 2002. The only good thing about that recession, as far as steel producers were concerned, was that it was not lengthy. With a significant reduction in capacity and improved economy, steel prices began to recover in 2003. The assets of Bethlehem Steel and LTV were purchased at a low cost, out of bankruptcy, by Wilbur Ross, under the banner of "International Steel Group," ISG, after the USW made major concessions in negotiations over wages and legacy pension and health costs. In 2005, Arcelor Mittal Steel acquired these assets from

ISG and combined them with Inland Steel to establish a North American beachhead. In the process, Arcelor Mittal cashed out Wilbur Ross, Franklin Mutual Shares, and other shareholders for $4.15 billion.

By 2003, the U.S. economy was on the rebound, although steel demand was still somewhat slack. With many mills having shut down, capacity utilization among the survivors increased, and this set the stage for a bull market in steel. By early 2004, iron ore and coke prices rose, as the world entered a major commodities squeeze. The rapid growth of the Chinese and Indian economies stimulated world demand for raw materials. The inventories carried by steel distributors, reduced by bankruptcies, were at very low levels. A mini-panic ensued, and steel prices shot up to levels never seen before in the industry.

In early 2004, the price of the steel benchmark, hot rolled steel, reached $400 per ton. In contrast to 2000 to 2002, there now was a severe shortage of steel. How things had changed! Mills began to allocate steel only to their best customers. By the end of 2004, prices for hot rolled steel reached a record $760 per ton. Incredibly, 2004 became the most profitable year ever for U.S. steelmakers and steel distributors.

The increasing profitability of U.S. steel companies was not lost on Wall Street. Steel firms suddenly became the darlings of stock analysts and bankers. Money was plentiful for any company on the prowl for acquisitions. Our company, Esmark, bought eight small companies during this bull market. Even so, we weren't the only ones. The Russian oligarchs also were paying attention, and they began to acquire U.S. steel assets as well.

Meanwhile, transportation costs, always a major factor when heavy, bulky materials must be moved, began to rise. Figure 4-1 depicts the value of the Baltic Exchange Dry Index (a rather arcane name for the popular index that measures international transportation costs) between 2002 and 2009. The "Baltic" leaped from about 1,800 in late 2005 to more than 11,600 in 2008. In the space of three years, international transportation costs skyrocketed by more than 500 percent.

Ordinarily, cost increases of any kind are problematic for firms. However, these price increases caused many U.S. steel operators to jump for joy. Why? Because these transportation price increases, along with the continued deterioration in the value of the U.S. dollar, combined to make foreign steel imports too expensive to compete in the U.S. steel market (see Figure 4-2). The upshot is that rising transportation costs and the falling dollar erected a cost barrier that foreign steel producers could not surmount. This had two visible effects. First, it enabled U.S. steel producers to raise their prices and increase their profitability because they no longer had to fear foreign competition. This was not a good development for U.S. consumers, but it introduced boom times for many steel companies. Second, it spurred foreign steel companies, such as Arcelor Mittal and those owned by the Russian oligarchs, to give

Figure 4-1 Baltic Exchange Dry Index

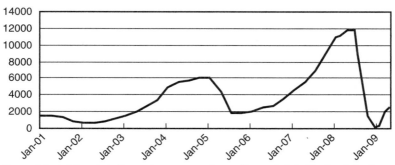

Source: Adapted from http://www. investmenttools.com/futures/bdi_baltic_dry_index.htm.

strong consideration to purchasing U.S. steel companies in order to leap over this cost barrier.

Another little recognized condition also profoundly influenced the steel market during these years. Relatively few individuals realize that the United States is one of a very few large countries that does not produce as much steel as it consumes. The gap between U.S. steel production and U.S. steel consumption has been roughly 20 million tons annually. Over the past few decades, this gap was always satisfied by steel imports. However, in 2007 and 2008, steel imports were realistically priced out of the U.S. market. Simply put, the demand for steel in the United States far exceeded available supply, as both the U.S. and world economies expanded. Predictably, this caused prices to explode upward. Prices for scrap iron, iron ore, and coking coal surged, and prices for hot rolled steel shot up even more, to an unprecedented $1,150 per ton for hot rolled sheet steel in the Midwest in ①

Figure 4-2 Steel Imports into the United States, 2005–2008 (millions of tons annually)

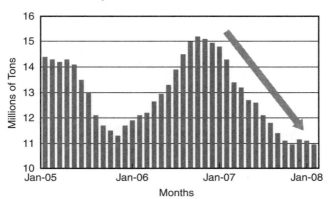

Source: Adapted from www.content.edgar-online.com/edgar_conv_img/2008.

Figure 4-3 Hot-Rolled Steel Plate Prices

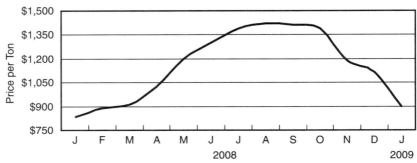

Source: Adapted from data at www.purchasingdata.com.

2008. Figure 4-3 shows this amazing inflation in steel prices, which occurred worldwide but which reversed itself in the last quarter of 2008.

Needless to say, this peculiar set of events made most U.S. steel companies and their stockholders happy. At the same time, however, these rather unusual circumstances made U.S. steel firms highly attractive targets for foreign steel producers who wished to penetrate the U.S. market. In some ways, it was the best of all worlds for foreign steel companies—U.S. steel firms were quite profitable, and, because of the weak U.S. dollar, they were priced inexpensively. America was indeed for sale as far as many foreign steel firms were concerned, and they did not permit this opportunity to escape. Foreign steelmakers, especially those located in Brazil, India, and Russia, began to make attractive bids for U.S. steel firms and steel suppliers. The Brazilians, Indians, and Russians were the hunters. U.S. steel firms became the hunted.

What was the impact of these developments upon the overall performance of the U.S. steel industry? Table 4-1 reveals that, between 2005 and 2008, the output of the steel industry expanded by almost 28 percent, even while industry employment contracted by about 10 percent. This reflects both the prosperity of the industry and its growing efficiency, at least with respect to labor productivity.

Table 4-1   Key U.S. Iron and Steel Manufacturing Statistics, 2005–2008

Performance Measure	2005	2006	2007	2008
Constant dollar revenue (2005 dollars)	$91.11 b.	$98.87 b.	$107.64 b.	$116.40 b.
Growth rate in constant dollar revenue	4.7%	8.5%	8.9%	8.1%
Change in employment	−6.2%	−1.6%	−1.4%	−0.7%

Source: Esmark, Inc.

WHO DID THE BUYING?

Let's take a look at who's been buying what in the steel industry. Table 4-2 provides a list of the 10 most significant North American steel assets that changed hands in the bull market of 2007 and 2008. Nearly $19 billion was spent on these 10 transactions from mid-2007 through 2008. U.S. buyers (Nucor and U.S. Steel) were involved in only 2 of the 10 transactions, and they paid approximately 11 percent of the total enterprise value of the deals. Fully 89 percent of the purchase money came from foreign firms.

NATIONAL SECURITY CONSIDERATIONS

Until recently, attempts to connect the steel industry to national security considerations were not treated seriously by most informed, neutral observers. After all, the U.S. steel industry was the largest in the world, it

Table 4-2   Acquisition of U.S. Steel Firms, 2007–2008

Acquiring Firm	Target	Date of Acquisition Announced	Effective	Selling Price
NLMK Russia	Beta Steel	09/04/08	10/31/08	$350 m.
Severstal Russia	Esmark, Inc.	06/25/08	08/04/08	$1,151 m.
Arcelor Mittal India	Bayou Steel	06/16/08	Pending	$475 m.
Nucor U.S.	Ambassador	06/12/08	08/26/08	$185 m.
Severstal Russia	WCI Steel	05/16/08	07/07/08	$331 m.
Severstal Russia	Sparrows Point	03/21/08	05/08/08	$810 m.
U.S. Steel	Stelco	08/26/07	10/31/07	$1,865 m.
Gerdau A. Brazil	Chaparral	07/10/07	09/14/07	$4,067 m.
Svenskt Stal Sweden	IPSCO	05/03/07	07/18/07	$8,151 m.
Essar Steel India	Algoma	04/15/07	06/20/07	$1,469 m.
			Total	$18,854 m.

Figure 4-4 Estimated North American Steel Market Shares, 2008

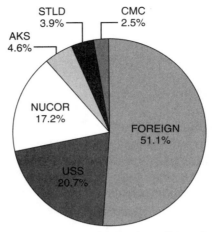

Source: International Business Information Services (IBIS), UBS, *Wall Street Journal.*

was U.S.-owned, and segments of the industry (the mini-mills) were demonstrably competitive, even in an international context. However, by 2002, four of the five largest U.S. steel producers had bitten the dust and were either in bankruptcy or had been bought out by other firms. The wave of foreign acquisitions of U.S. steel firms in 2007 and 2008 put an exclamation point on this process, because, as Figure 4-4 reveals, it resulted in slightly more than 50 percent of U.S. steelmaking capacity being owned by foreigners.

Here's why this matters. The Department of Defense depends explicitly upon steelmakers to supply it with timely, high-quality steel for its weapons and buildings. This dependence is hardly new. When Teddy Roosevelt and the Rough Riders splashed ashore on Cuba in 1898 during the Spanish-American War, the place they "liberated" first was the iron ore mine that fed the steel mill at Sparrows Point, Maryland. Sparrows Point later became the crown jewel of the Bethlehem Steel empire and eventually grew to be the largest steel mill in the world by the 1950s. Bethlehem Steel became the largest munitions maker in the world.

Today, the Sparrows Point steel mill is the only steel mill in North America that has its own access to a deep water port. Material easily can be shipped in and out of the port. Lakshmi Mittal, the Chairman and CEO of Arcelor Mittal, once told us in a quiet moment that, if he had to begin his company over from scratch in North America, the mill he would buy first would be Sparrows Point. Arcelor Mittal made an attempt to do so but was forced by the U.S. Department of Justice to divest itself of this mill, and, in August of 2008, the Sparrows Point Mill was purchased by the largest Russian steelmaker, Severstal. Russians now control the mill, as well as its attached port facilities on the Chesapeake Bay in Maryland.

It wasn't always that way. In 1945, as German and Japanese steel mills lay destroyed, the United States produced 2 of every 3 tons of global steel. How things have changed! Today we produce only about 10 percent of the world's total, and slightly more than one-half of our steel in the United States is produced by firms owned by foreigners (see Figure 4-4). Even Voltaire's legendary Dr. Pangloss, who always saw the rosy side of any situation, might be inclined to interpret these developments as a worrisome trend.

EXAMPLES OF STEEL USED IN MODERN AMERICAN WEAPONRY

Let's be more specific. Precisely how is steel used in our military establishment? There is more to national security and national defense than weapons; however, the reliance of weapons upon large amounts of steel visibly demonstrates the connections of the steel industry to national defense.

U.S. Army Weaponry that Consumes Large Amounts of Steel

- Abrams Tank: Each tank consumes 22 tons of steel plate.
- Light Armored Vehicle: Each vehicle consumes 8 tons of steel plate.
- Humvee: This staple of the U.S. Army uses large amounts of steel plate to ensure that explosives do not penetrate the shell. Many variations exist, but each version consumes at least 10 tons of steel.

U.S. Navy and U.S. Air Force Weaponry that Consumes Large Amounts of Steel

- Aircraft Carriers: Each fleet carrier consumes approximately 50,000 tons of steel plate. The steel for Nimitz class aircraft carriers must be able to withstand the impact of a 37-ton, F-14 Tomcat aircraft landing on the deck at 150 miles per hour, shield the ship's crew from radiation generated by onboard nuclear reactors, and take the impact of shells and other projectiles.
- Submarines: Each nuclear submarine consumes approximately 10,000 tons of steel plate.

- Guided Missile Destroyers and Cruisers: These ships vary substantially one from another, but each consumes substantial amounts of steel plate. DDG 51 class incorporates all steel construction. In 1975, the cruiser U.S.S. *Belknap* collided with the U.S.S. *John Kennedy*. *Belknap* suffered severe damage and casualties because of its aluminum superstructure. Subsequently, the decision was made that all future surface combatants would return to steel super-structure.
- Landing Platform Dock 17, San Antonio Class: This is the latest class of amphibious force ships. Each vessel requires 12,000 tons of steel. Notably, one of the ships in this class, the U.S.S. *New York,* includes 24 tons of steel recycled from the World Trade Center in memory of those who died in the terror attack.

THE PECULIAR AND POWERFUL ROLE OF THE USW

With 850,000 members, the USW is the largest industrial union in North America. It is the dominant union in the industries of steel, paper, forestry, rubber, plastics, aluminum, chemicals, oil, glass, cement, and energy. Clearly, the USW understands the power of consolidation. The USW has reversed the downward trend in its membership in recent years by merging with smaller unions and creating scale that caused Barack Obama and many others to court its support for their runs for the presidency. After being embarrassed by its formal support for failed candidate John Edwards in the Democratic Party primaries, the USW allegedly committed 500 people full-time to support the Obama presidential campaign in its final days leading up to the general election. Support from unions may well have been the winning edge in the general election, and it would not be a stretch to envision that political promises changed hands in 2008. Today, the USW is working hard to call in the chits that it believes it has earned. Its website trumpets the need to "Buy American," and it fully expects any federal stimulus package money to be spent inside the United States.

The USW maintains its international headquarters in Pittsburgh, but there are 13 districts that contain "local" steelworker organizations, several of which are tightly controlled by the "home office." The 13 districts are generously endowed with USW managers, who deal with union affairs.

Ultimately, the stated purpose of the USW is to protect steelworkers, maximize their compensation, improve their work conditions, and ensure job stability. Nevertheless, practically speaking, the USW ruthlessly pursues a business model that emphasizes maximizing payment of dues. Members' dues are the mother's milk of the USW. Dues fuel the organization. And, typically, the more unionized steel jobs that exist, the greater are the dues payments. On occasion, this means that the USW will sacrifice some goals (for example, the highest worker compensation or retiree benefits) in order to preserve or increase the number of USW members paying dues.

The USW management structure recently featured four individuals. Leo Gerard is the president and is acknowledged to be a clever, effective leader. Dave McCall and Tom Conway are two officers who stand out among the 26-member international executive board as most likely to succeed Gerard as the international president.

A fourth individual, Ron Bloom, was a staff member, but a very significant one, who is involved in crafting the union's strategy, legal positions, and issues that govern the all-important collective bargaining agreements with major clients. One should not miss the fact that Bloom is a Harvard Business School graduate who cut his teeth on Wall Street with Lazard Frères. Bloom's nickname is "the Cardinal," and he played a major role in causing steel companies to grow or shrink through mergers and acquisitions.

President Obama appointed Mr. Bloom to a position in the Department of Treasury to assist with the restructuring of the automobile industry, a move that was hailed by U.S. union leaders. However, he is no one's patsy, and, although the United Auto Workers will have an understanding ear in Ron Bloom, he has already extracted concessions from them, along with those from management and other constituencies.

One former union official is worthy of note. In the early 1980s, when the previously described wave of bankruptcies hit the steel industry and employment fell by hundreds of thousands of steelworkers, Lynn Williams, a Canadian, became the president of the USW and later became a member of the Esmark board of directors. The astute and savvy Williams so altered the mentality and strategy of the union that he may be remembered one day as the most important union president in U.S. history. Williams realized that the adversarial relationship of labor versus management had become counterproductive for the USW, which was losing paying members at a horrific rate. With union dues in a serious decline, he championed a new business model that emphasized consolidation of steel firms and the globalization of the marketplace. Williams wanted fewer, but stronger steel companies that would be willing to invest in infrastructure. He was cold to Wall Street-engineered deals and was willing to let in foreign steelmakers if he believed they would be dedicated industry participants.

Williams championed the new collective bargaining concepts known as the "Successorship Clause" and the "Right to Bid." These clauses required the USW to approve a sale of assets or change of control for any firm with which it had negotiated these provisions. Practically speaking, these clauses mean that the USW has the ability to bring its own favored bidder to the table when a steel company becomes available for sale. In fact, as exemplified by the sale of Esmark, the USW would consistently and coldly reject any suitor for a company that did not pay the USW appropriate homage and negotiate a deal with the union. The bottom line is that the USW acquired the right to veto any sale or purchase of a steel company whose workers were organized by the USW.

Does the Steel Industry Story Sound Familiar?

If the story of the steel industry sounds familiar, you should not be surprised, because most of the same issues exist among the Big Three automobile makers. The negotiations aimed at the momentary rescue of the Big Three in early 2009 revolved around labor costs, legacy pension and health costs, union veto power, and concerns remarkably similar to those of the steel industry.

The USW soon occupied a powerful role as broker in the international steel merger market. Because of its veto power, it also fostered the ability of the union to extract significant concessions from companies it supported in subsequent merger and acquisition wars. Williams pushed for seats for the USW on steel company boards, and he insisted the union begin to think more like a shareholder. This philosophy led the USW to the offer compensation and work rule concessions in exchange for equity in troubled steel companies. Through the Employee Retirement Benefits Association trusts that we describe in the following, the USW became a significant and powerful shareholder in many U.S. steel companies.

The USW also attempted to limit the "outsourcing" of jobs to lower-paid nonunion employees, placed emphasis upon building training centers to retool the skills of workers, and negotiated "job banks" for laid-off workers that required steel firms to pay large portions of workers' salaries even if there was no work for them. The USW also championed the concept of a Voluntary Employee Beneficiary Association (VEBA), a tax exempt trust fund into which companies contributed cash and stock as a means to guarantee endangered retiree benefits.

The USW was so successful with this approach to labor negotiations that many other unions began to copy its model. Unfortunately, there was a major downside to this success. These items led to a significant increase in labor costs for firms that agreed to them.

At the end of the day, one must acknowledge that the role of the USW in today's steel industry is huge. The union plays a role in large company governance, strategy, materials, financing, and discussions of mergers and acquisition. Obviously, this involves quite a bit more than wages and work rules!

In our view, the participation of the USW has had mixed effects in terms of the welfare of steel firms, their workers, and their customers. The Esmark buyout by Severstal illustrates some of the complications. Early in 2007, Esmark was considering making a bid to acquire the historic steel mill at Sparrows Point, Maryland. We visited with the chief negotiator for the USW to seek his opinion about the acceptability to the USW of the potential partners who might participate in such a deal. At that moment, Esmark was in discussions with Russian, Ukrainian, Mexican, and Brazilian companies about their joining us in our bid for Sparrow's Point. Before we proceeded, we wanted to know whether the USW would support foreign ownership of the mill. The USW's approval was required under the "successorship" clause contained in the seller's collective bargaining agreement (CBA). The response of the USW was that the steel world "had become global" and that foreign participation in our industry was destined to grow. And, if the foreign entities agreed to acceptable (hopefully rich) CBAs, then they would be welcome.

Our view at the time was that the Russian steel conglomerates were "new Russian," meaning "Westernized" firms with lots of cash. These companies were and are owned by oligarchs who were itching to take their new wealth and locate it out of the former Soviet Union. They sought reliability, security, and the rule of law that characterizes public markets in the United States and the United Kingdom. We also were of the opinion that the management teams of these companies contain significant operational, engineering and business talent.

The USW's view was essentially the same, and it was comfortable with the prospects that Russian oligarchs might acquire significant positions in the U.S. steel industry. The prevailing view was that this was not the Cold War and that Russians no longer were untrustworthy enemies. Publications ranging from the *Economist* to the *New York Times* signed on to this view of the world.

That was then, and now is now. The aggressive and petulant moves of Russia's Vladimir Putin (a former KGB executive) on a half dozen different fronts caused a painful, but major, alteration in the view that the Russian Cold War bear had disappeared. When the world financial crisis hit in the fall of 2008, it struck the Russian oligarch business leaders particularly hard. Several lost 80 to 90 percent of their wealth, and they were forced to take large loans from the Russian government. Table 4-3 discloses,

Agelbson

for example, that Alexei Mordashov of Severstal, which purchased Esmark, saw his wealth decrease from $22 billion to $3 billion in the space of only a few months.

We are not disposed to cry in sympathy for the Russian oligarchs. However, the problem is that the Russian government now owns substantial portions of their enterprises and has acquired the ability to make them sing to the Kremlin's tunes. Hence, the Kremlin now is a significant owner of a variety of U.S. business enterprises, including important portions of the U.S. steel industry.

Who Captures the Fruits of Steel Market Protectionism?

Mark Glyptis, USW local president in Weirton, West Virginia, argued several years ago that, "Someday when historians record the decline of the American steel industry, President Bush will have the infamous distinction of contributing to the decimation of our industry and the loss of American jobs" (http://thinkexist.com/quotes/mark_glyptis/). However, a variety of economists have found that the trade protections provided to the U.S. steel industry in the 1970s and 1980s did not improve steel firms' competitiveness. Instead, steelworkers' wages increased, and firms invested higher profits in other industries.

Table 4-3   The Russian Oligarchs Take a Financial Bath

| Name | Core Businesses | Net Worth | | Debts |
		Mid-2008	Early 2009	
Oleg Deripaska	Aluminum Raw Materials	$28.0 b.	$3.5 b.	$14.0 b.
Roman Abramovich	Oil Infrastructure	$23.5 b.	$3.3 b.	$ 2.0 b.
Vladimir Lisin	Steel	$22.2 b.	$3.1 b.	$3.3 b.
Alexei Mordashov	Steel	$22.1 b.	$3.5 b.	$0.2 b.
Vladimir Potanin	Commodities	$21.5 b.	$2.1 b.	N.A.
Mikhail Prokhorov	Commodities Finance	$21.5 b.	$1.3 b.	N.A.

Source: Financial Times, Forbes, New York Times, USA Today, Wall Street Journal.

The Kremlin loaned the oligarchs an estimated $78 billion before New Year's Day, 2009. "Some of them [the oligarchs] will definitely lose their property, either to the state or to investors," said billionaire Alexander Lebedev, 49, in an interview on December 8.[2] It seems almost inevitable that several of the oligarchs will bite the dust, because they collectively lost an estimated $300 billion in equity in late 2008 and early 2009. Either they will sell their assets, go bankrupt, or both. In either case, the Russian government will assume the position of the most powerful influence in their businesses.

The implications of these moves for U.S. national security cannot be ignored. We do not believe it is in the best interests of the United States to permit substantial Russian ownership of the U.S. steel industry. Note that our strong preference for a healthy majority of U.S. ownership of the U.S. steel industry is not the same as endorsing protectionist policies, which we reject. Most of our U.S. steel industry should be U.S.-owned; however, it must also be competitive and efficient. The identity of our steel industry's owners is an issue separate from import quotas and tariffs on foreign steel. True, U.S. steel companies will often argue that protectionist policies by the United States are necessary to maintain U.S. ownership, but we do not agree. It is possible to operate a competitive, efficient steel company in the United States, as Nucor and other firms have demonstrated. Even so, long-term survival may dictate a steel industry model that is not based upon the USW ground rules that have evolved over the past few decades.

THE FUTURE OF THE STEEL INDUSTRY

Sadly, there are only four truly American steel manufacturers left: Nucor, U.S. Steel, AK Steel, and Steel Dynamics. All are publicly traded companies. U.S. Steel and AK Steel are organized on the traditional integrated business model; Nucor and Steel Dynamics are mini-mill operators, reliant on scrap iron as their major input. AK Steel and U.S. Steel have higher operating costs and much more significant legacy costs for pensions and health care. Nucor and Steel Dynamics are not unionized. They control their sources of scrap from previous acquisition activity, and they will fare better than their competition in the current recession because of their lower costs and greater labor force flexibility. The wages of Nucor's workers are usually based upon production levels and worker productivity. As a consequence, during the steel industry slowdown in 2008, when weekly steel production dove from 2.10 million tons on August 30 to 1.2 million tons by the end of December, the weekly take-home wages of a typical

Nucor worker fell by approximately 50 percent. This did not happen at U.S. Steel, nor could it have happened at Esmark.

One often-ignored aspect of the cost superiority of the mini-mills is their ability to throttle back production. Their electric arc furnaces can be turned on and off much more easily than blast furnaces. Consequently, they suit the cyclical nature of the steel industry better.

We believe that Steel Dynamics and AK Steel will have great difficulty surviving as independent companies in the current milieu. They are obvious candidates for acquisition, probably by foreign investors in Brazil, China, India, and Russia, if the U.S. dollar deteriorates substantially. Nevertheless, Nucor would be a natural predator for Steel Dynamics, because the parties know each other well and neither Nucor nor Steel Dynamics is constrained by a union agreement. Steel Dynamics, perhaps the best steel company in the world, pound for pound, is just small enough to fit the budget of all the world's major steel investors. Steel Dynamics' stock price fell by over 75 percent in the second half of 2008, which only increases the company's vulnerability to takeover.

The same foreign "pack" could be interested in AK Steel, which also was humbled in the stock market. AK is also a well-managed company with excellent plant facilities. U.S. Steel faces legacy costs, but it is rumored to be interested in bidding for AK, given sufficient recovery in the U.S. steel industry. When the dust settles, we would expect foreign ownership of the U.S. steel industry to have increased well beyond the 50-percent level.

Nucor is now such a large and well-capitalized entity that we don't believe anyone will take a run at acquiring it in the near future. U.S. Steel may be a different story, because the "pack" has been eying U.S. Steel for a number of years. Although it was a richly capitalized entity when its stock traded at $180 per share, U.S. Steel's share price had fallen to $35 in July 2009. Thus, it is vulnerable. Its strong facility in Kosice, Slovakia, is an asset that could be worth as much as $5.0 billion when the steel market and stock market recover. U.S. Steel's tubular steel business—providing pipes and tubes for a wide range of tasks, ranging from oil and gas to construction and furniture—is attractive and could be spun out. Its Posco joint venture with Korea's Pohang Steel Company is divisible as well. Thus, what is today the United States Steel Corporation could be swallowed whole or broken into bits if the "pack" is allowed to continue its binge. The probability of this occurring will increase as the value of the U.S. dollar decreases. We do not believe this would be in our nation's best interest. It is one thing to have foreign steel companies acquire marginal, almost failing steel producers. It is quite another thing to have them take over the few core U.S. steel production firms that remain.

Chapter 5

Esmark on the Attack

Companies are owned by shareholders, and the management work for shareholders! It's their capital.

Warren Buffett

And David put his hand into his bag and took from it a stone and slung it, and struck the Philistine on his forehead. And the stone sank into his forehead, so that he fell on his face to the ground.

1Samuel 17:49, The Holy Bible

Let's review the story of Esmark, Inc., the dynamic but diminutive steel company whose history we outlined briefly in Chapter 1. James and Craig Bouchard founded Esmark in 2003, with a cash investment of $750,000, a loan of $1.9 million, and an abiding faith in their ability to thrive in the steel services industry. Jim Bouchard had more than a modicum of experience in this arena; he was substantially responsible for turning around U.S. Steel's steel plant in Kosice, Slovakia, and making it a profit machine. Craig Bouchard had extensive experience and valuable contacts in financial markets around the world.

The Bouchards began a systematic program of acquiring small- and medium-sized steel service centers in the Midwest. Ultimately, they acquired ten firms and maintained or increased the profitability of all of those firms under the flag of Esmark. In 2006, they decided that they would try to bite off a much bigger piece of the industry—the Wheeling Pittsburgh Steel

Corporation, traditionally one of the five largest firms in the North American market.

Wheeling Pitt, however, was not interested in being acquired by Esmark, and its board of directors not only turned down Esmark's overtures but also voted to pursue a deal with the large Brazilian steel firm, Companhia Siderúrgica Nacional (CSN). For most individuals, the matter would have ended there, but not with the Bouchards. They proceeded to orchestrate the first hostile reverse tender merger in U.S. history. This involved merging the privately held Esmark into the hostile target, the publicly traded Wheeling Pitt. This could happen only with an affirmative vote of Wheeling Pitt's stockholders, and so, in November 2007, everything came down to a vote of Wheeling Pitt's approximately 2,200 stockholders. This vote ousted the then-current board of directors and substituted a new slate of directors organized by the Bouchards, which would then fairly evaluate a potential deal with Esmark.

Although Wheeling Pitt had thousands of stockholders, the largest among them were Tontine Partners and Wellington Management and organs of the USW, which had acquired large blocks of stock as a reward for agreeing to concessions regarding wages and fringe benefits in collective bargaining. Ultimately, both of these critical stockholder constituencies voted in favor of the Bouchard director slate, and the Wheeling-Pitt board was ousted, along with the company's senior management. Esmark was merged into Wheeling Pitt, and the combined entity was renamed Esmark, which name the firm carried until it was sold to Severstal. The "new" Esmark now consisted of the "old" Esmark (a downstream steel-services operation) plus the newly acquired Wheeling Pittsburgh Steel Corporation.

SETTING THE STAGE

Wheeling Pitt had led a charmed life over the past 20 years. It had declared bankruptcy twice and survived only with financial help from the U.S. government and the state of West Virginia. However, even during good times, Wheeling Pitt typically struggled and carried almost a half billion dollars of debt as the credit crunch of 2007 unfolded. Of the 15 banks and financial institutions that somehow were "new" Esmark creditors, 14 asked for and received repayment of their loans during the credit crunch, leaving G.E. Finance as the only bank to show full confidence and support for the company's management team and strategy. Needless to say, G.E. Finance's attention was welcomed, but these circumstances also conferred substantial financial leverage on G.E. Finance, and it appropriately insisted on favorable terms to it.

By all odds, Esmark was vulnerable to a takeover, hostile or otherwise. Although Esmark owned some impressive assets and portions of the firm, such as the "old" Esmark service centers, were profitable, it was not vertically integrated in the fashion of many successful steel firms, it was almost a basket case financially, and it badly needed owners who could plunge considerable capital into the old Wheeling Pitt portion of the company in order to bring its often-outdated plant up to date. Only a great optimist could have regarded the negotiating clout of Esmark and the Bouchard brothers as high at this time.

Nevertheless, despite these negatives, during 2008, the Bouchards were able to stimulate and manage an international battle for Esmark's assets. In the event, in August 2008, Esmark's investors reaped an incredible price for its shares ($19.25 per share after the stock had traded at $10 only months earlier), while steel company stock prices around the world began plummeting to record lows. Was this superb ending the result of brilliant strategy on the part of the combative Bouchards and Esmark's talented board of directors, or was it just good old-fashioned luck? Immodestly, we believe skill and superb analysis were involved much more than luck. Regardless, the Esmark episode is an entrepreneurial U.S. story worthy of note. It also supplies an exclamation point to the story of the sale of U.S. firms and assets.

EARLY DEVELOPMENTS

The stories of Wheeling Pitt and Esmark are interesting in their own right. Even though the authors are still bound by confidentiality agreements, we can rely upon public documents and media reports to reconstruct what happened. Let's go back in time to set the stage.

1999

Jim Bouchard was a rising star in the U.S. Steel organization. Still in his mid-thirties, after stints in sales, operations, and strategic planning, Jim became a senior member of the four-person executive team U.S. Steel sent to Kosice, Slovakia, in the late 1990s. U.S Steel had acquired the Slovakian National Steel Company (VSZ), a 7,000-employee mill known as much for its financial problems and its conspicuously shady Eastern European business dealings as it was for making steel.

The rapid improvement of the Kosice mill under U.S. Steel ownership startled the industry. Jim Bouchard became widely credited with the successful commercial restructuring of the steel mill and, subsequently, of U.S. Steel's operations more broadly across the European continent. Within two years of its acquisition by U.S. Steel, the Slovakian mill became the jewel of the global U.S. Steel empire at a time when the firm actually was still struggling for survival. The Kosice mill was bought for $160 million. By 2008, it was worth $5 billion. Not surprisingly, Bouchard was named vice president-commercial for all of U.S. Steel in Europe.

2002

Jim Bouchard flew from Europe to meet his brother Craig in Naples, Florida, to discuss a career decision. Ready to bring his wife and three children home from Slovakia, and with politics in Pittsburgh blocking him from the most senior positions at U.S. Steel, Jim was convinced that it was time to leave U.S. Steel and run his own company. He had concluded that he was unlikely to enter the favored queue to lead U.S. Steel.

Craig had spent his career in international banking, mergers and acquisitions, and financial trading. He had made a successful career change after his banking years to become the CEO of a respected software firm on Wall Street. Jim went to Naples to talk with Craig about a change that could define his career. Craig listened to his logic and suggested that he was setting his target too low. He considered his brother the brightest strategic mind in the steel industry. More than that, he felt his brother was a natural born leader. "Don't run that company," insisted Craig. "Buy it!" That was the night that the company that would become Esmark, Inc., was conceived.

The strategic ideas that powered Esmark flowed from Jim's background. Distribution of steel in the United States was ready for consolidation. There were thousands of small "steel-service center" companies ripe for acquisition. Service centers are companies that buy raw steel from steel mills, cut it or coat it in some fashion, and then sell those products to a manufacturing customer base. The service centers control large groupings of downstream steel customers in the United States, and this leverage makes them some of the most important customers of the major steel mills.

Most of the downstream steel-service companies were profitable and had been spun off from the large U.S steel mills in the 1970s, as the industry attempted to recover from one of its frequent down cycles. The advice given to steel company executives by the management consultants of that era was to "focus" on production and give up the customer-intensive distribution component of the mills. They did so and sold out to a variety of individuals, mostly entrepreneurs aged 30 to 50.

The fortyish Bouchards and Esmark stepped into the picture some 25 years later. Most of the steel-service center owners now were in their mid-seventies and ready to retire. Jim Bouchard recognized the opportunity and added a second clever idea. Hot rolled steel represented the largest and most desired segment of the domestic sheet market. Cold rolled steel was the step child. Cold rolled steel was more costly to produce and less in demand by the customers. Bouchard designed Esmark to focus on cold rolled steel. It was counterintuitive, but brilliant. The mills sold as much hot rolled steel as they produced each year without difficulty. However, value-added products, such as cold rolled steel, were typically in oversupply, and this kept prices for cold rolled steel depressed. This was projected to continue well into the future.

In this milieu, the Bouchards developed a plan to buy enough distribution capacity for cold rolled steel in the Midwest to become coveted by the mills as a source of distribution for product that the mills most needed to sell but, in the past, had often not been able to sell. The Bouchards' hope was to command a much better price from the mills as a large volume buyer than as a splintered set of small individual competitors.

This strategy had never been attempted and therefore met with curious reactions from steel executives, bankers, and customers. Many were doubters. It made for great conversations at the water coolers around the industry. Three years later, however, it was clear that this strategic gamble had worked and was making investors in Esmark rich.

The Bouchards bought their first two companies in Chicago with little more than their private cash reserve and a bit of help from their friends. The first acquisition was ECT, an Electro Galvanizing facility in East Chicago, Indiana. ECT was losing money and was bought out of bankruptcy for $2.4 million in mid-2003. The second, Sun Steel Company, in Chicago Heights, Illinois, was purchased for $11 million in February 2004 from a retiring owner whom Jim knew well from his U.S. Steel days. Its earnings in a good year were less than $3.0 million. Naysayers opined that the Bouchards overpaid for both of these acquisitions. However, fueled by a strategic and operational makeover and the strong steel market of 2004, these two companies achieved eye-popping operating incomes that were 400 percent above those of the best years in their histories.

Esmark's success caught the attention of bankers. J.P. Morgan Chase became the lead commercial bank in financing Esmark. G.E. Finance, UBS and Raymond James would later join the list. Industry leaders, such as Arcelor Mittal Steel, Steel Dynamics, and U.S. Steel, provided liberal trade credit, because they thought Esmark would eventually become an important customer.

Capitalizing on these successes, the Bouchards toured private equity firms on Wall Street and raised $115 million of preferred stock in mid-2004 from Franklin Mutual Advisors and another $50 million from Franklin later in the year. This money fueled their next seven acquisitions, all of which occurred in a hectic two-year period. Esmark quickly became known as a leader in the national consolidation of the service center industry. The strategy, focused on cold rolled, Midwestern steel, yielded strongly positive financial results. Revenues, which had been $4 million at the end of 2003, grew to more than $400 million by the end of 2005.

However, the Bouchards were not thinking small, and now set their sights on transforming Esmark into a major player in the U.S. steel industry overall—by means of a controversial gambit. Put simply, their new strategic objective was to undertake vertical integration of their growing steel distribution network by means of acquiring the largest steel mill they could afford to buy. To the surprise of many, this turned out to be the Wheeling Pittsburgh Corporation (WPC), the publicly traded 86-year-old steelmaker headquartered in Wheeling, West Virginia.

THE BATTLE FOR WHEELING PITTSBURGH STEEL

The Wheeling Pitt saga began one evening in May 2005 when the Bouchards were riding in a car with Jim Tumulty, their investment banker from Raymond James. Tumulty was a steel specialist and well connected to both hedge funds and the USW union. The USW often relied on Tumulty as an informal steel industry analyst.

Tumulty posed a question to the Bouchard brothers. Would they be interested in working with the USW to find a better home for Wheeling Pittsburgh Steel, Algoma Steel (a Canadian mill), or both? The USW had concluded that both firms needed management and strategic changes if they were going to survive. Jim Bouchard's response was immediate. Yes, Esmark would have interest in Wheeling Pittsburgh Steel, but not in Algoma because of its remote location in Ontario, Canada. Swiftly, Tumulty was on his cell phone, relaying this message to Ron Bloom at the USW headquarters in Pittsburgh.

Jim Bouchard believed that he could translate his impressive performance in Kosice, Slovakia, with U.S. Steel to the United States. In Kosice, a large steel-service center had been built inside the mill to replace more than 100 brokers of steel that had been draining the mill of profitability for years. The strategy had been an incredible success and had made the Kosice mill profitable nearly overnight. The Bouchards felt the time was right to bring this model to the United States. By then, consolidation was beginning to occur among steel-service centers, even while steel mill con-solidation in North America was nearing completion.

Pragmatically, Wheeling Pitt was the only U.S. steel mill left that was even remotely "affordable." This term, of course, was relative. At that time, Esmark was a private company nearing $400 million of revenue. It had several hundred employees and minimal debts. Wheeling Pitt, on the other hand, was a public company with $1.6 billion of revenue, 3,000 employees, and more than $400 million of debt spread across 15 banks, most of which were guaranteed by the U.S. government's Emergency Steel Loan Guaranty Board (ESLGB). This board was a little known U.S. government entity that had helped Wheeling Pitt fund its new electric arc furnace and escape bankruptcy in 2003. The bottom line is that the ESLGB guarantees selected loans that financial institutions make to distressed steel companies, thereby enabling the steel companies to benefit from lower interest rates and perhaps even to obtain a loan at all. Ironically, this typifies the very kind of government subsidy of steel companies that U.S. steel companies object to when foreign countries have behaved in an analogous fashion. Regardless, Wheeling Pitt needed such a lifeline because it already had been in and out of bankruptcy twice.

Few thought that an organization as small as Esmark could take on a project of this complexity and scale and swallow Wheeling Pitt. However, Franklin Mutual Shares, the large mutual fund company and largest share-holder of Esmark, believed Esmark could pull it off. So did the USW, after several follow-up meetings with the Bouchards. Both Franklin and the USW essentially bought into the strategic vision, personal charisma, abil-ity, and promise of the Bouchard brothers. Perhaps most important, the Bouchards themselves had no fear and were brimming with confidence that they could pull this off. After appropriate handshakes, they asked Jim Bradley, the CEO of Wheeling Pitt, for a meeting in June 2005.

To say that Bradley was surprised to hear about the Esmark "swallow the whale" idea is an understatement. He knew very little of Esmark and kept asking the Bouchards how big their company was. Either he did not understand what he was being told, or he simply did not like the answer. Bradley was an older-generation steel guy, and, to him, this meant that steel mills were the kings of the hill, whereas steel-service centers were the equivalent of the used car dealers in the auto industry.

Bradley had seen his company enter bankruptcy and exit with a strat-egy that was his personal baby. With the help of Senators Robert Byrd and Jay Rockefeller of West Virginia, he convinced the U.S. government to guarantee $250 million of new bank loans to enable Wheeling Pitt to build a massive electric arc furnace to go along with its old blast furnace. This made Wheeling Pitt a steelmaker that was one-half mini-mill and one-half

In the 1970s, U.S. Steel Mills Had Become Distant from Their Customers

The mills dealt primarily with large customers, such as automobile manufacturers and large OEM appliance manufacturers. U.S. Steel Corporation had fewer than 200 significant customers for their steel sheet products. It was up to the steel-service centers (owned by others) to deal face-to-face with the thousands of smaller steel customers. Jim Bouchard thought it was a mistake when the mills divested their service centers and gave up control of these customers. Service centers tend to hold too much inventory and when that happens, steel prices weaken. Service centers in Europe and Japan hold much lower inventories because they are confident of supply from strategic mill partners. Jim Bouchard brought a philosophy of operating much closer to the European/Japanese model with close connections with customers and mills. This reduced risk.

traditional blast furnace-driven. Bradley was convinced his strategy would give Wheeling Pitt operational flexibility and result in a lower cost structure. Unfortunately, the new electric arc furnace was turned on only after months of delays and unexpectedly high transition costs. Even so, he now felt ready to prove the worth of his strategy. Although Bradley knew that Wheeling Pitt was overleveraged and needed fresh capital, the last thing he wanted to do was hand his company over to the Bouchards, and he said so flatly. Hence, in his view, they would not darken his door again.

The Bouchards felt differently. They immediately assembled senior executives of Franklin Mutual Advisors and J.P. Morgan, along with Esmark's legal teams of McGuire Woods, in Pittsburgh, and Patzic, Frank and Samotny, in Chicago. After checking again with the USW and confirming its support, Franklin committed $200 million of fresh capital, and J.P. Morgan worked on assembling a bank financing group with senior executives at G.E. Finance. The Bouchards went to Europe, hunting for partners who could provide low-priced steel slabs for the Wheeling Pitt hot-strip mill, after the USW confirmed it would allow foreign slabs to be imported to Wheeling. The Bouchards found potential partners in Duferco, a Swiss steel conglomerate, and IUD Donbass, a Ukrainian steelmaker.

Although Wheeling Pitt was a twice-bankrupt mill and the highest-cost, large-scale producer of steel in the United States, the Bouchard brothers thought nonetheless that it had considerable potential:

- They believed that Wheeling Pitt had the opportunity to evolve into a mini-mill. The Bouchards were confident they could alter the mill's cost structure dramatically with an electric arc furnace and low-cost steel slabs imported from locations such as Ukraine. They thought the pursuit of this strategy would eventually enable them to shut down the high-cost Wheeling Pitt blast furnace.
- Wheeling Pitt had an extraordinary hot-strip mill, with an annual capacity of 3.0 million tons—that was 1.0 million tons larger than the mill's own caster capacity. This meant that Wheeling Pitt could not operate that hot-strip mill at a near-capacity rate without obtaining an outside source of steel slabs to feed into it. Hot-strip mill capacity in the U.S. was in demand in 2005–2006, because a number of foreign steelmakers desired a place where they could export their cheaply produced steel slabs. The Bouchards concluded that replicating this hot-strip mill from scratch anywhere in the United States would cost a steelmaker $500 million, and this mill probably was therefore worth close to this amount. This meant the value of the Wheeling Pitt hot-strip mill by itself was greater than the depressed market cap of the company they sought to purchase.
- Wheeling Pitt, in a joint venture with Severstal, owned excellent coking facilities near its mill in Steubenville, Ohio. Both Wheeling Pitt and Severstal received 600,000 tons of coke per year from this joint venture. In Wheeling Pitt's case, this was enough to fuel its blast furnace without forcing it to rely on outside suppliers, a valuable situation given the rapidly inflating prices of inputs such as coke.

Furthermore, it was hardly irrelevant that the production of coke frequently creates environmental problems, and building a new facility inside the United States was therefore next to impossible. As the price of coke began to skyrocket in 2005–2007, the Bouchards understood that, if they shut down the Wheeling Pitt blast furnace and then sold its annual 600,000 tons of coke on the open market, then the resulting cash flow would be greater than what they could achieve by operating the entire steel mill. So, in their view, they would acquire a second asset that also was worth more than the market cap of the company itself.

- In Wheeling Nisshin, a joint venture between Wheeling Pitt and Nisshin Steel of Japan that focused on steel coating, Wheeling Pitt owned a valuable interest of 35.7 percent in perhaps the most successful Japanese-American joint venture operating in the United States. Wheeling Nisshin was consistently quite profitable and had a large cash balance but no debt. Paradoxically, however, Wheeling Nisshin seemed to produce no incremental value to the stock price of Wheeling Pitt. The Bouchards concluded they should sell it (and eventually did so for $71 million in 2008).
- One of Wheeling Pitt's subsidiaries was a corrugated steel firm, Wheeling Corrugated. Wheeling Corrugated maintained offices in roughly 20 states, enjoyed a top-three rank in the U.S. corrugated market, and sported annual

revenues of approximately $400 million. In the view of the Bouchards, it was woefully managed and that was why it made little or no profits. The Bouchards thought this asset could be carved off and could stand alone as an independent operation that would require no subsidies from its parent. Indeed, they believed that a change in the management of Wheeling Corrugated would result in a steel distribution company that could generate profits similar to those of the Esmark steel-service centers.

In sum, when the Bouchards looked at Wheeling Pitt, they believed its assets were worth more than twice its traded value, if it were reconstructed, were well managed, and were not handicapped by a very weak steel market. Simply put, they believed the sum of the value of the parts was greater than the current value of the whole company. Quietly confident, they were determined to acquire Wheeling Pitt and make it the centerpiece of the Esmark operation.

In 2006–2008, steel-service center companies traded in the market at a multiple of 7.0 to 8.0 times their EBITDA (earnings before interest, tax, depreciation and amortization—a widely recognized measure of the profitability of a firm). Steel mills, on the other hand, were selling at multiples of 3.0 to 5.0 times EBITDA. At the end of the day, Esmark's financial strategy was to gobble up the Wheeling Pitt mill and bury it inside the growing service center company. They hoped that, within a short time, the entire entity would trade at a 7.0 multiple, creating a large return for shareholders. It was a clever but untested idea, although the risk was reduced by the substantial value of Wheeling Pitt assets, such as the hot-strip mill and the coke supply. If things got tough, these parts could be spun off and sold separately, they reasoned.

On March 26, 2006, after acquiring support from its investors and banks, Esmark returned to Jim Bradley with a written proposal to merge Wheeling Pitt with Esmark. Then the fun started. The Wheeling Pitt board of directors reacted strongly, even a bit frantically, in opposition. Because the proposed merger would have enriched Wheeling Pitt's stockholders, aligned Wheeling Pitt with a profitable, expanding company (Esmark), and received the endorsement of the USW, the Wheeling Pitt board's strenuous opposition appeared to reflect other considerations. It was not irrelevant that each Wheeling Pitt board member was receiving almost $100,000 in annual compensation as a director, and, arguably, this encouraged some board members to oppose the merger.

In fact, Wheeling Pitt recently had looked unsuccessfully for partners that might provide it with capital, because it was in a liquidity squeeze. It was running out of money and did not have an ability to borrow more from financial institutions at anything other than unattractive terms. Thus, at this point, Esmark appeared to be the only game in town. However, CEO Jim Bradley bought some time. In a meeting in the Wheeling Pitt boardroom with Esmark and Franklin Mutual, Bradley shook hands with Jim Bouchard on a rough deal and stepped in the next room to discuss taking care of his management team. The Esmark team went home thinking they had made a deal. However, nothing had been signed, and it turned out there was no deal.

Jim Bradley was invited to the home of Jim Bouchard for a business dinner, to bond with his apparent new partners and talk strategy. He was offered a senior position in the new company. Present at the dinner were the Bouchards, Bradley, senior executives from Franklin Mutual, Leo Gerard and Ron Bloom from the USW, Victor Rashnikov, the owner of Magnitogorsk Iron and Steel Works (MMK), one of the largest Russian steelmakers and a potential steel slab partner for Esmark, and legendary hockey star Mario Lemieux, Jim Bouchard's neighbor and owner of the Pittsburgh Penguins. The business discussions that evening were pleasant, with all present expressing interest in building a brand-new company together.

> **Esmark and Jim Bradley** (the CEO of Wheeling Pitt) were adversaries in the battle for control of Wheeling Pitt. However, they also turned out to be allies when Wheeling Pitt later collected $260 million in a court suit against Massey Energy. Mr. Bradley, by then gone from Wheeling Pitt, testified very effectively on behalf of Esmark and was instrumental in Esmark's legal victory. He need not have done so, and earned the respect and appreciation of many for his efforts.

Rashnikov took a tour of the mill during his visit. He had interest in a potential partnership with the Bouchards, whom he had met in Turin, Italy, at the Olympics just a few months before. Rashnikov also had a non-steel agenda. Lemieux had acquired the draft rights to a young Russian Olympic hockey star named Evgeny Malkin, reputed to be the best hockey player in the world not yet playing in the National Hockey League (NHL). But Malkin's rights were controlled by Rashnikov, who also owned the best hockey team in Russia.

Lemieux came to the dinner wearing a smile. He hoped to encourage Rashnikov, Malkin's hockey employer, to surrender his rights to the young player. Rashnikov was not interested in giving up his star, but, in the fashion of Russian oligarchs, he thought it might be very nice to own an NHL team and perhaps a steel mill as well in the same geographic location. Such were the kinds of plans that had made him rich and famous in Russia. At that moment, the value of Rashnikov's business holdings exceeded $8 billion.

The USW in turn was interested in finding new ownership for Wheeling Pittsburgh Steel. Gerard and Bloom worked the room that night in their normal, politically astute fashion. The conversations were fascinating, and all seemingly left the dinner that evening in the mood to make something good happen.

All but one person, that is. The dinner ended with Esmark and Franklin Mutual thanking Bradley for supporting their proposal. Bradley returned the good cheer, but he carefully omitted mentioning the fact that the next morning he would board a plane for Sao Paulo, Brazil, where he would meet with representatives of Companhia Siderúrgica Nacional (CSN), one of the world's largest steelmakers. Ultimately, he would cut a very different deal with CSN, and it would result in CSN attempting to purchase Wheeling Pitt. This would leave the Bouchards, Franklin Mutual, and the USW out in the cold. Business dinners and toasts were just fine with Jim Bradley, but the Bouchards concluded later that he wasn't about to sell his company to a bunch of service center guys. Also, he probably did not care much for the aggressive Bouchards, whom he likened to a pair of Doberman pinchers nipping at his heels. In addition, if he succeeded with his gambit with CSN and was careful, then he probably would serve as Wheeling Pitt's CEO for several more years.

More Dinner Intrigue

Shortly after the dinner at Jim Bouchard's home, Malkin secretly left Russia and wended his way to Pittsburgh, where he joined the Penguins. This resulted in an unsuccessful lawsuit, launched by Rashnikov against the Penguins and the NHL. Malkin became an instant star in the NHL.

As soon as Jim Bradley's intent became clear, the fight for Wheeling Pitt was on, even though Mr. Bradley did not know this immediately. On April 7, 2006, confidential proposals were submitted both by Esmark and CSN to acquire a majority ownership in the company. To the Bouchards' chagrin, the proposals looked remarkably similar. This caused Ron Bloom of the USW to spring into action, with his trademark process of attempting to get all parties to cooperate and thereby produce an acceptable happy ending. He arranged a dinner between the Bouchards, Franklin Mutual, Benjamin Steinbruch, the largest investor and CEO of CSN, and Bob Greenhill, Steinbruch's financial advisor. The dinner took place at the Duquesne Club in Pittsburgh, an old and staid private club famous for the incubation of steel deals. The

Bouchards hoped to convince Steinbruch to join them in a transaction that would combine CSN's North American assets with those of Esmark and Wheeling Pitt. The Bouchards had in mind a partnership, not surprisingly, with Esmark the majority partner at 51 percent.

Jim and Craig Bouchard liked Steinbruch right off the bat. He was obviously a tough guy, but he was intelligent and charming. He brought his teenage daughter on the trip so he could spend time with her. They liked that and even more so that he actually listened to their ideas and asked probing questions. He didn't waste time and came directly to the point in each component of the discussion. He avoided talking down to the upstart brothers, who obviously did not rival his status in the steel business. The Bouchards felt Steinbruch was a winner. The Franklin people listened and liked him as well.

Steinbruch's financial advisor, Bob Greenhill, spoke next and suggested that, if Esmark withdrew from the fight, CSN would find a way for Esmark to become a 10-percent partner in the deal. Greenhill frankly gave small Esmark no chance of defeating CSN in a tussle for Wheeling Pitt. Greenhill evinced the sense that his offer of a 10-percent share was generous, if not charitable. Franklin Mutual took this in and quickly caucused with the Bouchards. After a quick discussion, these two parties returned to the conversation and politely responded, although with some chutzpah, that if CSN would withdraw, Esmark would give CSN a 10-percent piece of the deal! This response reflected the conclusion of Franklin, one of the world's largest investors, that Greenhill was grandstanding. The dinner ended at least semiamicably, with each party wishing the other good luck in the fight.

The Wheeling Pittsburgh board of directors, with Bradley as its chairman, moved methodically forward toward acceptance of the CSN proposal, despite not having the approval of the USW. The Wheeling Pitt board knew that the USW's approval probably was necessary but must have thought they could obtain the union's nod later. Unfortunately for them, the USW was unimpressed with the existing Wheeling Pitt board and leadership and let those feelings be known to Bradley and the board.

On April 18, 2006, the lead director of Wheeling Pitt asked his board to meet directly with Esmark, following a chat with Ron Bloom of the USW. Bloom asked the board to set up special counsel, specifically to provide a fair evaluation of the Esmark proposal. Bloom, however, was convinced this was a charade and that the Esmark offer was not being taken seriously. This was the beginning of a continuously escalating effort by the USW to convince the Wheeling board that the Esmark proposal was the best one for shareholders, as well as for employees.

Having the support of the USW's Bloom, Dave McCall, and Leo Gerard was a powerful card, perhaps even a trump card, for the Bouchards to play.

But the union exercised this power in its typically indirect, incremental fashion, grabbing an inch in negotiations, then a foot, then a yard, then a mile, then Wheeling Pitt's throat. We invite readers to conjure the image of a boa constrictor. The USW international leadership seldom rushes in for the kill. Instead, like a boa constrictor, it slowly puts a legal hug on its target and starts to squeeze. In the end, it is confident that its adversaries will end up in its tummy.

The Wheeling Pitt board and Jim Bradley, having watched the USW in operations over the years, had some understanding how the boa constrictor strategy worked, and this was sufficient to make them very uncomfortable. However, CSN, with its trusted New York financial advisor Greenhill calling the shots, did not yet fully comprehend how it was going to be squeezed.

 Teams from Esmark and CSN both flew to Pittsburgh on April 25, 2006, to make presentations to the 11-person Wheeling Pitt board of directors. Two of the directors were USW designees, so it is fair to say that the USW was represented in most of the closed door meetings of the board. On May 2, 2006, the USW declared by letter to the Wheeling Pitt board that it was not ready to enter into a new collective bargaining agreement with CSN. It also stated that it would not waive its "Successorship Provision" under its existing collective bargaining agreement with Wheeling Pitt that is triggered if and when the company changed control. The CSN offer had the Brazilian firm acquiring a 64-percent interest in the combined company, and so there was no dispute that this was a change in control. It did not take Albert Einstein to understand the USW's position vis-à-vis CSN—win our approval first or go home to Brazil! Without union approval, there would be no deal.

Alarmed, but not deterred, Bradley and CSN went away to craft a new proposal that they hoped would disarm the union Successorship Provision. On June 23, 2006, they revealed their answer. CSN changed its proposal to one in which it would acquire a 49.5-percent interest in the merged company. The notion was that the CSN would acquire majority control at some date in the future, presuming that, as time passed, the USW would come to accept CSN's skill and legitimacy. Cleverly, this appeared to bypass the rights of the USW under the Successorship Provision. Wheeling Pitt and CSN gave the union time to invoke its "Right to Bid" for control of the firm (required by the collective bargaining agreement), which allowed the union to enter its own purchase proposal. However, Wheeling Pitt and CSN were confident that the USW was not in a position financially to make a bid. They were correct, and the momentum clearly shifted to the Brazilians.

The USW and Esmark, now sailing in the same ship, were angered by these machinations and girded for action. They were helped when the Wheeling Pitt board made its first bad decision. In light of the possibility that a stockholder meeting would be required to approve the transaction with CSN, and such special shareholders meetings were expensive, the board decided to announce that the annual meeting scheduled for August 2006 would be delayed to some later date.

Esmark retained a Pittsburgh-based law team from McGuire Woods as its counsel for the fight. McGuire Woods put forward a baby-faced, pleasant, very competent lawyer named Scott Westwood. Although not yet a feared Wall Street counselor, Westwood proceeded to overwhelm his opponents with nonstop clever legal parries and defenses that were generated by his 12-hour workdays. He gathered the Bouchards in a legal war room in Sewickley, Pennsylvania, and began to educate them on the difficulties they would face. The Bouchards had never been in a similar Wall Street fight, and Westwood knew it would be draining. He told the brothers this fight could potentially wreck the small, but profitable company they had built. He pointed out that the cost of an extended proxy battle requiring SEC approvals would run into the millions of dollars. But he also had a few interesting stratagems to share.

The Bouchards remembered both the handshake Bradley had offered and the dinner at Jim Bouchard's house shortly after. Soon after, they had learned of Bradley's trip to Brazil. They asked each other what their dad, a 35-year veteran of steel wars at Inland Steel, would have done. The senior Bouchard had been a tough, savvy guy and had mentored both the sons until his death in the late 1970s. They instinctively knew he would have taken up the challenge. Yet they also understood that the behemoth CSN, with its well-known Wall Street advisor, Bob Greenhill, had pushed them into the corner and that they were now on the defensive. And it was clear the Wheeling Board sided with CSN.

The Bouchards spent that long night discussing risk and return, how much energy they had left after making nine grueling acquisitions over three years, whether they had a management team supporting them to be successful, and whether both Franklin Mutual, their largest shareholder, and the USW were likely to stay by their side. When the wine glasses finally turned over that night at the Edgeworth Club in Sewickley, the Bouchards went to sleep determined to initiate a hostile takeover of Wheeling Pittsburgh Steel.

The cat and mouse game continued. On July 12, 2006, Esmark sent a letter to Wheeling Pitt confirming it intended to move forward with its proposal. The letter asked the board to reply by July 14. However, the Wheeling Pitt board did not reply. No doubt, it was beginning to dawn on more than a few board members that their fiduciary responsibilities were paramount and that litigation was a possibility if they did not behave properly. Wheeling Pitt did not carry a large insurance policy for directors and officers, and this made some directors nervous.

Also, on July 12, the USW sent Wheeling Pitt a letter alleging violations of the collective bargaining agreement. This turned the heat up another notch, as Wheeling Pitt was suffering liquidity problems and was hardly in a position to fight the substantial union that represented 80 percent of its employees.

On July 16, 2006, Esmark announced publicly that it would contest the election of the Wheeling Pitt directors and also that it intended to elect a slate of new directors at the next annual meeting. This news met with a yawn in the stock market. After all, such an unseating of a complete board of directors in good standing of a large public firm had never happened before. In fact, most people thought it was not a doable proposition.

The delay of the annual Wheeling Pitt meeting had given the Bouchards the proverbial window of opportunity. There was now just enough time to get their story out to Wall Street and win a proxy fight. Furthermore, the "standstill agreement," which they had executed one year earlier when talking with Wheeling Pitt and which prohibited them from making a hostile takeover attempt, would expire in time for them to pursue their takeover strategy.

Meanwhile, Scott Westwood had discovered that the terms of the members of the board of directors of Wheeling Pitt, which had once been staggered so that board members were elected in different years, had become unstaggered when Wheeling Pitt exited bankruptcy in 2003. "My God," thought the Bouchards the day they heard this remarkable news. All of the directors could be put up for a shareholder vote on a single day, couldn't they? All of a sudden, the unthinkable was within the realm of possibility. The entire membership of the existing Wheeling Pitt board could be thrown out on a single day if the votes were there to do it.

On August 3, 2006, Wheeling Pitt announced that its annual meeting would be held on November 17, but many believed the Wheeling Pitt board would delay the meeting if they did not feel it was going to be successful. On August 31, Esmark filed suit to require the company actually to have the meeting on that day in order to force the board election. Otherwise, the Bouchards would be shooting at a moving, disappearing target. The suit was successful, and this eliminated some of the wiggle room for Wheeling Pitt's existing board.

On September 19, Wheeling Pitt announced that the annual meeting would indeed be held on November 17, but the CSN deal would not be on the agenda. This was an attempt to neuter the Esmark strategy, but it also reflected the reality that they were not yet ready to do so. No matter, the Bouchards concluded, because, if the board election were held on that day, lack of consideration of the CSN proposal would help the Esmark case.

Retrospectively, Wheeling Pitt's lack of readiness to put the CSN proposal to a vote was a stroke of good fortune for the Bouchards. Had a tangible, credible CSN deal been placed on the Wheeling Pitt agenda on November 17 and subjected to a vote of shareholders, it would probably have been approved, and our story would be truncated and hardly of interest. However, the Wheeling Pitt board and management forfeited their opportunity, and the intrigue continued.

On October 13, 2006, Jeffrey Gendell of Tontine Partners, the largest institutional, nonunion shareholder in Wheeling Pitt (9.5 percent) and an investor held in high esteem in the hedge fund community,[1] wrote a public letter to the board, saying that neither the CSN offer nor the Esmark offer conveyed enough value to stockholders. But the kicker in Gendell's letter was that he encouraged the board to replace the existing management team. This letter slowed the CSN momentum and gave Esmark room to refine its proposal and talk to shareholders. Esmark felt that winning over Gendell and Tontine could be worth as much as 20 percent of the shareholder vote, should a vote become a reality. Many large shareholders paid attention to Gendell, who is widely considered to be a near genius in commodity investing.

Esmark began distributing its proxy materials in mid-October for the annual meeting. The Esmark war room was now full of lawyers, accountants, bankers, and securities specialists. Craig Bouchard spent nearly every waking hour working on proxy materials and visiting bankers and investors. Jim led the steel company, worked the press, and joined his brother at times in New York, Boston, or Chicago in an attempt to win the investor base over to their side.

Esmark also announced a head-turning slate of highly regarded candidates for the board positions that garnered instant credibility for the Bouchard's efforts:

- Albert G. Adkins, former vice president for accounting at Marathon Oil.
- Clark Burrus, former comptroller of the City of Chicago and former chairman of the Chicago Transit Authority. Clark was an unofficial advisor to the Daley family running Chicago politics and one of the most accomplished African American leaders in the country.
- C. Frederick Fetterolf, the retired chief operating officer of Alcoa.
- Dr. James V. Koch, former president of Old Dominion University and a highly respected economist.
- George Muñoz, Harvard Law School graduate and former undersecretary of the U.S. Treasury, one of the most distinguished Latino businessmen in the United States.
- Joseph Peduzzi, the owner and manager of TF Asset Management, a successful hedge fund, and the youngest member of the slate.
- James A. Todd, former CEO of the Birmingham Steel Corporation.

By this time, the media had made the Esmark pursuit of Wheeling Pitt a national story. If successful, these seven individuals, plus the famous retired USW leader Lynn Williams and former AFL-CIO executive James L. Bowen, would join the Bouchard brothers on a new, 11-person Esmark board.

On October 25, the Wheeling Pitt board responded to these thrusts by formally entering into a transaction with CSN and began the strenuous and lengthy path through the SEC to obtain shareholder approval. This marked the point of no return for Esmark. It now had to convince Wheeling Pitt's shareholders to throw the existing slate of directors out of office at the annual Wheeling Pitt meeting on November 17, 2008. This was now less than one month away. They needed shareholders to understand that a vote for the Esmark slate was a mandate to cancel the CSN deal and to negotiate a merger with Esmark. If elected, then the new Esmark-Wheeling board would vote to cancel the CSN deal, approve the Esmark offer, and begin a multimonth journey through the SEC to a shareholder vote. It was a lengthy and daunting task, to say the least.

The days leading up to the annual meeting were tense on all sides, and the strategic moves by each party were critical. Wheeling Pitt had more than 14 million shares outstanding, and its almost 3,000 distinct stockholders had, by this time, received numerous letters and documents from both sides. The most critical votes would be cast by the largest stockholders. However, the odds were long. Large institutional investors on Wall Street rarely support hostile party takeovers.

The Esmark Offer Was Often Described in the Press as a "Hostile Reverse Tender Merger"

Three-year-old, privately held Esmark, with $400 million of revenue and several hundred employees, was attempting to force a public company with nearly $2.0 billion of revenue and 3,000 employees to buy Esmark, while simultaneously handing over the management keys and firing its board of directors! The firm allied with the Wheeling Pitt board, CSN, was one of the largest steel companies in the world, dwarfing the combination of Esmark and Wheeling Pitt by a factor of 10. Grizzled veterans walking the halls of J.P. Morgan, UBS, Credit Suisse, Goldman Sachs, Raymond James, and Franklin Mutual all talked about this transaction. Not only was it a classic case of David vs. Goliath, but also a hostile reverse tender merger such as this never had been successfully accomplished on Wall Street. All of these Wall Street parties were intrigued by Esmark's gambit, and most were sympathetic, but few were predicting success.

Who were the major stockholders? The largest single Wheeling Pitt stockholder was the USW-negotiated Voluntary Employee Benefits Association (VEBA) plan, which was represented by U.S. Trust Company in Washington DC. Other large investors included asset managers, such as such as Tontine, Wellington, Fidelity, Mellon, Wells Fargo, State Street, Samylyn Capital, Cobalt, Charlestown Capital, Praesidium, and a score of U.S. hedge funds. Small individual investors in midtown America made up less than 10 percent of the share ownership.

The end game of this financial chess match began to play out in the days immediately leading up to the annual meeting. Esmark knew the stockholder vote was likely to be close and decided to add a sweetener. On October 26, it surprised all onlookers, as well as the board of Wheeling Pitt, by dramatically changing its offer. Esmark announced that Franklin Mutual Advisors would underwrite a $200 million "rights offering" for Wheeling Pitt investors. This offering would allow existing shareholders

---

A Voluntary Employee Benefit Association trust plan is a financial organization owned and controlled by unions that is designed to pay for retired workers' health care benefits. The USW VEBA was created when the union made concessions to allow Wheeling Pitt to exit bankruptcy in 2003. The USW and other unions have worried that poorly performing or bankrupt firms will not be able to fund the pension and health care benefits they have agreed to in previous collective bargaining contracts. Hence, they have created VEBAs, into which the firms have placed assets, often in the form of company stock. It is employee ownership in a form not dissimilar to that found in Europe. This is how the USW ended up as Wheeling Pitt's largest stockholder.

---

the right either to sell roughly one-half of their existing shares back to the company at a price of $20 per share at the eventual closing date (to be many months later) or to purchase additional shares in the company at the closing for $19 per share, a $1 discount to the price being paid by Franklin Mutual Advisors. Franklin committed to buy a minimum of $50 million of new stock to a maximum of $200 million, depending on how many new shares the existing shareholders asked for at closing. This was a massive new investment by a highly respected financial house, which would, in all scenarios, own more than 50 percent of the company's stock when the dust cleared.

The precise details of the newest Esmark initiative were less important, in some ways, than the logic. Some shareholders had complained that the Esmark and Franklin combination was, in effect, stealing Wheeling Pitt for too low a price. They felt a financial deal that valued the Esmark assets at nearly the same amount as Wheeling Pitt assets placed far too low a value on Wheeling Pitt's assets. Now those investors that held this view had the option to buy in at a price lower than that at which Esmark itself could purchase shares.

On the other hand, other investors believed that Wheeling Pitt was being overvalued and did not want to "stay in the deal." These investors now had an option to cash out half of their shares at $20 per share. Months before, the Wheeling Pitt stock had been trading at nearly $10 per share. Hence, most of these investors were won over with the rights offering concept. This feature was attractive to Tontine in particular, whose votes and influence turned out to be critically important.

The next day, October 27, Jeff Gendell of Tontine Partners, perhaps coincidentally again, went public with a letter to the board of directors of Wheeling Pitt. The letter challenged the company's ability to stand independently, asserted that the CSN proposal continued to be unattractive, and argued that the Esmark proposal with the rights offering attached was preferable to the CSN option. Absent further changes to the dynamics, Tontine intended to support the Esmark board slate!

Gendell's letter had a very large impact on the market. Gendell's Tontine owned 9.5 percent of the company, and Jeff Gendell had a near cult following with other funds in the investor community. Gendell had lost confidence in Bradley and his management team. To make matters worse,

---

Interestingly, Wikipedia reports that "A tontine is a scheme for raising capital which combines features of a group annuity, and a lottery" (Wikipedia, 2009).

Tontine Partners, founded in 1997 and led by Jeff Gendell, tends to take positions in broad commercial or industrial groups that it believes will prosper. Reportedly, Tontine earned profits in excess of 100 percent on its invested capital in 2003 and 2005.

Bradley had hired a financial advisor named Bob Miller, for a reported $1 million, to double up with the much higher-paid CSN advisor Bob Greenhill in order to set strategy and chase investors. This was another mistake. Miller's approach was not well received by Gendell. After a visit by both

Bouchards, a meeting in which they described their strategy for turning the company around and after learning of the rights offering, Tontine picked its horse in the Wheeling Pitt stakes. It was Esmark.

Shocked by the Tontine letter following the meeting with Bob Miller and now visibly worried for the first time, CSN lurched into action. It announced major revisions to its offer on November 5, just 12 days before the annual meeting. This was timely, because most investors still were analyzing the two offers and considering their voting decisions. CSN added $50 million of cash to its offer, offered to redeem shares at $32 per share four years later, lowered the debt component in their offer, and included their own "rights offering." Once again, CSN's offer structure seemed to mimic the most important features of the Esmark proposal, while avoiding the USW Successorship Provision.

From that point on, the two combatants worked 24 hours a day to win votes. In the week before the vote, CSN learned that Fidelity and Mellon, two large shareholders, were voting with it. CSN felt it had an inside track with the union VEBA trustee, because intuition suggested that USW retirees would prefer the larger and more financially stable Brazilian bidder having financial responsibility for their health care and pension benefits. The roughly 2 million shares controlled by the VEBA Trust would likely swing the entire election, because it was the largest block of shares in the election. U.S. Trust took its fiduciary duties very seriously. In spite of the fact that the VEBA was related to the union and the USW was obviously supporting Esmark, U.S Trust (which administered the VEBA) was leaning toward voting for the CSN/Wheeling Pitt slate of directors. Jim Bradley had hired U.S. Trust, and CSN was definitely the more bankable entity. U.S. Trust's duty was only to the VEBA retirees, not to the USW itself.

Leading the U.S. Trust team was a senior banker named Norman Goldberg. Norman was known for holding his cards very close to his vest. He called both contesting parties frequently, to probe them and to attempt to motivate a higher share price. Both competitors were called together for a conference call a few days before the vote to state their best offers. Goldberg wanted to spark an auction environment for his shares, and the presumption was he would vote for the highest bidder. Bob Greenhill spoke for CSN and Craig Bouchard spoke for Esmark, as large teams of lawyers, bankers, and advisors on both sides listened in. The telephonic meeting took hours, and both sides made their respective pitches. The meeting became somewhat rancorous, because both parties knew that if the U.S. Trust voted with CSN/Wheeling Pitt, the contest for control was effectively over. (Note: the contents of this meeting are covered under the wrap of confidentiality, so we cannot provide additional details here.) Goldberg stated that he would not divulge his choice until the actual day of the vote.

The annual Wheeling Pitt meeting would be held at the White Palace Ballroom in a park outside Wheeling, West Virginia. The company normally held its annual meetings at the Airport Hyatt in Pittsburgh. This was a convenient location for investors as well as for directors to fly in and attend. Although the proxy vote could be accomplished electronically or in person, Bradley chose to move the meeting to Wheeling, apparently to diminish attendance from people out of state. The Esmark team decamped in Wheeling two nights before the meeting and set up a large war room in offices volunteered to them by Arcelor Mittal Steel at the nearby Weirton Steel mill facility. A team of individuals from Esmark, Franklin Mutual Advisors, and Raymond James manned the telephones, answering questions for investment committees throughout the country. Scott Westwood monitored all of this closely to ensure compliance with SEC rules.

On the evening of November 15, the electronic results of the vote began to trickle in. At 8 p.m., the Bouchards were floored when they learned that Wellington, one of the largest five stockholders in Wheeling Pitt, had cast roughly 1.0 million votes in favor of the CSN/Wheeling Pitt slate of directors. They knew that this vote, combined with a loss of the U.S. Trust vote, would lose the election for them. The war room went quiet, and the participants sat in a state of near-despair for 30 minutes.

By this time, the Bouchards and Esmark had invested over $3 million and 18 months of work in this venture. They had already learned that Fidelity and Mellon were voting against them. However, the pall was broken with a call from their proxy monitoring firm. U.S. Trust had cast its vote for Esmark, which elicited a huge cheer in the halls of Weirton Steel. The positive VEBA vote meant the two contestants were running neck and neck.

The Esmark team boarded vans the next morning and departed for the White Palace. They did not yet know what was in store for them. They had made a last minute telephonic plea to Wellington the night before. But the chances for such a reversal were given a close to zero chance of success by their advisors. Jim Bradley would be running the meeting. An agreement had been grudgingly struck that would give Jim Bouchard five minutes, and not a second more, to address the shareholder audience before the final manual vote took place. On the way up the long driveway to the White Palace, Craig Bouchard asked his brother Jim to have the van pull over so he could get out and finish an animated discussion he was having on his cell phone. Jim followed him out of the van and waited impatiently for the news. Craig hung up and hugged his brother. Tontine had just advised him that Wellington might have reversed its vote, taking 1 million votes away from the Wheeling slate of directors and adding 1 million to Esmark's count. If so, the battle had been won. They speculated that Jeff Gendell had made the difference.

Moments later, Jim Bradley began the crowded meeting in the presence of managers, union employees, local residents, local TV and radio personalities, and national publications, such as *Forbes Magazine*. There was a buzz in the room that few had ever experienced. Bradley was cool, but he politely extended his hand to Jim Bouchard before the meeting started. Then he began to talk to the crowd, first with formalities, then with time-consuming tidbits that seemed not to matter. Then, just before the vote, he called for a recess. The Bouchards and their advisors caucused. Bradley was stalling! Clearly, he was trying to pull off a last-minute negotiation with some large investor before calling for the vote officially.

Whatever the goal of Bradley's stratagem, it failed. He returned to the room slowly and calmly, called for the official vote, received it, and announced that Esmark had won! This set off a roar in the hall and ignited a media circus in the back of the room. Newspapers, journals, and broadcast outlets in the Ohio Valley, in Chicago, in New York, and in Brazil seized on this news and trumpeted it. The message was unmistakable—David's slingshot had knocked out Goliath.

At USW international headquarters in Pittsburgh, there was a celebration of power. Everyone knew the investment of prestige and influence that had been made in this deal by Leo Gerard, Dave McCall, and Ron Bloom on behalf of the USW. The defeat of CSN equated to a quantum boost in power for the union and for its legally hazy concept of the Successorship Provision. True, the clause had not been tested in the courts, but the major parties in the Wheeling Pitt episode had acted as though it were real. And, if the Successorship Provision were real, then the USW possessed an absolute veto power over who owned all steel firms organized by the USW.

The financial world marveled that a behemoth had been slain. It was not lost on them that the USW had been absolutely instrumental in this revolutionary result. The union's clout increased significantly as a consequence, and its success in this battle arguably had something to do with the USW's Ron Bloom eventually being appointed by President Barack Obama to help lead the restructuring of the Big Three U.S. automobile producers.

The "old" board of directors of Wheeling Pitt, excluding the two union-designated board members, immediately lost their positions. In their place came the new board of directors slate, endorsed by the Bouchards and the USW. Jim Bradley and many senior managers would soon lose their jobs. Query at this moment whether Mr. Bradley had cause to regret backing out from his earlier verbal understandings with the Bouchards and Franklin Mutual.

At the end of the day, diminutive Esmark and two youngish U.S. entrepreneurs had bucked the trend toward foreign ownership in the steel industry and won control of one of the largest U.S. steel companies. In the process, they pulled off the first reverse hostile merger in U.S. history. It was an upset of gargantuan proportions.

Not This Time

"Management always wins the close ones," reported Listokin when the managements of existing corporations are challenged in stockholder votes. Esmark's reverse hostile merger was indeed an unusual event.

Source: Yair Jason Listokin, "Management Always Wins the Close Ones." *American Law and Economics Review,* 10 (2), 2008, 159–84.

Chapter 6

Hunted by the Pack

Butch Cassidy and the Sundance Kid, which first hit movie screens in 1969, is ranked #50 on the American Film Institute's list of the best films of all time and continues, 40 years later, to generate income for Twentieth Century Fox and several of the actors. There are many memorable scenes in the film (for example, Butch and Sundance leaping off a cliff into a swiftly flowing stream hundreds of feet below), but there is one that speaks directly to theme of this chapter—being hunted by the pack. Bank robbers Butch and Sundance are being relentlessly pursued by a tireless posse that just won't quit. Finally, an exasperated Butch mutters to Sundance, "Who ARE those guys?"

The Bouchard brothers (Jim and Craig) felt much the same way in 2007 and 2008, as a variety of large, international steel companies began to circle their fast-growing U.S. steel firm (Esmark) for purposes of acquisition. Jim was chairman and CEO, and Craig (one of the authors of this book) was vice-chairman and president. The other author of this book, James Koch, was a member of the board of directors of Esmark. Collectively, they felt the hot breath of the wolves on their necks, as several international steel conglomerates competed to buy out Esmark and add it to their burgeoning holdings of U.S. steel companies. The prospective acquirers represented several different continents (Europe, South America, and Asia).

After a fierce public battle, Esmark sold out to Severstal ("Northern Steel"), a Russian firm, in August 2008. This chapter outlines the reasons why. Severstal is the second largest steel producer in the former Soviet

Union and operates 20 mills in five European countries (and now the United States). Severstal is highly diversified and is involved in the production of automobiles and timber, plus holdings in education and insurance. It is led by a brilliant individual named Alexei Mordashov, who easily qualifies as a Russian oligarch. In 2008, Mordashov was ranked by *Forbes Magazine* as the 18th wealthiest individual in the world. Prior to the 2008 financial meltdown, he was worth more than $21 billion.

THE BUILDUP

Exactly three years before, Jim and Craig Bouchard sat on a private plane headed for Edinburgh, Scotland, to meet with Vladimir Lissin, another Russian steel oligarch. They intended to discuss whether his company, Novolipetsk, had an interest in partnering with Esmark to make a possible run at taking over U.S. Steel. As they flew over the frozen North Atlantic, the Bouchards' discussion turned to predicting the future of the North American steel industry. Naturally, their speculation started with the fabled U.S. Steel Corporation, but it also included Nucor and Steel Dynamics. Together, these three firms control roughly 45 percent of domestic steel production.

Yet both of the Bouchards instinctively knew where the conversation was headed. They soon began to discuss a list of "steel barons," most of whom have not been and never will be household names in the United States. Table 6-1 summarizes the major players in this arena.

These are the men who wanted to own the steel industry in North America. Most still harbor that desire, although recent financial reverses have forced them to put those notions on hold. They are not "employees" like John Surma, Dan Dimicco, and Keith Busse, the CEOs of U.S. Steel, Nucor, and Steel Dynamics, respectively. To be sure, these American gentlemen are excellent managers and wealthy guys. Dimicco and Busse would also be widely considered great entrepreneurs as well. But their equity ownerships are minute relative to institutional shareholding in their companies.

The steel magnates on the international list in Table 6-1 are owners and entrepreneurs. They are experienced, tough, and savvy, and their wealth can be humbling. Lakshmi Mittal, who is the major owner of the largest steel company in the world, was ranked the fourth wealthiest individual in the world by *Forbes Magazine* in 2008. The rest of them were not that far behind! To put this in context, several of the well-known U.S. names on the *Forbes* billionaire list were T. Boone Pickens at #368, David Rockefeller at #428, and Ted Turner at #524.

On the plane that night, Craig listened quietly while Jim cut to the chase: "These guys are the 'pack' that will run us down and eventually

Table 6-1   The Steel Barons

Name	Firm	Country	International Personal Wealth Rank and Estimated Mid-2008 Wealth	
Lakshmi Mittal	Arcelor/Mittal	India	#4	$45.0 billion
Roman Abramovich	Evraz	Russia	#15	$23.5 billion
Alexei Mordashov	Severstal	Russia	#18	$21.2 billion
Vladimir Lissin	Novolipetsk	Russia	#21	$20.3 billion
Shashi and Ravi Ruia	Essar	India	#43	$15.0 billion
Viktor Rashnikov	MMK	Russia	#73	$10.4 billion
Benjamin Steinbruch	CSN	Brazil	#667	$1.8 billion
Jorge Jean Peter Gerdau	Gerdau	Brazil	Unranked (but should be)	

Source: Adapted from *Forbes*, "The World's Billionaires," www.forbes.com (March 5, 2008).

own the industry." Craig was struck by the fatalistic confidence of this statement. Jim then described the reputation of the oligarchs with a sense of respect that somehow sticks with people who begin with nothing, deal masterfully in the grey areas of business, and end up with a great deal of wealth.

During the next three years, the Bouchard brothers met and negotiated with nearly all of the members of the foreign "steel pack," regarding possible cooperative purchases of other steel companies or, later, the sale of Esmark. They met not just with their lieutenants, but, on many occasions, directly with them personally. Some of these discussions were defensive, and some were offensive. They were always humbling and thrilling experiences. Craig and Jim met them in places as far flung as New York, Baltimore, Pittsburgh, London, Turin, Edinburgh, Kiev, and Mumbai. The Bouchards were attempting to maintain the incredible growth of Esmark, the company they had founded and took to the NASDAQ through the hostile takeover of Wheeling Pittsburgh Steel. The oligarchs viewed them as an avenue to expand their march into North America.

Perhaps it doesn't really matter, but the Bouchards thought nearly all of the members of the "pack" were decent people, albeit driven individuals with voracious appetites for adding to their domains. In addition to being intelligent predators, the leaders of the pack were all very likable. We thought this despite the fact that one of them, Lakshmi Mittal, subsequently sued Esmark for $525 million over a botched attempt to sell Esmark his Sparrows Point steel mill. That law suit recently has been settled by Severstal. However, to this day, the Bouchards consider Lakshmi

Mittal the icon in the industry and a role model for what they would have wished to achieve.

Yet, that's the steel business, where things change constantly. Craig hasn't forgotten the electricity created when he sat across the negotiating table from the world's 4th richest man, or, on other occasions, the 18th richest, the 21st, 43rd, or 73rd richest—or even the 667th richest! At some point, one gives up trying to understand how much money $1 billion really is. The steel industry has made many men rich.

As Craig met them, one by one with his brother, he could see the future unfolding as Jim had outlined it that evening in the plane. It was clear from our discussions that each of the foreign oligarchs intended to own at least 10 million tons of steel capacity in North America. This made the math simple. If they achieved their goals, 70 percent of the U.S. domestic steel industry would be in the hands of foreigners. As of early 2009, approximately 51 percent of the U.S. steel industry was owned by foreigners, although the foreigners have paused to get their breaths because of the worldwide economic contraction.

We already have noted that quite a few of these foreigners, by the way, are Russians— we used to aim guns at them just a few years ago. Currently, the Russians are sailing their steel warships through the Panama Canal for the first time and docking at ports in Cuba and Venezuela.

THE PACK TRIUMPHS

The Esmark board, staring directly into the evolving worldwide credit crisis and seeing its effect upon Esmark's liquidity, viewed the eventual sale of Esmark (traded on NASDAQ as ESMK)—to a larger, better-funded international firm—as a virtually inevitable outcome. It ended up having two viable choices—Severstal or Essar, a well-regarded Indian firm that held assets throughout the world in steel and many other basic industries. The board's stated preference for Essar started the fireworks. Both the USW and Esmark's largest shareholder, Franklin Mutual Shares, objected and instead supported Alexei Mordashov and his Russian company, Severstal. In the end, this "pack"—Severstal, the USW, and Franklin Mutual—closed in, outbid Essar, and paid $1.3 billion to put the Bouchards into temporary retirement. In the process, Severstal consolidated its position as the dominant steelmaker controlling nearly the entire East Coast market of the United States.

But all of this did not occur easily for Severstal. The Esmark sale to Severstal closed in August 2008 after a convoluted and hostile process that might have passed for colorful fiction had it not actually occurred. The media served up this juicy story of intrigue on a daily basis to an international court of public opinion. Some of the coverage was accurate, but most was off base. We will set the record straight on a few topics in the following pages and focus on the issues that really matter in the odd, but interesting case of the sale of Esmark, Inc., which we regard as a metaphor for the times.

Among the issues we touch upon are the following: (1) How dominant should the role of management be in the sale of a public company? (2) How much influence should boards of directors have? (3) Should large, majority shareholders such as Franklin Mutual call the tune? (4) Is it appropriate for a labor union such as the USW to possess veto power over a merger? (5) Who should look out for the public interest (perhaps even a national security interest) if it conflicts either with the shareholder interests or with what is best for the employees?

The Short Reign of Esmark at Wheeling Pittsburgh Steel

When Esmark assumed control of Wheeling Pitt on December 4, 2006, it had been over a year since the Bouchard brothers had received any relevant information about the situation inside the company. The adversarial relationship that had developed with Wheeling Pitt CEO Jim Bradley virtually guaranteed this. In general, this is a problem associated with hostile takeovers.

After they walked through the door and began their jobs, the Bouchards were taken aback by the poor financial health of the company. The company had almost no sales orders booked for the first quarter of 2008. Its borrowing facilities were dangerously close to default, and it had shut down its electric arc furnace to preserve liquidity. Wheeling Pitt had shortly to pay more than $10 million to a Chicago-based contractor who was finishing work on a refurbishment of Wheeling Pitt's coke batteries. However, the *coup de grâce* was the approximately $30 million in payments Wheeling Pitt was obligated to make to CSN within a few weeks for steel slab orders, cozily arranged in the prior year at prices that, by this time, were considerably higher than the going market price.

This was a rude awakening both for the ambitious, new management and new board of directors. It was like buying a used car that was in good shape when the deal was made but turns out to be a lemon when finally delivered. Truth be told, Esmark had no cash balances available to make these payments. Jim Bouchard discussed with Craig the idea of putting the company in bankruptcy to allow itself the room to negotiate a solution with its creditors in order to get the company on the right track. However, this would be a third and perhaps terminal bankruptcy for

Wheeling Pitt, and the brothers rejected it as a course of action. Instead, they called each of the creditors and told them candidly that Wheeling Pitt could not pay them. Then they started from scratch, negotiating critical changes in terms.

There were other major problems, including an explosion in the electric arc furnace, and a hostile federal ESLGB that had grown tired of Wheeling Pitt and wanted that headache removed from its agenda. The ESLGB, however, was an absolutely critical piece of the puzzle, because many of the company's creditors relied on these government guarantees to support their otherwise untenable loans to the company. Hence, this threat from the federal government was yet another possible path to bankruptcy. In spite of direct appeals from West Virginia Senators Byrd and Rockefeller, the administrators in this relatively unknown federal office played hardball with Esmark and threatened to eliminate the loan guarantees.

At about the same time, the Bouchards also discovered that Wheeling Pitt had been drained of cash by debatable dealings with scrap vendors, energy providers, and banks on Wall Street. This included discovering that the company had paid the Royal Bank of Canada (RBC) an unending series of finance and "consulting" fees totaling almost $20 million since the bankruptcy, including an astonishingly large fee for a simple introduction to the steel firm CSN. RBC had squirmed its way into favor with the ESLGB and earned fees for risk management consulting with that agency concerning Wheeling Pitt. The agency then passed these invoices back to Wheeling Pitt. This aggravated the sorry state of Esmark's finances.

Even while they dealt with these issues, the Bouchards received another financial body blow. Ukrainian company IUD Donbass, which had provided a commitment letter to deliver slabs to Wheeling Pitt, now chose to renege on this deal. Donbass had suffered huge cost increases on its iron ore purchases back home because it was being squeezed by rival Metinvest, a group of 23 industrial companies that controlled the iron ore industry in the Ukraine. That meant that the Bouchards had to search for another supplier of slabs to fill up the Wheeling Pitt hot-strip mill.

They found themselves an answer when Mittal Steel put up its Sparrows Point Mill for auction, but only after being ordered to do so for anti-trust reasons by the U.S. Department of Justice. The Department of Justice supervised sale began with 12 potential buyers for Sparrows Point. They were progressively whittled down to 6, then 2, and finally to 1: Esmark! Esmark once again had startled the steel world by emerging with a winning bid of $1.3 billion, with the debt component to be financed by GE Finance and a large syndicated commercial bank group, and the equity component by a group led by Franklin Mutual Advisors. CSN again finished second. The was one of several reasons why the Bouchards had met Benjamin

Steinbruch once again to see if a partnership at Sparrows Point made sense. However, CSN believed it would be selected as the winner and, after a nice dinner, declined any partnership possibilities. Esmark soon announced that Craig Bouchard would depart the company with a team of its best managers to take the reins of Sparrows Point after the sale closed.

Unfortunately, as the Sparrows Point transaction neared closing, it became clear that Mittal would not be able to meet the closing conditions of the deal. USW approval of this deal was needed once again, and the USW was asking Mittal for a large amount of money to make up for the loss of profit sharing that would occur when the Sparrows Point facility withdrew from the Master International Steel Group VEBA Trust. Like the Wheeling Pitt VEBA, this trust was set up to fund thousands of retirees' pension and health care benefits. The Bouchards did not want to cast these retirees onto the street, not the least because their own mother still collected her pension and health care from Arcelor Mittal, which had bought Inland Steel before the International Steel Group.

Arcelor Mittal, no doubt feeling excessively jockeyed by the USW, said no to this last-minute demand. The USW responded by withholding its approval and threatening Arcelor Mittal with litigation. Again, its bargaining chip was the "Successorship Clause" in the collective bargaining agreement. The bankers and investors connected to all of the parties watched this theater of horror, as the closing date came and went without resolution of the closing conditions. Ultimately, the deal fell apart, and Arcelor Mittal found reason to blame Esmark, which was seen as having a cozy relationship with the USW, for the whipsawing it had endured. We wish we could have explained this properly to Lakshmi Mittal and his lieutenant, Sudhir Maheshwari, both of whom we respect a great deal, but the lawyers took over, and it was not possible. Such is life in the world of steel mergers and acquisitions.

The Sparrows Point adventure was a side show, albeit a rather huge one, to the ongoing story of Esmark being hunted down by the pack. Arguably, if the Sparrows Point deal had succeeded, then Esmark, with the backing of Arcelor Mittal, the USW, and several European firms, might have been able to survive and prosper on its own. However, among other reasons, the timing of the Sparrows Point episode was bad. Already in July 2007, a cloud was beginning to form over Wall Street. Interest rates began to rise, lenders became much more demanding, and liquidity in the loan market began to dry up.

Compounding the problem, insofar as Esmark was concerned, this was happening as prices of oil, natural gas, iron ore prices, coal and scrap were rising at alarming rates. Esmark had successfully put together $1.3 billion of debt and equity commitments to fund the Sparrows Point deal. This included a large banking group and an investor club, which included the Brazilian company CVRD, plus IUD Donbass, Franklin

Mutual, and several hedge funds. However, as the deal neared closing, this group was now telling Esmark that there could be no hiccups.

These prospective lenders focused in particular on USW approval of the transaction. Initially, this was not problematic, because the DOJ, Mittal, and the investors were in agreement. When Arcelor Mittal failed to obtain USW approval and meet its closing conditions, the deadlines for the transaction passed, and CVRD and Donbass exited. The funding mechanism that the Bouchards had laboriously developed had dissolved into thin air.

Craig Bouchard looked around Wall Street and saw that no other similar transactions had been funded in recent months and that none was on the docket. This was amazing to Wall Street veterans. No one was lending money! Looking back, this was the first chapter in the credit crisis that has thrown the global economy into its current deep recession.

The world was now in the middle of a commodity price boom (soon to be referred to as a bubble). Jim Bouchard was very concerned about the effects of rising commodity prices (oil, natural gas, iron ore, and coal) on Wheeling Pitt. True, steel prices were rising to historic levels as well, but not sufficiently to cover what were extraordinary cost increases. Furthermore, because the demand for steel tended to be cyclical, Esmark could be caught with contracts obligating it to high input prices, even as steel demand reversed course and started to decline. Jim Bouchard looked at every opportunity to hedge away components of this operating risk, the prospect of which was unsteadying the nerves of both investors and the board of directors.

After the collapse of the Sparrows transaction, Craig Bouchard called his brother aside. He had become convinced that these abnormal movements in the credit market were an even bigger menace to the company than the rise in commodity costs. After all, Esmark had over $400 million of debt. This was not chicken feed. He wanted to make sure that his brother, the CEO of the company as well as the chairman of its board, fully understood the implications of a credit crunch. Their discussion was thorough, and Jim asked many questions. What were the data? What were the options? Shortly thereafter, the brothers began discussing with the board of directors their intuition that Esmark needed a strategic partner that could help it withstand the oppressive commodity price increases it was now paying. Failing that, Esmark should look for a buyer for the company from among the circling pack of potential buyers. Esmark could not risk standing alone.

The Move toward a Sale

On January 23, 2008, the Bouchards attended a meeting that had been quietly organized by the USW at a mutual friend's condominium in frigid downtown Chicago. Senior representatives of the USW, Esmark, Raymond James, and Franklin Mutual gathered for a discussion of Esmark's future, given the credit crisis. The union was worried about Esmark and its vulnerable financial position. Sparrows Point was, by this time, up for rebid by Arcelor Mittal, and the USW encouraged Esmark to partner up with a larger firm and bid again.

In essence, Esmark, with knowledge and forethought, was helping organize the pack that ultimately would devour it. The motivations of parties in attendance at the meeting were transparent. Esmark wanted a reliable, steady source of steel slabs and felt Sparrows Point was the best place to obtain them. The USW wanted Esmark on more stable financial ground in order to preserve steelworker jobs and union dues, but the union also wanted to be in the position to pick the winner of the Sparrows Point auction. Franklin wanted to ensure the stability of its common stock investment in Esmark, which, by this time, had grown to a remarkable $400 million. Raymond James smelled a large fee, while continuing its traditional role as union advisor.

The group collectively identified CSN, Severstal, and Essar as the ideal candidates to backstop Esmark or even purchase it outright. Each had interest in expanding in North America. Sadly, there was not even one U.S. steel company that qualified for consideration. Nucor and Steel Dynamics were not willing to join in a discussion with the USW, let alone entertain the notion of partnering with or buying a unionized mill. AK Steel and U.S. Steel were deemed poor strategic fits. More important, the USW, which was perceived to hold veto power, wasn't impressed with either at the time.

Duties were assigned to specific individuals at the meeting to contact each of the foreign parties and determine their levels of interest in Sparrows Point, Esmark, or both. All three companies expressed significant interest; however, the two that stood out were Severstal and Essar. Both were known as efficient steelmakers, and both were expanding aggressively. Esmark already owned a joint venture on its coke battery with Severstal and respected its management. Essar had recently bought the Algoma steel mill in Ontario, Canada, as well as the iron ore mines in the Mesabi Range that operated under the rubric of Minnesota Steel. Both Severstal and Essar would have strategic interest in obtaining the hot-strip mill and coke batteries of Wheeling Pitt, and both would likely be interested in the Wheeling Pitt electric arc furnace.

From that point forward, events become frenetic. Feeling that a sale now was inevitable, because deteriorating financial markets were making it very difficult for Esmark to finance its debt, the Bouchards flew to Mumbai at the beginning of April to meet the Ruia family, which owned Essar. Meanwhile, the USW and Franklin Mutual wooed Severstal. Both apparently did a good job in their flirting and dating rituals. As a consequence, two prospective brides showed up at the wedding. On February 25, 2008, Severstal sent Esmark a nonbinding proposal to acquire Esmark for $15 per share. Esmark's board was unimpressed with the price because the merger of Esmark and Wheeling Pitt had been consummated not that long before at a theoretical valuation of $20 per share. The board was worried about being sued by shareholders if it sold for a materially smaller amount in what was still, in early 2008, a strong U.S. steel market. Furthermore, they believed that this was only the first round of negotiations and that there was room for an improvement in Severstal's offer.

Successively, on March 31, April 8, and April 16, 2008, Essar submitted continually improved offers to purchase the key assets of Esmark, including the steel mill, for amounts ranging from $620 million to $700 million. With this amount of cash in hand, Esmark could retire all of its debt and survive as a smaller distribution intensive business. The board liked this idea. They found the Ruia brothers to be a breath of fresh air in the steel business. They were direct, positive, and brilliant in constructing their strategy to build a North American conglomerate. However, the USW and Franklin Mutual silently vetoed the idea.

Three days after the third Essar offer, Severstal, armed with union backing, increased its nonbinding offer to $15.50. Again the board was unimpressed, if for no other reason than that the offer was nonbinding. They preferred the Essar proposals, which now included an offer to lend the company $80 million or more so that Esmark could pay off its debt and negotiate an end to its headaches with the federal government's Emergency Steel Loan Guarantee Board.

On April 20, Ron Bloom sent a powerful e-mail to the Bouchards, stating that the USW was fully supportive of the Severstal offer, did not support the Essar offer, and, if necessary, would enforce its rights under its collective bargaining agreement with Esmark to prevent a transaction with Essar. With this e-mail, the gauntlet was thrown down. Even though a peaceful ending was still a possibility, it now looked as if hostilities were almost inevitable. Severstal engaged Skadden Arps and Merrill Lynch. Esmark engaged McGuire Woods, Patzik, Frank and Samotny, and UBS. The board of Esmark engaged Buchanan Ingersoll and Rooney, with Pittsburgh roots and long experience with the steel industry as its special counsel; Essar engaged Sherman and Sterling and J.P. Morgan. What had been cordial, even friendly discussions now had evolved into a classic Wall Street celebrity legal and financial slugfest! Teams had been chosen, and the contest would begin.

On April 25, Essar delivered a fifth proposal to Esmark. It now offered either to buy the Esmark's steel mill business for $775 million or to offer

$17.25 per share for all of Esmark's stock. Essar also offered to increase its loan to the company to $100 million.

Later that same day, Severstal confused everyone by upping its offer to only $16 per share and stated its willingness to lend the company $120 million, thus trying to negate the lending advantage enjoyed by Essar. Members of Esmark's board scratched their heads, trying to figure out how they could be expected to say yes to an offer $1.25 less per share than the offer they had from Essar. Visions of shareholder lawsuits danced before them if they did not move in Essar's direction.

As the Esmark board thought about the two offers, Franklin Mutual made the decision even more complex. On April 28, Franklin delivered a statement to the board in support of the Severstal offer, despite its lower price. Franklin owned roughly 24 million shares, which translated to 68 percent of the firm's stock. Without question, it was the majority and dominant stockholder. This was not what Esmark's board hoped to hear! Franklin identified the USW support of Severstal as influencing its decision.

To some, this may have appeared to be an unexpected alliance of interests—a Russian steelmaker, a U.S. investment manager, and the USW. Perhaps it was a strange "pack," but it was a powerful one, and the participants had done deals together before. In simple terms, it appeared that the USW and Franklin felt the USW's Successorship Clause permitted them to insist upon an offer that was worth $1.25 less per share. The Esmark board was amazed by this representation, and its members wondered how the USW, whose retirees owned a considerable hunk of Esmark stock and Franklin Mutual, which owned 68 percent of Esmark's stock, could shoot themselves in the foot in this fashion. What else, they speculated, was going on here?

On April 29, 2008, Dave McCall, the president of USW Area 1, a very important union officer and likely successor to Leo Gerard as the next president of the USW, sent yet another powerful letter to the Esmark board reinforcing the statements of the earlier e-mail from Ron Bloom. The USW, which was accustomed to squeezing its opponents, was ratcheting up its pressure.

Later that evening, the Esmark board gathered at the Pittsburgh Airport Hyatt to hear the opinions and advice of its law firms, as well as the fairness opinions and analysis of UBS. Then, in a meeting that went well past midnight, they met with the senior representatives of Essar and Severstal to hear their latest proposals firsthand. Skadden Arps accompanied Severstal and stated that Severstal was not willing to move forward with its proposal that night. It stated that it had strong concerns over the $525 million law suit that Arcelor Mittal Steel had filed against Esmark because of the collapse of the Sparrows Point transaction.

> **Coincidentally, Severstal had won** the thinly attended follow-up auction of Sparrows Point at a price that was exactly $525 million less than Esmark's prior bid. It would be, punsters noted, a steal of a steel firm.

Severstal's pause, however, made the Esmark board of directors' job remarkably simple. For the time being, there was now only one bidder. The board voted unanimously to accept Essar's offer. Even the legendary Lynn Williams and strong-minded James Bowen, the two USW-designated directors, surprised Ron Bloom by voting in favor of Essar.

The next morning, Esmark and Essar executed a "memo of understanding" directed at completing the merger and signed a commitment letter for a loan of $110 million. These agreements included significant break-up fees and prepayment penalties that Essar would receive in the event the deals anticipated were interrupted by Severstal or others.

Story over? Of course not! This was Esmark, after all. The USW argued that the deal required its consent, and, under the Right to Bid provision in the collective bargaining agreement, the USW had the ability to mount a counter offer. Furthermore, if Severstal launched a public tender offer, Franklin Mutual, the majority stockholder, might support Severstal. The board insisted on and received a "Go Shop" provision from Essar. Such a provision meant that Esmark could continue to look for a higher price or better offer for a short period of time. This was the fiduciary duty of the Esmark board under most interpretations of Delaware Law, which was binding here. This enabled Severstal to up its ante if it wanted to continue to play, and therefore the provision was distinctly to the benefit of stockholders.

On May 16, Dave McCall of the USW again wrote Esmark's board of directors, arguing that Esmark had violated the Right to Bid provision. He demanded that Esmark withdraw from its agreements with Essar. The company refused to do so, in a letter to the USW a few days later, and stated that it did not believe the USW had the right to block the transaction under the terms of its Successorship Clause. Later that day, Skadden Arps delivered a letter to the board indicating Severstal's interest in increasing its offer to $17 per share, still less than Essar's $17.25 per share.

On May 22, Franklin Mutual delivered a letter to the board once again, supporting the bid by Severstal. The Esmark board of directors continued to be puzzled by this behavior. Why would Franklin Mutual and the USW, the two largest shareholders, sell themselves short? What else was going on here? Once Franklin Mutual's support of an apparently inferior offer was made public, most other institutional shareholders began flooding Craig Bouchard's office with calls with violent reactions to Franklin's apparent endorsement of a lower offer. May 30 was an eventful day. First, Severstal launched a $17 tender offer for Wheeling Pitt's shares. Clearly, they intended to make this a battle. Second, the USW took legal action against Esmark. The union filed a formal grievance surrounding the issues of right to bid, notice periods, and Esmark's alleged failure to enter into a confidentiality agreement with the USW. The USW asked the court to throw out the Essar agreements, including prepayment penalties and break-up fees. This initiative meant the USW and Esmark were headed to a binding arbitration that would decide the disputed issues.

Interestingly, the USW did not mention the Successorship Clause in its complaint. The inside word on the street was that it was worried about losing on this front. A loss to Esmark on this legally hazy concept could potentially threaten one of their most important levers over such major clients as U.S. Steel and Mittal Steel. Perhaps the USW did not want to risk such an outcome unless the stakes were larger. In any case, the USW and Esmark agreed to June 18 as the arbitration date, with an arbitrator's ruling scheduled two days before Essar and Esmark were scheduled to complete their merger agreement.

On June 5, Franklin Mutual agreed with Severstal to tender all of its shares to the Russian company. Pressure was building on Esmark to cave in and accept the Russian offer. Esmark's board felt all of these maneuverings were unfair and amounted to a three-way hostile attack on the board as well as the company. But they realized that all is fair in love and war and, perhaps, in the steel industry as well.

One of the reasons the board of directors was miffed was that the loan Essar had promised to Esmark had been funded. This placed Esmark on a solid financial footing. Furthermore, the Board felt that, without the Essar offer, Severstal would have purchased Esmark for $15 per share. Thus, in spite of the fact that its majority shareholder was demanding that the board accept the Severstal offer, and the organization representing 80 percent of its employees was demanding the same, the board felt this was not in the best interests of all shareholders. Essar had saved the company and had put forward a superior offer; hence, the board was not in the mood to back down.

Essar, however, realized that the chips were stacked against it. It realized that it had to offer something distinctly superior to Severstal or lose the battle. On June 6, Essar advised the board that it might increase its offer. On June 10, Essar increased its offer to $19 upon execution of the merger agreement, but it simultaneously increased its break-up fee to $24 million. Essar now had something valuable to gain, no matter what the outcome of the struggle.

Severstal, on the other hand, banked on the potential success of the arbitration hearing as a means to nullify the Essar deal. The stage was set for an exciting ending of Esmark's shocking rise to prominence in the U.S. steel industry. All those involved held their breath as they approached the arbitration.

Most, but not all, of the contending parties' chips were on the table. As Esmark prepared for the arbitration, its board of directors fired a shot across the bow of the USW. A majority of the members of the board was getting tired of being pushed around and believed that the board was being treated badly by the USW, which inexplicably did not appear to be acting in the best interests of its own members, a least with respect to share prices. Esmark filed a lawsuit under the National Labor Relations Act against the USW alleging multiple violations of federal labor law in connection with repeated claims that it could block the Essar acquisition. In

A Collective Bargaining Primer

Let's start with the Successorship Clause. The USW interprets this to mean that a company with whom they have negotiated such a provision cannot be sold without the USW's approval. That approval will not be forthcoming without a "Come to Jesus" meeting with the USW, in which the prospective buyer agrees to the USW's terms, which include perpetuating the Successorship Clause and other stipulations noted as follows. Buyers that do not agree with these terms face a strike on their first day of business, even if they somehow find a way to purchase the firm without USW approval. Hence, most prospective buyers, in their haste to get their deal done, "strike a deal with the devil" and agree to the USW's terms. Another key USW collective bargaining feature is a Right to Bid clause, which gives the USW the right to bid for the ownership of the firm when there is a change of control or (and this is crucial) to assign its right to bid to another firm it designates.

Yet another collective bargaining plank of the USW is its Neutrality clause, which permits the USW to attempt to organize other nonunion plants and shops owned by this firm, even those overseas. An additional favorite of the USW is its preference for a Card Check provision, which allows it to collect signatures of workers who say they wish to be represented by the USW rather than indicating that preference by means of a secret ballot. The USW considers secret ballots of workers to be a potential Achilles heel, and that is why it and other unions have pressed the Obama administration to eliminate secret ballots under the guise of the deceptively named Employee Free Choice Act. Frequently, there also is an Outsourcing clause, which requires a firm to use union labor for a wide range of jobs that do not directly involve steelmaking.

Finally, "upstreaming" restrictions prohibit a firm from transferring cash outside of that company. This can constrain the ability of a firm to purchase other firms, to grant dividends, and in general, to make the financial transactions it deems best for the firm. The USW has been successful in negotiating versions of these provisions with virtually all of the firms where it has collective bargaining. Others unions, for example, the United Auto Workers, have done the same. Such provisions give the unions truly significant power over the operation, life and death of the firms in these industries. It is not for nothing that President Obama has been paying lots of attention to such unions as he has contemplated how to restructure those industries. It is not clear, however, that the firms in these industries can be competitive internationally with such restrictions binding their conduct.

layman's terms, the board challenged the legal standing of the famous Successorship Clause.

The USW now faced a potentially high price for continuing the fray. Arcelor Mittal, U.S. Steel, and every large steel company in North America were watching this fight like hawks. The USW knew well that the NLRB was a Republican-dominated organization that did not perhaps have great sympathy for the USW. (Coincidentally, more than a few USW members turn out to be Republican when they enter the voting booth, but historically the USW has backed the Democratic Party through thick and thin.) The USW's Democratic Party heritage might not impress the NLRB. As a consequence, the USW now had to contemplate the possibility that it could lose the preeminent sources of power it had negotiated in collective bargaining agreements with the largest steel companies. Furthermore, this case now had implications beyond the steel industry, because the Successorship Clause had by now migrated to other unionized industries. Was Severstal worth this risk to the USW when compared to Essar, whose offer remained superior to that of Severstal?

The circumstances Severstal and Franklin Mutual found themselves in suggested that the game might be in the fourth quarter, but it was far from over. With Essar now offering $19 per share and Severstal only $17 per share, there was little question in the eyes of the members of Esmark's board about which proposal was superior. Nevertheless, both board members and investors anticipated that Severstal would improve its offer, and the board's two USW appointees fervently hoped that would occur. Furthermore, even though the Franklin Mutual tender at $17 was shocking to the point of being incomprehensible, it was amendable under Delaware law. Presumably, however, both Franklin Mutual and Severstal hoped that a favorable arbitration decision would take both of them of out of the hole they found themselves in. After all, if the arbitrator declared Esmark's offer null and void, then Esmark could be purchased for $17 per share by Severstal, and the Russians, at least, would be happy. Franklin Mutual still would look a bit silly for promoting a price that was lower than market sale, but the collapse of Essar's offer would enable it to be free and clear of Esmark and would also generate several hundred million dollars in cash for Franklin Mutual.

Nevertheless, even while most observers were waiting to see what Severstal would do, it was Esmark that struck next. With near-perfect timing, Esmark's board launched a tactic that approaches the status of a nuclear weapon on Wall Street. They announced a "poison pill." Poison pills erect significant financial barriers that discourage unwelcome suitors for a firm. Frequently, they involve commitments to minority shareholders that allow those stockholders to purchase shares of stock at significant discounts to the prevailing market price if an unfriendly merger occurs.

Poison pills had become less common on Wall Street in past few years because, in some cases, they were deemed to be shareholder unfriendly. And, there was something to this argument. Incompetent and unproductive management teams would erect poison pill defenses to discourage more efficient and productive suitors from acquiring them, thus ensuring their own continuation in their executive positions.

However, in this case, Esmark's poison pill was stockholder friendly. Its poison pill protected all shareholders, ensuring that either Essar would prevail in this battle at $19 per share, or Severstal would win by providing a superior offer. In both cases, shareholders, including especially the majority stockholder Franklin Mutual, stood to benefit.

Esmark's poison pill took the form of a "rights offering"—a euphemistic label often attached to poison pills to make them more attractive to the media. If a party deemed unfriendly launches a tender offer and obtains a large chunk of the company's stock, then the other shareholders have the "right" to purchase additional shares at a large discount. The effect of this is to dilute the value of the hostile party's acquired stock, and, by itself, this often kills the prospective deal. In Esmark's case, minority investors were accorded the right to buy $120 worth of new stock at a price of $60 per share. If many stockholders took this offer, then it would have diluted Severstal's acquisition massively.

Poison pills, despite sometimes being used to defend inefficient, unproductive firms, have stood the test of time and legal challenges in the state of Delaware (Esmark was a Delaware corporation). The Esmark board took great pains to structure its particular version of a poison pill to satisfy standards that have been set by previous legal challenges in Delaware courts.

The USW did not take this sitting down and quickly added the Esmark poison pill to the list of items to be ruled upon at the arbitration hearing.

The End Game

The arbitration hearing between the USW and Esmark was completed on schedule. The always cogent Ron Bloom led a New York legal team for the USW, and Craig Bouchard spoke for the Esmark, supported by Scott Westwood and a quiet but brilliant legal team from McGuire Woods. The minutes of the meeting are confidential; however, the press releases issued by the parties after the arbitrator rendered his decision provided an accurate summary of the positions of the parties and the arbitrator's decision on June 24, 2008.

In laymen's terms, the arbitrator spared the union the agony of dismantling the Right to Bid concept. He seemingly understood this was a crown jewel of the USW's collective bargaining platform. However, the arbitrator upheld the Esmark position that the union had been given sufficient time to bid. He therefore gave the union one day to issue a bid on its own behalf or instead assign their bid to Severstal, and he further intimated that a price of $19 per share should realistically be the floor for any new Severstal bid. The arbitrator also upheld the considerable break-up and penalty fees negotiated by Essar. Most important, he refused to set aside Esmark's poison pill, stating it did not violate the collective bargaining agreement. The bottom line was that Severstal now had one day to outbid Essar, or it had to go home. Esmark had won!

Esmark investors anxiously awaited Severstal's next move and were gratified the next day when Severstal raised its offer to $19.25 per share. Essar now acknowledged that it would never be able to live peacefully with the USW in Wheeling and declined to improve its bid. It withdrew to the sidelines, collecting approximately $40 million in break-up and prepayment penalty fees. This left Severstal alone on the field of combat. Severstal had emerged victorious, but the victory had been expensive.

When the sale of Esmark finally closed, Esmark had roughly 40 million shares outstanding. This meant that the $2.25 per share higher bid that Esmark procured from Severstal was worth $90 million ($2.25 × 40,000,000 = $90 million) to shareholders and $4.00 × 40,000,000 = $160 million more than Severstal originally offered. The lower number also was a first approximation of what the arbitration cost Severstal, although it now had additional costs to bear, including the break-up fees that were due Essar. Severstal repaid the $110 million loan from Essar and closed the acquisition of Esmark on August 4, 2008, after a final vote of approval from Esmark's shareholders.

After the Battle

The Bouchard brothers, who were the sixth and seventh largest investors in Esmark, exited from the steel industry, but they promptly purchased two private, non unionized oil companies in Nebraska and Oklahoma. With the price of crude having fallen from $147 to less than $40 per barrel, they had found another industry in ferment, where their ability to manage in turbulent times would be extremely valuable.

Severstal took control of Esmark and, presumably at the urging of the USW, sagely advised the NLRB that it was dropping litigation over the Successorship Clause. The USW thus dodged a potentially lethal bullet. However, given the political revolution that has taken place in Washington DC and the changes that have occurred in the NLRB's membership, the USW may not duck arbitrating this issue in the future. This time around, however, the apparent costs had exceeded the benefits.

With the acquisition of Esmark, Severstal became the fourth-largest U.S. steelmaker and firmly established its presence on the North American continent. Unfortunately for Severstal, less than two weeks after the transaction closed, worldwide steel markets began to experience problems. The implosion of the U.S. financial market and the accelerating contraction of the U.S. economy caused steel prices to plunge. Severstal's market cap, which exceeded $40 billion in its salad days, fell to $3.6 billion by early March 2009, a 91-percent decline. Severstal was forced to go hat in hand to the Russian government for bailout money, and it is now beholden to Vladimir Putin (as are many other major Russian firms).

LESSONS

What are some of the lessons to be learned by this meteoric rise of Esmark and its subsequent sale to the Russians?

- Hostile takeovers are generally not a good idea. They carry with them a host of problems. Ultimately, the assets acquired should carry with them a sign saying *caveat emptor*—let the buyer beware. The assets that are actually turned over to a hostile buyer often turn out to be far less valuable than supposed.

- The USW has regained its mojo in the past five years. Its collective bargaining strategies have rejuvenated it, and it has become a model for many other struggling unions in traditional manufacturing industries. The USW bet a huge stack of chips on the election of President Barack Obama and now is riding high. Ron Bloom's signal appointment is evidence of this. The mellifluous, but deceptive Employee Free Choice Act promoted by the Obama administration is another piece of evidence. Strictly judged on the basis of the competence of its leadership, the USW deserves a good fate. Its executives work hard and are savvy negotiators. They believe in what they are doing, although we remain unconvinced that their industrial model is one that will enable the United States to compete effectively in the long term on a worldwide basis. No doubt, this model may be good for those tariff-protected steelworkers who retain their jobs, but it also is a cost and price millstone around the necks of U.S. consumers. The several-inches-thick collective bargaining agreements that the USW has negotiated with steel companies are visible testimony to the costly shackles that the USW has placed around the activities of U.S. steel firms. We do not suggest that it is impossible for unionized U.S. steel firms to maintain long-term profitability in such a world, but we do argue this makes it much more difficult. Not only will unionized firms operate at disadvantage with respect to nonunionized mini-mills, but also they will usually be unable to compete with foreign steel mills unless they are protected by tariffs and other trade restrictions. We wish the history of the industry indicated otherwise, because we recognize that the USW has benefitted many workers over time and has brought a semblance of stability to the U.S. steel industry as well.

- Pursuing this point, the cost structures of such nonunionized firms as Nucor and Steel Dynamics are dramatically different (and much lower) than those of U.S. Steel, AK Steel and Arcelor Mittal North America. Union contracts with the USW make U.S. Steel and Arcelor Mittal uncompetitive. The nearest analogue in the industrial United States is the overwhelming difficulty that the Big Three automobile manufacturers have encountered in competing with the likes of Honda, Hyundai, Nissan, Toyota, and others, which we have noted previously. It is not simply a matter of the costs associated with wage rates and fringe benefits, although the legacy costs of the Big Three may drag them under financially. It also is the work rules and lack of management freedom that the United Auto Workers have imposed upon the Big Three automobile companies. The USW may have developed arguments for discounting the relevance of the decline of the automobile example to the steel industry. We have yet to see any that are persuasive.

- Based upon our experiences in the episodes involving Esmark, we believe Ron Bloom is well positioned to help President Obama restructure the Big Three in the U.S. automobile industry. Although we believe that only Ford has a realistic chance to survive as an independent firm, Mr. Bloom is both tough enough and pragmatic enough to coerce a workable solution, if there is one to be had. He understands and has experience with all sides of the situation—with credit markets, equity markets, management, and labor unions. If anyone can improve this situation, it is Ron Bloom.

- Why did Esmark's board choose to brawl with its largest shareholder, its union, and a respected global steelmaker? There were two reasons. First, Severstal's offer was inferior to Essar's offer. Stockholders would be $90 million better off if Essar's offer, or one that imitated it, were accepted. Second, the Bouchards felt they had an understanding with the USW, Franklin Mutual, and Severstal about how events could proceed. However, they were left out of the "handshake" deal that these three parties had made concerning Esmark. In any event, Esmark's board felt the trio's proposed deal undervalued its assets.

- Regardless, let's review what each apparently was attempting to defend or accomplish. For Severstal, Esmark was the final piece of a strategy that combined the North American assets of its mill in River Rouge, Michigan; Sever-Corr in Columbus, Mississippi; Sparrows Point; WCI in Warren, Ohio; and the scrap iron company it bought subsequent to its swallowing of Esmark. Severstal benefitted from truly significant assistance from the USW in putting this puzzle together. The USW dearly wanted a third large steel company in North America in order to improve its leverage in its negotiations position with Arcelor Mittal and U.S. Steel. Franklin Mutual had a very large investment to protect and had other large transactions involving the USW. These three parties shook hands, and all are good for their word. Unfortunately, the board of directors of Esmark wasn't in on this handshake. Esmark had been banished to the fringes, and this left the Bouchards and most Esmark board members believing they had not been treated appropriately. Whenever possible, deal makers should avoid such situations. Parties who feel aggrieved seldom fade into the woodwork if they believe they have the means to change things. Consequently, the energetic Bouchards came up with a better deal, one that created a new ball game.

- The Esmark board actually viewed Severstal and its management quite favorably, but that meant little when Severstal's early offers were not competitive. Severstal's executives, Alexei Mordashov, Gregory Mason, and Ron Nock, were straight shooters throughout the negotiations and earned the respect of all. Hence, when the Esmark sale finally closed, the transition was amicable (in contrast to Esmark's takeover of Wheeling Pitt). The struggles between the parties did not occur because of dishonesty; they simply reflected skilled negotiators knocking heads in order to do what they perceived to be best for their constituents.

- Two financial firms stood out in the events we have described. In our opinion, UBS Investment Bank ran circles around its competition, which included

J.P. Morgan, Merrill Lynch, and others. More important, there was one commercial bank whose support was absolutely critical in saving Wheeling Pitt and then Esmark and their investors: G.E. Finance. There were 15 international banks supporting the company when the sun was shining, but only G.E. Finance stuck with Esmark through the credit crunch, lending large amounts of money when Esmark needed it and providing brilliant ideas through the most difficult of markets. G.E. Finance believed in the Esmark management team and its strategy. The shareholders of Esmark, who received $19.25 for each of their 40 million shares, owe a debt of gratitude to this financial institution.

- When foreigners snap up our national assets, who will look out for the national interests of the United States? The CFIUS is charged with assessing ramifications for the national security. However, its relative anonymity is a tip-off that it has not often refused to approve foreign acquisitions of U.S. firms. At least partially, this is because the CFIUS has recently been deluged with applications from foreign investors who wish to purchase substantial U.S. firms. Because of the existence of CFIUS, the casual observer might be deluded into concluding that the barriers to foreign acquisitions of U.S. assets have been high. That is not the case, and we believe the various steel industry transactions involving Severstal in the United States (one of which involved Esmark) are evidence of this. We believe the charter of the CFIUS must be expanded and that the possible remedies it might pursue should be broadened and strengthened. We have much more to say about this in the final chapter.

Chapter 7

Winners and Losers

He was born on third base, but thought he had hit a triple.
An old U.S. political sarcasm usually aimed at the wealthy

Second place is just the first loser.
Dale Earnhardt Sr., U.S. race car driver, 1951–2001

In the real world, ensuring that nobody is disadvantaged by a change aimed at improving economic efficiency may require compensation of one or more parties.
Wikipedia entry for "Pareto Efficiency," www.wikipedia.org (January 9, 2009)

Bill Gates once memorably observed, "Your school may have done away with winners and losers, but life has not."[1] So also it is with economic life, which generates both winners and losers. However, because today's winners sometimes are tomorrow's losers and vice-versa, sometimes you need a program to identify the players. Witness "the Donald," Donald Trump, whose fortunes have risen, fallen, risen, and fallen in the space of two decades. Trump fell from his status as a billionaire in the 1980s and was saddled with an estimated $900 million in personal debts in the early 1990s, at which point several of his business ventures declared bankruptcy. By 2007, however, his circumstances had improved so much that *Forbes Magazine* estimated his wealth at $3 billion and The Donald was hosting a successful NBC-TV reality show, *The Apprentice*. Alas, for Mr. Trump, the financial crisis of 2008 once again put a serious dent in his wealth.

Nevertheless, Mr. Trump has not been the only economic actor to learn that winners and losers often change identities rapidly. Recall that Inbev, which agreed in July 2008 to purchase Anheuser-Busch for $52 billion in cash, was rudely shocked when the value of the U.S. dollar increased by about 20 percent between July and the deal's closing in November. Inbev had to eat this difference, because the euros that it was supplying to buy Anheuser-Busch now cost it about $62 billion rather than the $52 billion it had anticipated in July 2008.

Both the Trump and the Inbev examples serve to underline a central reality when we evaluate economic winners and losers. What's true today may not be true tomorrow, and this has been in evidence especially when foreign purchases of U.S. assets have been concerned. Changing conditions, ranging from rising and falling exchange rates to adverse weather, can totally alter the apparent distribution of gains and losses that accrue from economic activity. An economic crisis of the magnitude of the debacle in the fall of 2008 was guaranteed to scramble the identity of winners and losers.

Even so, it remains true that voluntary transactions between informed individuals usually make both parties better off. Otherwise, the trade would not occur. Nevertheless, this win-win situation truly reflects what the parties perceived to be true at the time of the deal. Perceptions often change.

There is at least one additional fly in the ointment when we calculate whether or not specific countries are winners and losers when assets are sold across borders. This relates to the allocation of gains and losses across the population, or the distribution of income, in economic jargon. The gains and losses generated by an economic transaction usually are not evenly distributed across the citizenry. In fact, an uneven distribution of gains and losses nearly always is the result in the case of countries. Consider that a tariff (tax) on textile imports into the United States may help preserve the jobs of textile workers in South Carolina but will force U.S. consumers to pay higher prices for T-shirts and socks. Of course, it also will hurt textile producers in Thailand and Malaysia.

Let's mull over Inbev's purchase of Anheuser-Busch once again. The sale was good for Anheuser-Busch's stockholders, who were paid a price premium of approximately 25 percent for the shares of stock they sold to Inbev. Unfortunately, the deal was not so good for Anheuser-Busch employees—thousands of them lost their jobs. Furthermore, the City of St. Louis also suffered from a diminution of the company's corporate presence and a reduction in charitable and volunteer activities by Anheuser-Busch and its remaining employees. Hence, even though the United States may have won, in an overall sense, in this transaction, some constituencies within the country were damaged.

ADDING UP GAINS AND LOSSES

Any attempt to calculate the economic impact of foreign purchases of U.S. assets must find a way, sooner or later, to place a dollar value on the various outcomes generated by the purchases. If one is doing this from the standpoint of the entire United States, the place to start is to identify the various constituencies affected by a purchase. They may include the following groups:

- Stockholders are primarily concerned with the price they receive for the shares of stock they sell.
- Employees focus overwhelmingly upon whether their jobs will continue and what their wages and benefits will be.
- Consumers are interested in the prices they will pay for products, the selection of products available, the continuation of service, and the possible loss of warranties and guarantees.
- Suppliers want to know if they still will be able to sell product to the new owners of the firm.
- Governmental units have strong interest in future tax collections, including income, property, and sales taxes, but perhaps also capital gains, franchise, and license taxes. Governments also may have concerns about national security and/or increased vulnerability of their governmental unit to political and economic intimidation.
- Financial institutions and intermediaries have an interest in being paid for any outstanding debts, but they may also have an interest in earning fees for handling foreign purchase transactions.
- Charitable recipients have concern over the pattern of future gifts and charitable contributions by the new owners (and any new employees).

In principle, dollar values can be placed upon all of these items. Setting aside questions of pride, face, perception, and reputation (none of which is irrelevant, but all of which are extremely difficult to assess in an economic context), one can determine whether a given asset purchase makes economic sense. This is classic benefit-cost analysis. One computes the measurable benefits and compares them to the measurable costs.

Actual computation of benefits and costs, however, is often easier said than done. First, the benefits and costs are usually spread over the years, well into the future. Pragmatically, this means two things. One is that estimation is often required, because actual data are not available. Another is that the present value (today's value)[2] of the future benefits and costs must be determined.

Perhaps the future stream of benefits and costs associated with an asset purchase is known precisely, but the reality is usually otherwise. As we have seen, fluctuating foreign exchange rates, input prices, and the like easily change unexpectedly, to say nothing of the onset of a worldwide financial crisis. The old maxim "Those who rely upon crystal balls are destined to eat glass" applies in spades here. Elegant statistical estimation models may turn out to have no relation to reality. Consider the adverse experiences of the sovereign wealth funds that plunged billions of dollars into U.S. assets. Collectively, they were the recipients of an unanticipated financial haircut in 2008 that exceeded $1 trillion. Risk does not disappear simply because an elegant estimation technique ignores or minimizes that risk.

Yet another problem with assessing future benefits and costs is that it immediately introduces a difficult question: How much should we value the future? Except in highly unusual circumstances, nearly everyone would agree that having $1 million in hand today is better than being forced to wait one year to receive the same amount. Nevertheless, how much better is a bird in the hand? Is it 5 percent or 10 percent? What we are speculating about here is the appropriate rate of discount that should be applied to deflate these future benefits and costs.

When future benefits and costs have absolutely no risk attached to them, they are often deflated (discounted) by the yield paid on U.S. government bonds. For example, if one is evaluating a risk-free 5-year stream of future benefits and costs, one probably would use the yield on 5-year U.S. government bonds. If that yield is 5 percent, the effect of using that rate is to deflate $1 million, which one will not receive until one year from now, to $1,000,000/(1.05) = $952,381.

But this exercise is not as easy as it may seem at first. Table 7-1 reports the yield on 5-year U.S. government bonds since 2000. In December 2000,

**Table 7-1   Yields on U.S. Government 5-Year Bonds,
December 2000–December 2008**

Year and Month	Yield
December 2000	5.17%
December 2001	4.39%
December 2002	3.03%
December 2003	3.27%
December 2004	3.60%
December 2005	4.39%
December 2006	4.53%
December 2007	3.49%
December 2008	1.52%

Source: Adapted from http://www.economagic.com/em-cgi/data.exe/fedbog/tcm5y.

that yield was 5.17 percent, but it fell to only 1.52 percent in December 2008. The difference is hardly trivial. If we discount the $1 million that comes to us one year from today at 5.17 percent, its value today is $950,841. But if we discount that $1 million at only 1.52 percent, its value is much higher—$985,027.

But our assessment difficulties don't stop there. What if the future stream of benefits and costs is uncertain and we can't really be sure when and if they will occur? In that case, we need to adjust our rate of discount to recognize this risk. If we had been leaning in the direction of a 5-percent rate of discount, we might add from 1 to 30 percent (or even more) to that rate of discount to take into account the uncertainty attached to the future revenues and costs. Rather than discounting future revenues and costs at, say, 5.0 percent, we might discount them at 10 percent, 20 percent, or by an even larger number. Table 7-2 reports typical rates of discount applied to investments in a variety of risky situations. In general, the greater the risk is, the larger is the add-on to the rate of discount to reflect that risk.

Even in situations without uncertainty attached to the actual receipt or payment of future revenues and costs (suppose we are absolutely certain that we will receive the $1 million), there are at least two other gremlins that will cause problems. The first is price inflation. If prices are going to rise in the future (and they nearly always do), then we must take this into account, because the real value of our scheduled future benefits and costs will turn out to be lower than it would be if there were no price inflation. Thus, if prices rise by 3 percent, then the $1 million that we aren't going to receive until one year from now will have only $1,000,000/(1.03) = $970,874 of spending power when we finally receive it. We must take this into account if we wish to avoid losing our economic shirts.

In general, if one expects 5 percent inflation in the future, one must include that expected inflation rate in the rate of discount. Nevertheless, note that most quoted rates of interest that are used to construct discount rates already reflect an expectation of some future price inflation. For example, in December 2000, the average yield on a 5-year U.S. government bond was 5.17 percent. Over the previous year, the consumer price index (CPI) for all items purchased in large cities rose by 3.37 percent.

Table 7-2   Representative Discount Rates when the 5-Year Bond Rate Is 5 Percent

Risk-Free Projects	5%
Low-Risk Projects	6–10%
Moderate-Risk Projects	8–15%
High-Risk Projects	12–25%

If 3.37 percent also reflected investors' expectations of future price inflation at that moment in time, then this revealed that investors were expecting a $5.17 - 3.37 = 1.80$ percent as the real rate of return on their investment in 5-year U.S. government bonds. Retrospectively, we can say that an estimate of 3.37 percent in price inflation for the succeeding five years would not have been terribly far off the mark in 2000. The CPI for all items purchased by consumers in large cities increased at a 2.49-percent compound rate between December 2000 and December 2005. (See Richard Razgaitas[3] for an illuminating discussion focusing on the determination of appropriate rates of discount. Razgaitas concentrates upon situations involving technology and intellectual property, but the principles he enunciates applies to all circumstances. For a more detailed and general exposition, see Goetzmann and Ibbotson.[4])

Still, blithely stating that we must consider price inflation in our valuations almost begs the critical question: What will price inflation actually be in the future? This requires that we make a forecast. Comedian George Carlin once offered an intrepid weather forecast for the evening: "It will be dark." Perhaps the now-deceased Mr. Carlin had potential as an economist. Any old economist can venture that prices will rise in the future, but by how much? Those who hope to evaluate the economic impact of foreign purchases of U.S. assets cannot issue a Carlinesque statement concerning price inflation; they must come up with a hard number.

Table 7-3 records the rate of increase in the CPI for all items purchased by urban consumers in selected years. It is apparent that price inflation rates vary considerably over time and that they can be illusive targets if we want to predict them. Even so, changes in the CPI tend to be much more stable than inflation rates for such essential basic commodities as oil and coal. Suppose the advisability of a purchase of a particular foreign asset critically depends upon the price of oil because transportation costs will be a very important part of the picture. Figure 7-1 records the monthly price per barrel of crude oil in the United States during 2008. Even though monthly averages iron out larger daily variations in crude oil prices, the monthly price per barrel averaged $84.70 in January, increased by 49 percent

Table 7-3   Changes in the Consumer Price Index (CPI), U.S. City Average in Selected Years, for All Items, December to December

Year	Change in the CPI
1979–1980	12.40%
1989–1990	6.17%
1999–2000	3.37%
2007–2008	0.09%

Source: Adapted from http://www.economagic.com/em-cgi/data.exe/blscu/CUUR0000AA0.

to $126.33 per barrel in June, and then declined by 74 percent to $32.94 in December.

How does one deal with such price volatility? With some considerable degree of amazement and humility. The reality is that any economic assessment of a foreign asset purchase that was based in any substantial way upon the price of oil in 2008 would have led to dramatically different answers in January, June, and December. A purchase that seemed to be a wonderful idea in January might have seemed untenable in June, but it was eminently doable in December.

Given these circumstances, it is no wonder that the public and the media pay attention to foreign purchases of U.S. assets on some occasions, but not others. Differing rates of price inflation and, in particular, differing expected future rates of price inflation make all the difference whether a particular purchase (or sale) makes economic sense. However, both the public and the media usually have short time horizons and act as though current conditions will endure as far as the eye can see. However, as we continue to point out, the world often refuses to cooperate and does not unfold in a linear, predictable fashion. As a consequence, when one concludes that a specific foreign asset purchase is good or bad, subsequent events frequently invalidate that judgment.

Let's consider an instructive example. Between 2007 and mid-2008, prices skyrocketed for many inputs used in steel production. Tremendous price increases confronted all steel firms for the materials they needed to make steel—coking coal, coke, iron ore, and steel scrap—and, in some cases, these prices increased by more than 100 percent within a year. The

Figure 7-1 Monthly Price Per Barrel of Oil in the United States, 2008

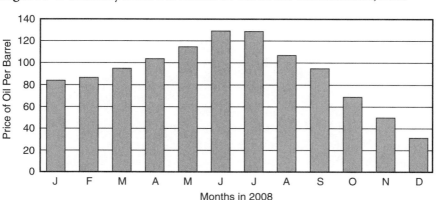

Source: Associated Press, *Business Week, Wall Street Journal.*

GFMS/Basic Metal Price Index, which covers primary aluminum, copper, lead, nickel, tin, and zinc, surged from about 175 in December 2005 to approximately 390 in February 2008 (a 123-percent increase). Stunned steel producers, in an attempt to deal with this situation, scrambled to acquire new, reliable, and predictable sources of input supplies. In this vein, several foreign producers, notably those from Brazil, India, and Russia, purchased U.S. and Canadian sources of supply, hoping thereby to ensure the continued profitability of their North American steel operations. India's Essar, for example, purchased Minnesota Steel, which owns a large iron ore field in the famed Mesabi Range in Northern Minnesota. Russia's NMLK (Novolipetsk Steel) acquired a unit of Duferco in Pennsylvania in order to ensure itself a destination for the slabs it produces in Europe. Severstal, which eventually purchased Esmark, bought 50 percent of a Wheeling Pittsburgh Steel coke battery several years previous in order to pin down a steady supply of coke for its steel mill in River Rouge, Michigan.

Finally, still another element of risk relating to foreign purchases of U.S. assets depends upon the behavior of foreign exchange rates. If non-U.S. currencies are involved (and this will nearly always be true when purchases of U.S. assets by foreigners are involved), then potential fluctuations (positive and negative) in foreign exchange rates must be taken into account. Any party to a foreign transaction that ignores potential changes in foreign currency values might just as well blindly place bets on matches of unknown teams in the Primera División of the Uruguay's major soccer league. The financial results are likely to be the same.

We already have predicted that another "America for Sale" episode is in the future for the United States. One of the major reasons we believe this will happen is because a fall in the value of the U.S. dollar relative to most foreign currencies will occur as a consequence of the U.S. government's financial rescue operations. We are convinced that the financial consequences of a doubling the U.S. monetary base within a few months in 2008 are going to be felt in many different ways, but one of the most important will be a significant decline in the value of the U.S. dollar relative to foreign currencies. We doubt that the Federal Reserve System will have the skill or political ability to be able to deflate the U.S. economy at precisely the right moment in order to avert this scenario. Chinese prime minister Wen Jiabao expressed such fears in March 2009, when he bluntly stated that he was "worried" about the dollar value of the $1.0 trillion U.S. Treasury debt the PRC held at that time.[5] The relevant point is that those who are evaluating the economic impact of foreign purchases of U.S. assets must take such things into account.

However, even if we are wrong about a future fall in the value of the U.S. dollar, it remains inescapable that significant changes in the value of foreign currencies occur every year, sometimes within the space of a week. Consider the relationship between the Japanese yen and the euro. On January 16, 2008, each euro was worth 158.73 yen. A year later, on January 16, 2009, each euro was worth only 120.48 yen, and the value of the euro relative to the yen had fallen by 24.1 percent. It is inescapable that such currency value fluctuations make a huge difference in whether specific transactions are smart or not. Any rational economic decision maker should give consideration to such possibilities.

The real question is whether foreign currency value changes can be forecast accurately, both in terms of direction and timing. We believe it is difficult to forecast foreign currency value changes with any degree of precision (although we believe the value of the U.S. dollar will fall relative to other major currencies in 2010 and 2011). As a consequence, when one is evaluating, say, the economic consequences of the purchase of a U.S. automobile parts supplier by a Japanese firm, an intelligent way to approach uncertainty over foreign currency values is to specify a confidence interval for currency values and other critical variables. That is, one should generate estimates that assume changes in currency values—perhaps 5, 10, and 20 percent—and do so for both appreciations and depreciations in value. It may turn out that even larger currency value changes are in store in the future, but such an exercise will allow decision makers and even casual observers to gain a sense of how their worlds could change when currency values move up and down. Those concerned about such changes can hedge their positions in futures markets and thereby insure themselves against adverse currency fluctuations. Yes, they will have to pay to gain this insurance, but such hedging may provide them with peace of mind and a more predictable future.

The bottom line is this: valuations of future benefits and costs are quite sensitive to the assumptions one chooses to make about what counts and what developments one sees in the future. General Dwight David Eisenhower (later a two-term U.S. president) is said to have commented that the best conceived battle plans are usually thrown out the window after the first hostile shots are fired. So it may also be with assessments of the purchase and sale of U.S. assets to foreigners. Things change, often unpredictably. Nevertheless, we can easily speculate that the world's sovereign wealth funds, which lost approximately $1 trillion in 2007 and 2008 on their foreign investments in the United States and elsewhere, wish they had proceeded on the basis of differing assumptions. Transactions that appeared at the time to be "steals" in their favor lead instead to their financial muggings.

There are several morals we can draw from this discussion. First, when foreign purchases of U.S. assets are concerned, it is ordinarily unwise for anyone to make extremely strong statements that they are either good or bad for the Americans, because subsequent events may turn that conclusion on its head. Impassioned statements, like those of Jim Cramer, predicting impending disaster often backfire.

Second, even when subsequent events do not change, the conclusions of most economic analyses of the benefits and costs that accrue to a particular purchase or sale of assets may be surprisingly susceptible to seemingly benign changes in assumptions about factors such as discount rates, inflation rates, or exchange rates. For example, when economists wish to devalue the future benefits and costs associated with an asset purchase or sale, they can achieve this by simply choosing a higher rate of discount. After all, $1 million that will be received five years from today has a present value of $783,526 today if it is discounted at 5 percent—but a present value of only $690,921 if it is discounted at 10 percent.

We are not arguing that anyone who desires a different analytical result than the one already in hand should simply hire a different economist who proceeds to make different assumptions about the future in order to alter the results. Although no absolute rules exist that require economists to choose one set of assumptions over another, there are accepted norms in economic analysis, both theoretical and empirical, that constrain economic assumptions and analysis. The choice of an obviously inappropriate rate of discount or a failure to take into account risk, price inflation, or fluctuations in the foreign exchange rate would cause a study suffering from those defects to be greeted with guffaws by knowledgeable economic and financial personnel. The conclusions of such a study would be quickly discarded, and it would soon end up in someone's fireplace.

Nevertheless, competent "straight as an arrow" analysts can arrive at different conclusions on the basis of reasonable but competing assumptions and models. Hence, when one reads or sees the report of a study of the economic impact of the sale of U.S. assets to foreigners, almost the first question should be, "What assumptions did they make?"

Ultimately, experience (and here this refers primarily to reliable empirical evidence) is the most powerful arbiter of the economic impact of foreign purchases of U.S. assets. Although generally accepted economic and financial theory might justify a range of different assumptions about benefits and costs and the future, over time it becomes evident that some assumptions are more useful than others because they underpin models that have superior predictive validity. To paraphrase Friedman[6] and others, the decisive test of a theory is its ability to predict and explain behavior. Simply put, economic studies that choose unrealistic rates of discount and do not take into account prospects for price inflation and variations in foreign exchange rates will not predict or explain well. Of course, a

Win-Win versus Pareto Optimality

Voluntary economic transactions between participants who have not been deceived nearly always make both parties to the transaction better off in their own eyes at the time. Contrast this situation to a transaction in which at least one party gains, and no other party loses (again, in their own eyes at the time). Such a transaction is "Pareto Optimal" and reflects many situations in which numerous individuals simply are not affected by a foreign purchase of U.S. assets.

major difficulty is that we may not learn until it is too late that such studies stink like the proverbial skunk. This is why, when a new study appears, we should immediately ask how benefits and costs have been computed and what assumptions have been made in the process.

EVALUATING THE ESMARK SALE

In Chapter 6, we described the sale of Esmark Corporation, a steel production and services firm, to OAO Severstal, a Russian firm. The deal was negotiated by Esmark's chairman and CEO (Jim Bouchard) and its president (Craig Bouchard) and subsequently approved unanimously by Esmark's board on June 25, 2008. The transaction was consummated on August 4.

Let's now evaluate how the major constituencies affected by the sale made out. That is, in the fashion of the previous section of this chapter, let's see if we can determine winners and losers.

- Stockholders

    We asserted earlier that stockholders are primarily concerned with the price they receive for the shares of stock they sell. More to the point, stockholders are generally pleased when they receive a price for their shares of stock that exceeds the price currently being quoted in equity markets. In the year prior to the sale, the nadir of Esmark's stock was $6.81 per share, and its maximum value was $20.55 per share. The final sale price to Severstal was $19.25 per share, up from the $17.00 per share that Severstal initially offered.

    Esmark's stockholders (there were 39.51 million outstanding shares at the time of sale) were generally delighted, because only six months previously (on December 17, 2007), the stock had closed at $9.28 per share on NASDAQ. The delight no doubt included such large institutional owners of Esmark stock as Franklin Mutual Advisors (which controlled more than 60 percent of total outstanding shares), Tontine Partners, Wellington Capital, and the USW. After all, on July 2, 2008, the frequently cited investment blog, Motley Fool, placed Esmark on a list of "5 Deathbed Stocks" and suggested that Esmark was a firm exhibiting a "financial death rattle," primarily because of the severe trouble it was encountering in financing its substantial debt. Until Esmark publicly went into play in April 2008, its share price was "putt-putting along" at about $12 per share (the pithy comment of a board member). The competition to purchase Esmark that came down to Severstal versus Essar, a well-regarded Indian firm, revised Esmark's share price, and, by June, it was trading in the $18 per share range, reflecting the fact that Essar had bid $17 per share (later raised to $19 per share).

Unfortunately for Severstal, the world steel market literally "went to hell" (the comment of another Esmark board member) shortly after Severstal completed its purchase of Esmark. The worldwide financial crisis that came to a head in October 2008 directly sabotaged whatever plans Severstal might have had for Esmark and one of Esmark's key units, the former Wheeling-Pittsburgh Steel Company. Severstal was forced to postpone enhancements to Wheeling-Pitt, shutter nearly all of its operations, and lay off workers, no doubt to the mortification of its erstwhile allies, the USW, which had strong armed Severstal forward as the final victor in the intense negotiations with Esmark's board and rival buyer Essar.

Using the enviable advantage of hindsight, it seems clear that Esmark would not have sold for $19.25 per share even a couple of weeks after the deal closed on August 4, 2008. There is general agreement among steel industry insiders that the $19.25 per share price Severstal paid for Esmark was the maximum price that Esmark would be capable of attracting for years to come. "Those guys wouldn't sell for $5 a share today," commented a stock broker in January 2009 who follows the steel industry. In fact, Esmark and most similar steel assets are no longer salable at virtually any price until the worldwide financial crisis is resolved.

The ultimate tale of this sale? Esmark's shareholders did very well, even "made out like bandits," according to the stock broker. Exquisite timing on the part of Jim and Craig Bouchard, their cold-eyed skill in playing off one suitor against the other, and a bit of good luck resulted in a sale of which nearly every shareholder approved. Retrospectively, rational Esmark stockholders would have to search hard for a reason to complain.

- Employees
Esmark employed 3,500 individuals at the time of the merger. Both physically and conceptually, the corporation is split into two parts: upstream steel production and downstream service. The upstream steel production portion of the company centers upon the venerable Wheeling Pittsburgh Steel Corporation, whose production employees are represented by the USW. Esmark's downstream service employees are located primarily in about a dozen firms, mostly dotted around the Midwest, that bend and fabricate

Figure 7-2 Esmark's Share Price Movement, 2007–2008

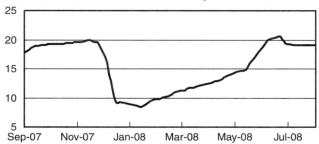

steel and serve many customers face-to-face. They are partially unionized and had no connection to Wheeling Pitt until Esmark purchased Wheeling Pitt in November 2007.

As noted in Chapter 6, the USW decided early on that it favored the sale of Esmark to Severstal, the Russian firm, rather than Essar, the Indian firm. USW leaders maintained this preference even when Essar offered objectively superior financial terms to Esmark's board and stockholders. The USW's position in this regard evoked questions because the union itself owned a large amount of Esmark stock as a part of its retiree VEBA Trust. Therefore, the USW's position seemed to some to be contrary to the best financial interests of its own membership. No doubt the USW had other issues to consider.

USW leadership attempted to rebut this criticism by arguing that Severstal would be the superior owner in the long-term, even though Essar initially offered a higher buyout share price and pledged more capital investment in Wheeling Pitt's plant. This disconnect between the USW's position and the apparent superiority of Essar's offer led to speculation that a non-public agreement had been reached between the USW and Severstal.

Regardless, USW leaders stated that they would not approve any buyout by Essar and that they were prepared to litigate their contention that the USW had the right to veto any purchaser of Esmark. The USW's two appointees on the Esmark board of directors consistently toed the same lines. They were to be disappointed by subsequent events. Although Esmark's board did indeed approve Severstal's bid, the rapid deterioration of steel markets, both in the United States and worldwide, led to nearly all of Wheeling Pitt's production facilities being closed and employees laid off. According to Helmer,[7] Severstal's Wheeling Pitt assets lost more than 80 percent of their value by March 2009.

Retrospectively, we can see that Esser has fared much better than Severstal in North America. It would be unfair to saddle Severstal and the USW with responsibility for the multiple economic misfortunes that afflicted nearly all steel firms worldwide in 2008. Hence, although Esmark's Wheeling Pitt employees are much worse off after the buyout than before, only some of this can be attributed to Severstal.

It remains to be seen how capable a steward Severstal will be over the years. Both Severstal and its CEO, Alexei Mordashov, face immense financial challenges. Indeed, virtually every Russian oligarch has struggled to maintain his economic empire, and the Russian government appears to have strong interest in renationalizing portions of their firms. By contrast, Essar appears to be much better situated financially and to have a greater ability to withstand the stiff economic winds confronting the steel industry. It is possible that Esmark's employees (especially those at Wheeling Pitt) and USW leaders may come to rue their preference in 2008 for Severstal instead of Essar. This provides an excellent illustration of the principle we enunciated earlier in this chapter: what is true in the short run may not also be true in the long run when purchases of U.S. assets by foreigners are concerned.

- Consumers

  Consumers nearly always are better off when significant numbers of viable, competitive suppliers exist in a market. If the sale of Esmark to Severstal maintains the Wheeling Pitt portion of Esmark as a viable competitor (there is no question that the downstream service portion of Esmark is viable), then consumers are likely to benefit. Realistically, this will require hundreds of millions of dollars of investment to modernize and improve Wheeling Pitt's facilities, a task Severstal pledged to undertake prior to the rapid deterioration of the steel industry. Severstal has also committed to maintaining Esmark's production selection and customer guarantees. It's too early for us render a judgment in this regard, and so, like a college professor grading a student who has not yet finished all of his or her work, we assign an incomplete grade. We'll know much more in a few yeas.

- Suppliers

  Understandably, the major concern of the firms that were supplying Esmark with inputs prior to the buyout was that Esmark should not go out of business afterward. As we have noted, there seems little doubt that downstream Esmark can survive and prosper; this group was consistently profitable prior to Esmark's sale. The general decline in economic conditions will reduce downstream profitability, but this division will survive. This is good news for firms that supply it with items ranging from rolled steel to food.

  The position of suppliers to the Wheeling Pitt portion of Esmark is not so clear. The ratcheting down of Wheeling Pitt's production already has reduced to zero its purchases of scrap iron and other essential inputs. Query whether Severstal will move to acquire its own sources of supplies of basic inputs; it has pursued that strategy elsewhere. If so, then existing suppliers to Wheeling Pitt could be pushed out. From the standpoint of public policy, this would not be an adverse development if Severstal can perform these jobs more efficiently. This remains to be seen, and so we assign another incomplete grade. The evidence thus far discourages that view.

- Governmental Units

Governmental units have strong interest in future tax collections, including income, property, and sales taxes, but perhaps also capital gains, franchise, and license taxes. Governments also may have concerns about national security and/or increased vulnerability of their governmental unit to political and economic intimidation. Without question, tax collections for governments at all levels have fallen because Severstal has contracted production and laid off workers. Even so, virtually none of this can justifiably be attributed to Severstal's purchase. If, years down the road, Severstal does not honor its commitment to reopen Wheeling Pitt facilities and the Wheeling Pitt portion of the business stagnates or fails, then Russian firm's purchase of Esmark will be judged harshly by nearly all observers. It remains to be seen if Severstal will live up to its commitments when worldwide business conditions improve.

- Financial Institutions and Intermediaries

Financial institutions have an interest in being paid for any outstanding debts, but they may also have an interest in earning fees for handling foreign purchase transactions. As a result of the Severstal purchase, all of Esmark's creditors were paid what they were owed. Hence, these entities must have been pleased with the sale, because some may have had reason to doubt that such payments ever would be made.

- Charitable Recipients

Charitable recipients want to know the pattern of future gifts and charitable contributions by the new owners (and any new employees). Their worry is that new owners, especially those not connected to their communities, will reduce their charitable contributions. There is evidence of this phenomenon in some other acquisitions and mergers. It is too soon to tell how Severstal will behave in this regard.

SUMMING IT UP

Who won when Severstal acquired Esmark in August 2008? Stockholders were clear winners, as were creditors. Stockholders received a price for their shares that easily exceeded market values over the previous year and which were dramatically larger than share prices that probably would have ruled had Esmark been sold only a few weeks later. Among these stockholders were several large institutional investors (notably Franklin Mutual Advisors) and the USW itself. The Bouchard brothers also emerged from the sale with attractive gains.

Esmark's creditors may have been the happiest constituency after the sale. All were paid what they were owed, and several breathed sighs of relief since the wretched state of U.S. credit markets had no doubt caused them to worry that Esmark might default on its debts. Creditors were unqualified winners.

Esmark's employees and suppliers were losers, at least in the short run. The general decline in worldwide economic conditions and the accompanying decline of the steel industry are the major villains here. The same conclusion applies to governmental units associated with Esmark.

It is too early to tell whether consumers and charitable recipients will be better or worse off because of the sale of Esmark. Events in subsequent years will determine the answer. However, Jim Bouchard did make a gift of $1.0 million to build a Little League baseball complex in Sewickley, Pennsylvania. Jim and Craig Bouchard also contributed the funds necessary to construct a fitness center at the high school they graduated from in Hinsdale, Illinois.

Finally, on the list of apparent losers, one must include Severstal, although a significant recovery in the steel industry worldwide could change this evaluation. Severstal paid generously for Esmark, and it seems evident that Esmark could not have attracted the same high share price even several weeks later. Severstal also had to compensate the ostensible losing bidder, Essar, in order to bring Severstal's purchase of Esmark to fruition. This amounted to at least $30 million. It will take Severstal many years to recoup these investments, and only dramatically improved steel markets will enable it to do so.[8]

Were we to reevaluate the Esmark transaction 5 or 10 years from now, we might arrive at different conclusions. If Severstal visibly prospers, then some might ask why the Bouchards and the Esmark board did not maintain faith but sold out in 2008. Within a few years, we will also know much more about how workers, consumers, governmental units, and charitable recipients will have fared.

English economist John Maynard Keynes once remarked that "in the long run, we're all dead"—in order to deflate critics who told him that, in the long run, the policies that he espoused were wrongheaded. Keynes ordinarily preferred to concentrate upon short-run consequences. We understand his point, but the truth is that most purchases of U.S. assets by foreigners cannot be evaluated fully except in the long run or, at the very least, until several years have passed. Our rendition of winners and losers is not final.

CHAPTER 8

If We Were Running This Country, We'd ...

Much of the self-righteous nonsense that abounds on so many subjects cannot stand up to three questions: (1) Compared to what? (2) At what cost? and (3) What are the hard facts?

Thomas Sowell, economist, 1930–

It is always the best policy to speak the truth—unless, of course, you are an exceptionally good liar.

Jerome K. Jerome, author, 1859–1927

Our moment of truth has arrived. We must now toe the line and outline what, if anything, we propose to do about foreign purchases of U.S. assets. We will start with general principles and then speak more specifically about core industries and technologies related to national security.

MOST FOREIGN PURCHASES OF U.S. ASSETS ARE NOT A PROBLEM

Most foreign purchases of private sector U.S. assets are not harmful to the U.S. economy. They represent efficient reallocations of capital and force U.S. firms to keep on their toes. In some cases, U.S. firms badly need the capital they acquire via foreign purchases. Does anyone doubt that bankrupt automobile producer Chrysler urgently required capital in 2009 when it sought to sell 35 percent of itself to the Italian automobile manufacturer Fiat? Similarly, is anyone unconvinced that such Wall Street financial firms as Citigroup and Morgan Stanley did not have a strong need for the capital injection they received when organizations from Abu Dhabi and Japan purchased stakes in them?

There are other ways that foreign purchases of U.S. assets can improve the welfare of U.S. citizens. Foreign purchasers of U.S. firms figuratively rattle the bars on the cages of quiescent, stagnant industries. The new foreign owners often cashier complacent or incompetent managers and turn around the performance of inefficient, unproductive firms. They increase efficiency, stir things up, and enhance competition. The example of the U.S. automobile industry is instructive. Who would argue against the proposition that the entrée of Japanese automobile manufacturers in the United States forced the previously unchallenged, somnolent Detroit Big Three firms to improve their efficiency? Would any knowledgeable observer maintain that this hasn't also been a good thing for U.S. automobile buyers?

Roughly similar competitive scenes have played out in industries as diverse as personal computers, steel, garden tools, food stores, and microprocessors. This is not the dreaded "foreign competition" that features imports entering the United States from countries such as China and India. Instead, this is foreign competition emanating from plants located inside the United States. These "domestic, yet foreign" competitors invest capital and employ U.S. workers who are compensated more on average than workers employed by "native" U.S. firms. The end result is that consumers benefit from more choices and pay lower prices. The new competition generated by these asset purchases may slice as much as 1 percent annually from the CPI.

Those who rail against foreign purchases of U.S. assets conveniently forget that the United States has been an active purchaser of foreign assets around the globe for more than a century. Even in 2007, when the "America for Sale" phenomenon peaked, Americans purchased almost $100 billion more of foreign assets than foreigners purchased assets in the United States. Hence, it would truly be a case of the pot calling the kettle black were we to object categorically to foreign purchases of U.S. assets. Furthermore, empirical evidence reveals that the United States earns higher rates of return on its investments abroad than foreigners earn on their investments in the United States. Simply put, we have had a good deal going for us, and we should not permit the flurry of foreign purchases of U.S. assets that occurred in 2006 and 2007 to confuse us.

Of course, not all foreign purchases of U.S. assets involve U.S. firms being bought out or the purchase of stock market equity. Foreign purchases of U.S. government debt have assumed increasing importance in recent years. Where foreign purchases of U.S. government debt are concerned, it is fair to say that the United States would be severely impaired if it were not able to sell debt to foreigners. Foreigners now own approximately one-half of all U.S. government debt that is not held by the federal government itself. Without this infusion of foreign funds, interest rates would increase and the U.S. government would struggle to fund even its routine operations. The U.S. government's financial rescue and stimulus packages in 2009 assume that foreigners are willing and able to purchase unprecedented billions of dollars of U.S. government debt annually, not only in 2009, but for many years thereafter. Indeed, the U.S. government has recently floated such massive amounts of debt that even friendly observers worry that China and other countries might refuse to accommodate the United States in this regard. After all, if you were China, would you want to purchase U.S. government bonds whose value is quite likely to decline because the declining value of the U.S. dollar will make each of the bonds worth less?

Ultimately, we believe the citizens of the United States should be unconcerned about most foreign purchases of U.S. assets. More precisely, if the British or the Germans own U.S. soft drink producers, or petrodollars are used by a Middle Eastern country to buy a professional U.S. sports team, or Japan decides to purchase a stake in Target in order to do battle with Wal-Mart, there is little for us to worry about over and above what would be true if these enterprises were owned free and clear by Americans. There are no national security concerns associated with such foreign purchases and, as noted previously, they may provide needed capital and make these industries more competitive.

True, some egos may be damaged when foreigners take over iconic firms with long, proud histories (witness Anheuser-Busch). This is understandable, and we are not prepared to discount such feelings as irrelevant. It is not for nothing that Pittsburgh's National Football League team is named the Steelers. The nickname reflects the industrial heritage of the Pittsburgh area, and only the foolish overlook such connections.

Even so, if the stockholders—the owners—of a firm decide willingly and knowledgeably to sell that enterprise to a foreigner purchaser, we must assume that they at least perceive the deal to be a good one. Others usually gain as well, although, as we saw in the case of the sale of Esmark to Severstal, it does not follow that all other constituencies (employees, governments, suppliers) will also perceive themselves to be better off. On occasion, some individuals lose their jobs and entire small communities are devastated when new owners decide to move in different directions. How should we take such things into account? There is a tendency for interested parties to issue analyses that either paint unrealistically blue skies or function as jeremiads that warn of impending doom. Ultimately, there is some art, judgment, and informed extrapolation, as well as science, in analyses that focus on whether a specific foreign purchase is beneficial.

We readily acknowledge that specific transactions with foreign buyers can go badly astray. It is, however, usually difficult to predict such disasters ahead of time because of the many critical assumptions that must be made in order to attribute costs and benefits to constituencies other than stockholders.

WHAT WE REALLY SHOULD WORRY ABOUT

Foreign purchases of U.S. assets often provoke heated emotions. When events subsequent to a purchase do not turn out well, finger-pointing and hostility nearly always result. Witness DHL's ill-fated purchase of Airborne Express in 2003 and the demise of that venture in 2008. The negative impact upon Wilmington, Ohio, was overwhelming—this small town of 12,500 citizens lost 7,000 jobs.

DHL's pledge to pay more than $260 million in severance benefits to those it laid off diminished the immediate economic blow to the town, but it did little to diminish the criticism of foreign asset purchases in general and DHL's purchase in particular. Wilmingtonians scored DHL for inefficient management. Many came to believe that DHL, owned by Germany's Deutsche Post, would have treated German workers differently.

Similar episodes exist on both sides of the Atlantic. Nonetheless, after all the dust has settled and dispassionate analysis takes over, we must conclude that most purchases of U.S. assets by foreigners are not a problem. They supply the United States with needed capital, invigorate management and operations, increase competition, and often lower prices. All of these are good for consumers; they constitute the fruits of increased economic efficiency.

MARKETS FOR CONSUMER GOODS AND SERVICES

What if a foreign investor were to make a successful bid to do one of the following?

- Purchase Hershey Chocolate   Giardelli
- Buy a significant stake in Wal-Mart
- Purchase Educate Services, which runs Sylvan Learning and other private sector educational providers
- Acquire Dreamworks, which produces film, television, software, and music.

> **In general, if entry barriers into a market are low, there is little for us to worry about** if and when a foreign investor acquires a U.S. firm or set of assets. Misbehavior or inefficiency will soon be disciplined by the entry of new competitors.

Would such events constitute something we should worry about? Probably not. There is little reason for any American to object if a foreign company were to make successful bids for any of these enterprises, or, for that matter, if a foreign competitor purchases the neighborhood corner grocery store or dry cleaning establishment. Such acquisitions would have minimal impact upon the welfare of Americans and might well improve the situation.

We chose these examples deliberately. All involve firms competing in consumer goods and services industries, and none of these transactions has occurred or, to our knowledge, even been seriously contemplated. We are prepared to assert that such purchases ordinarily make both stockholders and consumers better off. Stockholders frequently benefit either from their ability to sell their shares at an attractive price or from superior new management that generates higher profits and therefore increases the value of their shares. Consumers often benefit from innovation and lower prices.

Lurking behind our judgment, however, is the notion of barriers to the entry. In most consumer goods and service industries, it is easier for a new competitor to enter than it would be in a capital-intensive industry such as automobile production or steelmaking. This is crucial because, if entry barriers into a market are low, then any foreign investor that acquires a U.S. firm and subsequently misbehaves will soon be chastised by the market. Foreigners that attempt to reap monopoly profits will attract entry from new competitors (domestic and foreign), and this dynamic will eliminate supranormal profits in a hurry.

We don't mean to imply that there are no barriers that discourage new competitors in consumer goods industries. On occasion, branding and product differentiation are so great in consumer goods markets that this deters new firms from entering. The strength of such brand names as Amazon, Canon, Cheerios, Coors, Gillette, Google, Pizza Hut, and Tide creates problems for prospective new competitors. Rational investors would consider the circumstances carefully before they would make a decision to take on such firms head-to-head in competition. Similarly, the entry of new firms could be discouraged by the existence of pervasive economies of scale that would require a firm to grow to large size in order to be efficient. There is also the possibility that restrictive patents, franchises, zoning, and licenses could shower cold water on the entry of new competitor firms.

Nevertheless, we can generalize: the easier it is for new firms to enter an industry, the less we need to worry about foreign purchases of firms or assets in that industry. Our reasoning is straightforward—if the foreign purchaser gets out of line, it will attract the entry of new firms and ultimately be punished (economically speaking) for its behavior. Investment capital is notoriously mobile when profitable opportunities appear.

Digitizable Goods Are Different

There is, however, one category of consumer goods and services presenting special problems: intellectual property in the form of computer software. Software, such as Microsoft's Windows Vista operating system or Intuit's TurboTax program, has peculiar cost characteristics. The development and production of software is usually accompanied by high fixed-costs of development, but low variable-costs in production. Microsoft and Intuit must expend considerable money and time developing their software packages. Microsoft reported that it spent $6.0 billion to develop its Windows Vista operating system. Furthermore, it had to make this investment prior to selling a single unit. The $6.0 billion represents a classic "sunk cost"—funds that have been spent and can never be retrieved.

Once developed, however, the marginal (additional) cost of producing one additional copy of Windows Vista is quite low. Even when packaging costs are included, the marginal cost of generating an additional salable copy of either program appears to be less than $1.00. This has direct implications for Microsoft's cost structure. As it produces additional copies of Windows Vista software, the average cost of each additional unit falls rapidly because Microsoft spreads the $6.0 million in development costs over these additional units of production. In the jargon of economics, Microsoft's long-run cost curve declines significantly as its Windows Vista production increases.

Hence, Microsoft realizes tremendous economies of scale with respect to the production of a piece of software such as Windows Vista. Figure 8-1 explores in simplified fashion how this phenomenon translates to Microsoft's average unit production costs for Windows Vista. If the development costs are $6.0 billion and each copy costs $1.00 to produce at the margin, at a production level of 1.0 million, the average total cost per unit is $6,001. However, at a production level of 100 million, average total cost per unit falls to $61 per unit. At a production level of 180 million (a good number to keep in mind because Microsoft had this many Windows Vista licenses outstanding in the summer of 2008), average total cost per unit falls to $34.33.

> **High fixed-cost industries can evolve in an oligopolistic fashion** and become dominated by two or three firms that soak up all the sales. A ready illustration of this phenomenon is the market for tax preparation software, which is dominated by Intuit's TurboTax and H&R Block's TaxCut. Markets for Internet browsers, computer operating systems, and computer games also often exemplify this circumstance. The reality is that the basic economics of these markets (symbolized by the declining long-run average cost curves of each firm) make it unlikely that large numbers of firms will compete and survive over time. Nevertheless, if entry into these markets is relatively easy, we need not worry about foreign ownership or any other change in ownership.

We might not pay much attention to such economies of scale here except for two reasons. First, cost efficiencies of this sort place a premium on firms becoming large in size and push them to do so quickly. The larger each firm's production is, the lower their average unit production costs are and the greater their competitive advantage is over firms that produce less output. For example, in Figure 8-1, if Microsoft produces 180 million

Figure 8-1 Windows Vista Long-Run Cost Curve

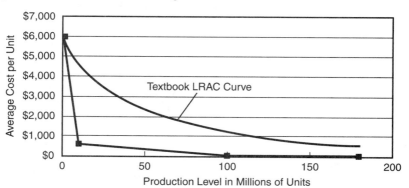

Production Level	Total Production Costs	Average Cost Per Unit
1,000,000	6,001,000,000	$6,001.00
10,000,000	6,010,000,000	$601.00
100,000,000	6,100,000,000	$61.00
180,000,000	6,180,000,000	$34.33

Source: Microsoft, Inc.

units, but a competitor firm producing identical software produces only 100 million units, Microsoft will enjoy a per unit cost advantage of $61.00–$34.33 = $26.67. The implication is that firms should grow large quickly and attain that large size before their competitors, who will be forced to produce and sell at higher costs because they have not attained large volume.

Small firms in industries with high fixed-costs but low variable-costs tend to bite the dust, because they operate at distinct cost disadvantages. In some cases, only one monopoly firm will survive. Hence, there may be a natural tendency toward monopoly or oligopoly in such markets, not unlike what we observe with public utilities.

We should be aware that foreign investors may occasionally seek to purchase an already existing natural monopoly position. Typically, in the United States, the prices and profits in such markets (for example, electricity, natural gas, and cable television) are constrained by some public regulatory body. On the face of it, therefore, U.S. consumers are no more disadvantaged by a foreign-owned and regulated monopolist than one whose owners are domestic. Nevertheless, some fear that an obstreperous foreign-owned natural monopolist (viz. Vladimir Putin) might rake U.S. consumers over the coals.

No one we have heard, however, is talking about selling portions of our natural gas system to the Taliban or selling an electrical utility to Hugo Chávez. However, would ownership by a British firm of a utility supplying natural gas be acceptable? It probably would be, and that is why blanket prohibitions of foreign ownership in this arena are inappropriate.

Another important implication of a high fixed-cost, very low variable-cost situation is that prices often tend to be driven toward zero. If the marginal (additional) cost of producing a unit is very low, there is a strong tendency for competition to push prices down to that level. After all, if I can produce an additional unit for $1.00, but your price is $5.00, I can easily undercut your price in order to gain market share. This dynamic frequently produces a race to bottom in terms of pricing, because rival firms continuously undercut each other's prices. Competition usually is strenuous, and therefore we typically have little to fear from any new firm that enters the market.

When the barriers to entry by a new competitor are high, we often see a prospective new foreign competitor seeking to purchase a U.S. firm outright and, in the process, vault over the barriers to entry. Frequently, this is less expensive than it is for that same foreign investor to start his or her own new firm in the United States. Once established, foreign firms in such situations are difficult to dislodge, even if a U.S. competitor comes along with the proverbial better mouse trap. Nevertheless, the citizens of the United States are no more disadvantaged by barriers to entry exploited by foreigners than they are by the same barriers to entry used by domestic producers.

Digitized products often can easily be copied or stolen and transmitted in a millisecond to any corner of the world. Music, movies, television, and otherwise proprietary data all fall into this category. In essence, the ubiquitous, almost-zero cost copying of digitized materials effectively reduces entry barriers to new competitors to zero. Constant threats of entry by new competitors and cutthroat pricing reductions are not a recipe for long-term financial success. Hence, we usually have little to fear from foreign purchases of firms or assets in such situations. If foreign firms wish to jump into such a bubbling pot, then we have no reason to discourage them and perhaps should welcome them.

CORE INDUSTRIES AND CRITICAL INFRASTRUCTURE

The tenor of our analysis changes its tone when we analyze foreign purchases of firms or assets in markets that are central to the overall infrastructure and viability of the U.S. economy. Here we refer to firms that produce key inputs used throughout the economy, including national defense-oriented industries. Examples include electricity, natural gas, public utilities, computer networking and search, sensor and laser-based technologies, a variety of telecommunications and satellite technologies firms, steel, aluminum, copper, and a variety of semiexotic metals such as molybdenum and titanium.

However, the list of firms worthy of concern also must include those that are substantially process-oriented in that they produce superalloys and advanced composite materials. Superalloys typically have a nickel, iron, or cobalt base and are designed for machines and equipment that must maintain exceptional strength at very high temperatures. Military aircraft and missiles often rely upon superalloys, but so do private sector turbine engines and steel production facilities.

Advanced composite materials combine two or more dissimilar materials or elements in order to produce something new. An easily understood and uncomplicated version of a composite material is steel-reinforced concrete, but fiberglass, porcelain enamel, and wear-resistant vehicle tires also are included. The goal is to generate lighter, tougher materials that are resistant to fatigue and corrosion. Aircraft, submarines, tanks, and body armor are among the unclassified military applications. Virtually all of these materials, however, also have civilian spin-off counterparts.

Key Inputs: Basic Industries

There are three major classes of cases within the broad "key inputs" rubric that we have just developed. Class one consists of such important intermediate inputs as steel and aluminum, which are used throughout the remainder of the economy for purposes that are primarily non-military. Steel, for example, is used to produce buildings, automobiles, industrial equipment, and a wide variety of other products. Of course, it has military and national security uses as well.

It is worrisome that foreign firms now own slightly more than 50 percent of the U.S. steel industry (please review Figure 4-4). If this share of U.S. steel output were to continue to climb and if just a few firms from a single adversarial country dominated this list, then our worry would evolve into a clear and present danger. Such an ownership pattern could bring into question the willingness or the ability of the U.S. steel industry to perform in the time of need in order to support the rest of U.S. industry and the U.S. military establishment.

Let's be specific. It is not comforting to know that Russia's Vladimir Putin might be lurking in the background, calling signals for the Russian oligarchs who now own more than 30 percent of the U.S. steel industry. Mr. Putin and the Russian government have been progressively exercising much greater control over the major Russian industries. Using the financial crisis of 2008 as a fulcrum, the Russian government has made large loans to the financially vulnerable oligarchs, and it now owns a significant stake in many large Russian firms. It is generally conceded that the Russian government has not always been adept in its actions. The bankrupt Russian oil firm Yukos currently has a case pending before the European Court of Human Rights in which it asks for more than $42 billion in damages because of what it alleges was a politically motivated attack upon it by the Russian government.

If Prime Minister Putin harbors a nasty wish to throw a wrench into the works of the U.S. economy, then he now has acquired the means to do so because of significant Russian ownership within the U.S. steel industry. He could take obstructive actions that could hobble many firms that either supply the steel industry or buy its products. Even so, although Mr. Putin's behavior marks him and Russia as major concerns, our focus is less upon Mr. Putin's specific peregrinations and more upon the underlying question of how much foreign ownership of key assets and inputs is advisable.

As we have seen, the movement of the U.S. steel industry into foreign hands continued in 2008. Russia's Severstal defeated Essar Steel of India in the battle for Esmark we already have described. Severstal also acquired Ohio's WCI Steel and took control of the new SeverCorr mill in Mississippi. Meanwhile, Evraz, yet another Russian company and one of the largest vertically integrated steel, mining, and vanadium businesses in the world, continued its expansion in North America by acquiring IPSCO Tubulars from Sweden's SSAB. Evraz also spun off IPSCO's U.S. tubular and seamless business to another Russian company, TMK, but held on to IPSCO's Canadian plate and pipe business. Evraz also purchased Claymont Steel in Delaware, complementing its plate-making operation on the opposite coast at Evraz Oregon Steel Mills.

Although we believe that most foreign ownership is relatively benign, we also believe that it is not in the best interests of the United States to allow most foreign countries to acquire very large proportions of the assets of core U.S. infrastructure. We have relatively little concern over foreign ownership that constitutes 25 percent of less of an industry's output. When that ownership share rises to between 25 and 50 percent, we should begin to examine such instances in detail and clearly take into account the identity of the purchaser. All purchasers are not equally virtuous, and so the home countries of all purchasers is a relevant consideration.

When a foreign purchase would drive foreign ownership of an industry above 50 percent of U.S. output, we believe the burden of proof must be upon the purchaser to demonstrate that this transaction is benign. The CFIUS, which focuses upon the probable effects of foreign asset purchases on national security, should regard such purchase proposals in such situations with a skeptical eye.

Ultimately, however, it is behavior that counts, and we therefore believe that many such foreign purchases be subject to divestiture provisions. The foreign purchaser must agree that, in the future, the U.S. government could, at its discretion, order the sale of this firm or portions of its assets to another entity, probably a U.S. entity, and possibly to the U.S. government itself. Essentially, the divestiture provision would operate like a call provision on a bond, and the U.S. government could exercise eminent domain.

Despite the travails of the Big Three automobile manufacturers in the United States, we do not regard the "traditional" U.S. automobile industry dominated by the Big Three as one of the critical input markets that the United States should defend. Nor apparently does the CFIUS, probably because it recognizes that the United States actually boasts a two-segment automobile industry now—the Big Three in Detroit and the foreign-owned automobile producers, located mostly in the southern, nonunionized reaches of the country. We are not convinced that the survival of the Big Three carries with it national security implications. Indeed, we believe that the "southern model" may well provide a realistic road map for the future survival of the Big Three, but only after a tightly managed set of Big Three bankruptcies has been negotiated successfully. We believe this must be the eventual task of Ron Bloom, the highly talented, driven USW staff member with whom we dealt at Esmark, who has been appointed by President Obama to help "restructure" (a euphemism of the first rank) the automobile industry.

Key Inputs: Critical Technologies

There is considerably greater reason for us to be apprehensive about a second class of basic inputs, namely, critical technologies that have specific military and national security applications. Ordinarily, it is not in the best interests of the United States to allow majority foreign ownership in firms that are producing (as an illustration) superhard steel alloys or exceptionally durable and strike-resistant armor. CFIUS should place the burden of proof upon any foreign investor in such instances.

In some cases, selective foreign ownership (for example, by NATO allies) may be allowed, and, in others, the appropriate criterion may be ownership that is limited only to long-term allies such as Canada and Great Britain. In other instances, hardheaded analysis might generate the conclusion that foreign ownership is allowed but is subject to divestiture provisions, as previously noted. In yet other cases, foreign ownership of a firm or its assets should be denied completely. It would be foolhardy, for example, to permit an Iranian firm to acquire ownership in a U.S. firm producing highly advanced sensors. Even if the Iranians did not attempt to exercise control, their access to the science related to such developments would be destructive to national security.

Judgment calls are in order, and a revitalized CFIUS with a somewhat broader imprimatur is the best available means to promote these judgments. We recognize that the lists of U.S. friends and enemies changes over time. Today's friends may be tomorrow's enemies and vice-versa. We also understand that the status of a particular technology, or even the centrality of the activities of a particular firm, can change over time. For these and other reasons, judgments about what constitutes a national security risk may change as events unfold. For that reason, it is not possible to write a set of rules that will cover all situations, and we should resist calls to do so.

> **Strategic materials laws** have existed in the United States since 1939, when the Strategic Materials Act of 1939 allocated $100 million to establish a stockpile of strategic raw materials. By 1989, 62 different materials were being stockpiled and had an estimated value of $9.6 billion. This law and its relatives have been amended and expanded several times but do not directly address questions of foreign ownership of vital resources. It is the CFIUS that has responsibility in this latter arena.

What is required is strong analytical work carried out by knowledgeable individuals who are capable of accurately assessing the extent to which real or potential problems actually exist. We believe that more resources must be devoted to the CFIUS, because the issues relating to foreign purchases of U.S. firms and assets are often exceedingly complicated. In addition, because we predict another wave of "America for Sale," CFIUS business is going to increase dramatically over the next few years.

Key Inputs: Defense Production Firms

We take it as self-evident that the CFIUS should place the burden of proof upon anyone who argues that foreign control of U.S. firms is appropriate when those firms are involved in military production and national security tasks (see Table 8-1 for a list of the 10 largest U.S. defense contractors in 2007 ranked by dollar volume). Yes, in some cases,

Table 8-1   The 10 Largest U.S. Defense Contractors by Dollar Value, 2007

Firm	Total Value of Defense Contracts, 2007
Lockheed Martin	$27.32 billion
Boeing	$20.86 billion
Northrup Grumman	$16.77 billion
General Dynamics	$11.47 billion
Raytheon	$10.41 billion
KBR	$ 5.97 billion
L-3 Communications	$ 5.04 billion
United Technologies	$ 4.57 billion
BAE Systems	$ 4.50 billion
SAIC	$ 3.40 billion

Adapted from http://www.govexec.com/features/0807-15/0807-15s3s1.htm.

shared production of military weaponry or technologies may be appropriate, as when the United States and its allies decide jointly to produce an interchangeable fighter airplane. Except in unusual cases, however, meaningful foreign ownership or control of military contractors is inadvisable. The CFIUS should exercise its judgment in this area, but it should be abundantly clear that the hurdles such acquisitions must overcome are elevated.

Setting aside joint projects with our major allies, it will seldom be in the best interests of the United States to allow meaningful foreign ownership or control of U.S. defense contractors, such as Northrup Grumman (which produces aircraft carriers and nuclear submarines) or Lockheed Martin (military aircraft). Let's be clear about what we mean in this arena. We have few worries about a German citizen who owns 10 or even 100 shares of Northrup Grumman stock. By way of contrast, everyone should be concerned about any foreign stockholder who owns a meaningful proportion of Northrup Grumman stock, which we define as 5 percent or more. The accumulation of foreign ownership is also relevant. The sum of all foreign owners' stockholdings should not be large, and sovereign wealth fund ownership of U.S. defense contractors ordinarily should be prohibited. We define large in this situation as 10 percent. Where permitted and wise, foreign ownership must carry with it a contractual understanding that the CFIUS retains the power to mandate divestment of that stock in the future.

Furthermore, in no case should ownership (by either Americans or foreigners) at any level carry with it an automatic right to inspect the defense company's intellectual property or its production facilities. Exceptions to these rules should require the approval of the CFIUS.

Should General Motors be considered a defense contractor?

This should be a CFIUS call. However, GMC was the 40th largest defense contractor by dollar volume in 2007, with $806 million of business, not an insignificant amount. If GMC's activities are confined to producing generic trucks, engines, and the like, the risks associated with foreign ownership appear to be small. If GMC is producing military fighting vehicles that boast the latest technology, this is another matter. This example underlines the extent to which the interlocking worlds of foreign ownership and military contracting are complex and not easily governed by hard and fast rules.

Ultimately, foreign ownership of U.S. defense contractors carries with it two risks. The first is that ownership potentially might enable the foreign owners to direct the defense contractors to undertake actions that are not in the best interests of the United States. At the limit, these directions could involve unsubtle refusals to produce or deal, but they would more likely involve failures to bid, lack of timeliness, problems with quality and interchangeability, and the like.

A second potential risk relates to the disclosure of valuable intellectual property, including national security secrets. This is a more complicated issue than it may first appear to be, especially when telecommunications and computer technologies are concerned. How worried should we be about advanced computer technologies that have, nonetheless, begun to age or have, at least, been duplicated in other countries? Such technologies can be used in many potentially dangerous weapons systems. Even so, the identity of the purchaser makes a difference. If Poland wishes to acquire such technology, should we regard it differently than we would Bolivia, which currently is led by a government that is distinctly left of center and even anti-U.S.? In some case, the identity of the purchaser is ultimately more important than the actual technology in question.

The previous examples only scratch the surface of possibilities, but they serve to emphasize the crucial role of judgment in determining what is in the best interests of the United States when foreign ownership of defense contractors is concerned. It would be splendid and it would satisfy our need for order if we were able to offer intelligent, easy-to-translate rules that clearly specify what is permissible and what is not. Alas, the real world is too complicated for this, and no set of rules can capture all of its nuances. This is why the minimal set of rules we have put forward in this arena operates primarily as a set of trip wires designed to focus attention.

All foreign ownership is not identical, either with respect to the countries involved or the firm or technologies involved. The United States would be ill-served if it were to rule out all foreign ownership of U.S. defense contractors and firms involved in national security-related activities and research. In an increasingly multipolar world, this is an unproductive direction in which to move. Instead, wisdom and judgment are required, and that is what the CFIUS should supply.

INVIGORATING AND EXPANDING THE CFIUS

The CFIUS is (or should be) one of the most important agencies in the United States government. It is an interagency committee within the federal government, chaired by the Secretary of the Treasury (currently

Timothy Geithner), but it includes representatives from nine U.S. government agencies. The list of agencies reads like a list of the most powerful on the planet and includes the Departments of Commerce, Defense, Energy, Homeland Security, and State. Other vital individuals, such as the director of National Intelligence, are also included in its deliberations.[1]

The CFIUS was established by presidential executive order in 1975, but its existence has since been codified several times, most recently by means of the Foreign Investment and National Security Act of 2007 (FINSA). FINSA significantly expanded the authority, scope, and size of the CFIUS and added several dollops of additional congressional oversight. CFIUS exists to assess the national security implications of foreign investments in U.S. companies, infrastructure, technologies, and operations. The 1988 Exon-Florio amendment to the Defense Production Act explicitly gave the president of the United States the authority to investigate the impact of proposed mergers, acquisitions, and takeovers of U.S. firms and operations by foreigners. If CFIUS decides to proceed with a full investigation of a proposed purchase, then it must conclude its initial review in 45 days, after which it submits a recommendation to the president, who has 15 days from the date of referral to clear, prohibit, or suspend a transaction. Since the passage of Exon-Florio, CFIUS has launched 45-day reviews in only about two dozen cases.

Between 2005 and 2007, foreign investors filed 313 notices of transactions that were potentially within the bailiwick of the CFIUS. Approximately 8 percent (or 24) of such notices were withdrawn during CFIUS's review, 5 percent (15) resulted in a CFIUS investigation, and less than 1 percent (2) resulted in an eventual decision by the president. The number of notices more than doubled between 2005 and 2007. What kinds of markets were potentially affected by the notices? Table 8-2 reveals that almost one-half (47 percent) of all notices were in manufacturing industries and 36 percent were in information provision and technology.

Table 8-2 Focusing on CFIUS Notices, 2005–2007

Total Notices	313	(100%)
Manufacturing	148	(47%)
Computer and Electronic Products	51	(16%)
Transportation Equipment	30	(10%)
Information	112	(36%)
Mining, Utilities, and Construction	27	(9%)
Wholesale Trade	25	(8%)
Other	1	(0%)

Note: Industry definitions overlap, and hence the sum of the industries affected is greater than the total number of notices.

Table 8-3   Originating Countries of Foreign Investors Supplying Notices to the CFIUS, 2005–2007

Total Notices	313	100%
United Kingdom	79	25%
Canada	35	11%
France	25	8%
Australia	18	6%
Israel	16	5%

Foreign investors seeking to purchase U.S. firms home in on manufacturing, especially manufacturing involving computer technologies such as semiconductors. Who are the interested parties? Table 8-3 discloses that the United Kingdom led the pack with 79 notices, followed by Canada with 35, France with 25, Australia with 18, and Israel with 16. This is not a list of terrorist nations. A total of 15 notices emanated from Middle Eastern oil-exporting countries, 4 from China, 2 from Pakistan, and 2 from Russia. These data do not portray a deliberate, intensive thrust by rogue or adversarial nations to buy their way into the United States. Of course, in some cases, espionage provides a less-expensive, less-obvious, and perhaps preferred way to obtain desired technological information. Potemkin-like shell corporations established in friendly foreign countries may represent another way.

The most recent annual report of the CFIUS (December 2008) contains repeated statements similar to this: "There is no credible evidence of a widespread coordinated strategy among foreign governments or corporations to acquire critical U.S. technologies through the use of foreign direct investment" (CFIUS, 2008, p. 32). CFIUS maintains a Critical Technologies List: 1,073 deals involving 56 companies and 67 transactions that focused upon critical technologies were analyzed in 2006 and 2007. Thompson Corporation of Canada and RAB Capital led the way with 10 transactions each. Together, Canada and the United Kingdom accounted for 43 percent of all transactions. Their transactions focused upon information technology, but CFIUS did not detect significant problems.

SHOULD THE CFIUS BE REDIRECTED?

The basic intent of the CFIUS is appropriate and necessary. It is in the best interests of the United States to examine the national security implications of foreign investments in the United States. In general, the current CFIUS structure brings to the table the necessary players to evaluate the consequences of proposed investments. However, we have several suggestions for improvement:

- Currently, it is up to foreign investors to notify CFIUS of their proposed transactions. Although it is ordinarily in the best interests of them to do so, sometimes quite the reverse is true, and otherwise unacceptable buyers would prefer to proceed in a clandestine fashion, perhaps through a shell company in a less risky country. The CFIUS should become more active in examining actual controlling ownership and intent, matters that it now often tends not to investigate closely.

- The CFIUS should give special attention to sovereign wealth funds, which, even if they do not exhibit strong interest in national security-oriented assets, can accumulate political and economic muscle with sufficient acquisitions.

- The CFIUS needs additional authority to reopen previously approved transactions and, as we have suggested, have the ability to reverse them. In a world full of change and uncertainty, circumstances change, and a transaction that was noncontroversial when consummated may, only a few years later, be seen to be quite detrimental. Divestiture provisions should be inserted as a condition of approval when the long-term implications of a foreign purchase cannot be known until many years have passed. As we have seen, except for stockholders, it is often difficult to assess the economic impact of many foreign purchases of U.S. firms and assets. Mistakes can be made, and divestiture may become appropriate. Divestiture provisions must be clearly understood by all concerned, in which case foreign investors who accept divestiture by their actions declare that the deal is, nonetheless, a good one for them.

- Actual divestiture (as opposed to specifying it as a possibility) is a remedy that should be open to CFIUS, subject to the prior approval of an appropriately qualified specialist federal court panel. Divestiture is a strong remedy that would violate commonly accepted property rights, and it therefore must be subject to judicial review by a specially situated court. An analog to this is the process of federal judicial inspection and preapproval of federal wiretapping requests. Except in unusual circumstances, divestiture should be confined to cases in which the investor has agreed ahead of time to this possibility as a requirement for purchase approval. The United States should support open-capital markets and accept the discipline of freely operating capital markets until such point as the benefits are outweighed by dangers to national security in the eyes of the CFIUS.

- CFIUS should pay additional attention to such critical infrastructure as transportation and port facilities, public utilities, energy resources and production, and core industrial activities, such as steelmaking, that it does not currently consider to be critical infrastructure.

- It may be too late to declare that the nation's financial infrastructure is critical to the United States in the long-term, but control over financial information should continue to be a concern. Several financial industries are "old," in the sense that frequently they do not involve cutting edge technologies. Nevertheless, they are key to the proper functioning of the U.S. economy and our collective welfare. As we have argued throughout, some foreign ownership of such assets may be desirable, because it injects both capital and enhanced competition. CFIUS must judge when these benefits are outweighed by foreign influence over their use and future development.

- CFIUS should not ignore the anticipated impact of an acquisition upon the major constituencies we have identified when acquisitions are analyzed: stockholders, employees, customers, suppliers, governments, etc. Heretofore, CFIUS has focused primarily, if not exclusively, upon the national security implications of foreign purchases of U.S. firms and assets. This is too narrow a perspective, and, if necessary, it needs to be cured by a change in the law. After all, some acquisitions may have minimal national security implications but, all things considered, be ill-advised for the United States in a benefit-cost sense. Of course, the reverse can also hold true. Some acquisitions may benefit stockholders, consumers, and the other constituencies but have adverse effects upon national security. Rationally, CFIUS should take both classes of factors (national security and U.S. constituencies) into account, and it is well-positioned to do so. Heretofore, its mission has been more limited.

SUMMING IT ALL UP

Nobel Prize-winning author and philosopher Albert Camus once pungently observed, "We are not certain, we are never certain. If we were, we could reach some conclusions. We could, at last, make others take us seriously."[2] Camus's observations are salient. Information is an economic good, and quality information is scarce. We can never be completely certain about the critical aspects of reality in the world we inhabit. This certainly applies to our economic universe. Anyone who boasts of having forecasted all of the unusual economic events that transpired worldwide in the fall of 2008 is either a masterful savant worthy of many kudos or a liar—perhaps a very accomplished one.

The reality is that we don't yet completely understand major past events (for example, the Great Depression), and hence we definitely can't predict future developments with certainty. Risk is omnipresent. Incomplete information, deceptive information, and even blatantly false information define the world in which we operate.

Faced with imperfect and even false information, risk, and differing sets of values, each of us tends to flee to models and modes of thinking that we believe will allow us to categorize information usefully and explain and predict the world. Our personal pillars are economic theory and principles, the empirical evidence that economists have accumulated over time, and the hard knocks of practical entrepreneurial and management experience. We see the world through these lenses, and they inform the conclusions and predictions we have offered here.

Nevertheless, as Camus noted, those who fail to reach substantive conclusions may not be treated seriously. The tendency of the public to ignore commentators who say they don't know, or who refuse to make predictions, pushes some analysts to reach conclusions that sometimes are not merited by the evidence. It leads some experts to attempt to shock their readers and listeners and to utter bombastic warnings and prophecies. We have attempted to avoid such excesses in this book.

We believe our major conclusions constitute logical implications of experience, available evidence, and economic theory. We recognize that others may see things differently, but we are prepared, as always, to put our vision of reality on the firing line. By no means are we infallible; however, we have assembled documented records of past success, and we willingly subject ourselves here to the market test.

We have made three very significant predictions within the confines of this book. First, we predict that the value of the U.S. dollar relative to most major currencies is going to plunge. This is an inevitable consequence of the recovery and stimulus policies that began in the fall of 2008. Huge federal government deficits and rapacious monetary policies will make this outcome very difficult to avoid.

Second, we believe that the "America for Sale" phenomenon will reemerge in 2010. We will once again see foreigners making numerous bids to purchase large hunks of U.S. assets. We've already pointed out that much, probably most, of this is not a bad thing. Indeed, most foreign purchases of U.S. firms and assets are either beneficial or they have minimal effects on Americans. Even so, the intensity of the next "America for Sale" cycle will exceed that we observed in 2006 and 2007, will surprise many, and will probably have national security implications.

Third, the United States has transitioned into an extremely challenging period, economically speaking. We believe the typical American will confront a stagnant or lower standard of living in the next half decade because of our collective actions over the past few decades. One of the most fundamental principles of economics is that meaningful actions always have costs associated with them. For the next half decade, we will be paying the costs of unwise past decisions. Older Americans may avoid some of these costs, because current U.S. government recovery and stimulus policies involve borrowing and therefore passing huge costs on to future generations. Nevertheless, when our children and grandchildren figure this out, many of them will come to rue what we perceive to be an intergenerational financial transfer of historically large proportions.

Can the Fed Do It?

"In essence, then, the bond market has to trust that the Fed can, and will, apply the brakes at just the right time-a skill the central bank hasn't mastered in recent years. If the Treasury isn't careful, the current skirmish with investors could yet turn into another rout."

Source: Peter Eavis, "The Fed Risks Burying the Treasuries." *Wall Street Journal*, 253 (February 3, 2009), C10.

Nevertheless, those who understand the events that have transpired and those events that are poised to occur in the future not only have the ability to survive, but also to prosper in the coming years. Individuals who have conquered the material presented here will be able to ride the current economic tsunami in the fashion of a veteran Banzai Pipeline surfer riding a huge wave elegantly to the shore in Hawaii.

One can easily hear the booming crescendo of the economic waves in the background. Grab your board. Have a great ride!

Notes

CHAPTER 1

1. See Biskupic's article in *USA Today* as one example out of many how the machinations of the West Virginia Supreme Court captured the popular imagination. Biskupic, Joan. 2009. "At the Supreme Court, a Case with the Feel of a Best Seller." *USA Today*, 27 (February 17), 1A, 2A.

2. http://blog.synthesis.net/2008/06/11/when-it-comes-to-us-real-estate-arabs-are-the-new-japanese/.

3. This is more than idle speculation since Chrysler and Chevy have been discussing a joint venture. See http://industry.bnet.com/auto/1000174/if-us-auto-market-looks-tough-now-wait-til-the-chinese-get-here-soon/.

4. http://en.wikipedia.org/wiki/Dubai_Ports_World

5. Under a limited number of circumstances, individuals who are coerced to trade could emerge better off. Modern behavioral finance posits circumstances in which forced membership in a 401-(k) plan or forced savings may make individuals better off even though the same individuals would not have done so if left to their own devices. Fifty years ago, Richard Musgrave talked about a broad class of "merit" goods that government might provide that would improve citizen welfare even though the citizens themselves might not vote for such goods. (Musgrave, Richard A. 1957. "A Multiple Theory of Budget Determination." *FinanzArchiv*, N.S., 25(1), 33–43; Musgrave, Richard A. 1958. *The Theory of Public Finance*. New York: McGraw-Hill.)

6. Roger Simmermaker (Simmermaker, Roger. 2008. *How Americans Can Buy American: The Power of Consumer Patriotism, Third Edition*. Orlando, FL: Consumer Patriotism Corporation) as reported in http://www.businessweek.com/globalbiz/content/jul2008/gb2008079_984183.htm.

7. Suppose 100 million beer drinkers exist, and each purchases six six-packs annually. Each beer drinker therefore saves $0.60 per year, and the total savings to U.S. consumers are $60 million.

8. http://en.wikipedia.org/wiki/Newton_Minow.

9. This also is the same Mitsubishi that, in late October 2008, had to raise $10.7 billion of capital in order to shore up its own balance sheet. This was done primarily in response to falling Japanese equity prices.

10. "Private" U.S. government debt is that debt not held by agencies of the U.S. government itself. U.S. government agencies, such as the Social Security Administration, hold large amounts of U.S. government debt. Hence, one arm of the government owes another.

11. http://www.cnnmoney.com. "Government: U.S. Needs Foreign Cash." March 5, 2008.

12. Eduardo Porter, "A Dicey Safe Heaven," *New York Times*, 158 (December 17, 2008), A28.

13. James K. Jackson, "Foreign Ownership of U.S. Financial Assets: Implications of a Withdrawal," Congressional Research Service (Washington, DC, January 14, 2008).

14. James K. Jackson, 14.

15. "The Rise of State Capitalism," *Economist*, 388 (September 20, 2008), 22.

16. *Economist*. 2008. "The Rise of State Capitalism." 388 (September 20), 22–5.

17. Ronald J. Gilson and Curtis J. Milhaupt, "Sovereign Wealth Funds and Corporate Governance: A Minimalist Response to the New Mercantilism," (February 18, 2008), Stanford Law and Economics Olin Working Paper No. 355, http://ssrn.com/abstract=10950923.

18. Gilson and Milhaupt, 21.

19. Job 1:20–21 (King James Version of the *Holy Bible*).

CHAPTER 2

1. Of course, many other factors also account for the increase in the value of the U.S. dollar relative to the Canadian dollar (the "loonie") in 2008. We already have noted the "flight to safety" (that is, to U.S. government debt) that the international financial crisis stimulated in 2008.

2. Ariana E. Cha, "Weak Dollar Fuels China's Buying Spree of U.S. Firms." *Washington Post* (January 28, 2008).

3. "Economics Focus: The Resilient Dollar," *Economist*, 389 (October 4, 2008), 84.

4. Tom Fitzpatrick of Citigroup Global Markets, as quoted in Min Zen, "For Dollar, December Blues," *Wall Street Journal*, 252 (December 14, 2008), C2.

5. The personal savings rate is defined here as the percentage of household disposable income that is saved rather than consumed.

6. Tom Zeller, "India Shopping for U.S. Coal, Mines," *New York Times* (October 23, 2008), http://www.nytimes.com/timesreader.

7. Vernon Smith, "The Clinton Housing Bubble," *Wall Street Journal*, 251 (December 18, 2007), A20.

8. Nassim Taleb, as quoted on his website, http://www.fooledbyrandomness.com.

9. http://en.wikipedia.org/wiki/American_International_Group.

10. "U.S. Treasuries: A Safe Harbor in Tumultuous Financial Times." http://www.scrippsnews.com/node/36797.

CHAPTER 3

1. "'A Bittersweet Day' for A–B," *St. Louis Post-Dispatch* (November 13, 2008), http://www.stltoday.com/stltoday/business/stories.nsf/developmenteconomy/story/B8EFEDBFDFB678B88625750000154E67?OpenDocument.

2. "Herb Stein's Unfamiliar Quotations." http://www.slate.com/id/2561/.

3. Robert Lucas, as quoted by Drake Bennett, "Paradigm Lost," *Boston Globe* (www.boston.com/bostonglobe/ideas/artiacles/2008/12/21/paradigm_lost?mode=PF (December 21, 2008).

4. β is the ratio of the covariance between this security "i" and the market "m" as a whole, divided by the variance of the market as a whole, where the R's could be asset prices or rates of return:

$$\beta = COV(R_i, R_m)/VAR(R_m)$$

CHAPTER 4

1. John W. Miller, "U.S. Steelmakers Seek More Tariffs to Fight Imports." *Wall Street Journal*, 253 (February 20, 2009), A8.

2. Bloomberg News, "Oligarchs Seek $78 Billion as Credit Woes Help Putin (Update2)," http://www.bloomberg.com/apps/news?pid=20601109&sid=aM71GKiXdzZ8&refer=home.

CHAPTER 5

1. Jim and Craig Bouchard became the sixth- and seventh-largest shareholders in Esmark, respectively.

CHAPTER 7

1. Bill Gates, quoted at http://thinkexist.com/quotation.

2. The present value (PV) of a stream of future benefits (B) and costs (C) spread over "n" years and discounted at rate "r" is: $PV = \sum (B_t - C_t)/(1 + r)^t$ as t = 1, 2, ..., n

3. Richard Razgaitas, *Valuation and Pricing of Technology-Based Intellectual Property*. New York: Wiley, 2003.

4. William N. Goetzmann and Roger G. Ibbotson, *The Equity Risk Premium: Essays and Exploration*. New York: Oxford, 2006.

5. Michael Wines and Keith Bradsher. "China's Leader Says He Is 'Worried' over U.S. Treasuries." *New York Times* (March 14, 2009), www.nytimes.com/times-reader.

6. Milton Friedman, "The Theory of Positive Economics," in Friedman, *Essays in Positive Economics*. Chicago: University of Chicago, 1953, 3–43.

7. John Helmer, "Severstal Writes Down American Asset Value, As Russian Steel Mills Subsidize Mordashov's Follies." http://johnhelmer.net, March 19, 2009.

8. Severstal is hardly the only firm in the steel industry that has been flogged by the worldwide economic decline. Arcelor Mittal, the largest steel producer in the world, lost more than 80 percent of its market cap by the spring of 2009, and U.S. Steel lost more than 90 percent.

CHAPTER 8

1. See http://www.treas.gov/offices/international-affairs/cfius for additional information.

2. Camus wrote words very similar to these in *The Fall* (1991). Since then, his words have been rephrased in many publications and websites to make them more readable, and we use a rephrased version. (Albert Camus, 1991. *The Fall*. Justin O'Brien, trans. New York: Vintage. Originally published in 1957.)

Index

About the Authors

CRAIG T. BOUCHARD founded Esmark with his brother Jim in 2003. Esmark acquired 10 steel companies throughout the Midwest states through 2008, including the celebrated hostile takeover of Wheeling Pittsburgh Corporation which made Esmark a publicly traded stock on the NASDAQ. From 1998–2003 Craig was the President and Chief Executive Officer of New York based NumeriX, a high level mathematics based software company known as the risk management gold-standard to Wall Street's global trading institutions. Craig was a Senior Vice President and the Global Head of Derivative Trading at the First National Bank of Chicago (1976–2005). In the 150-year history of the bank Craig was the second youngest individual ever to rise to the level of Senior Vice President.

Craig holds a Bachelor's degree from Illinois State University (1975), a Master's degree in Economics from Illinois State University (1977) and an MBA from the University of Chicago (1981). He has been a member of the Board of Trustees of Boston University, and the Foundation of the University of Montana. He is an alumnus of Leadership Greater Chicago.

JAMES V. KOCH is Board of Visitors Professor of Economics and President Emeritus at Old Dominion University. Dr. Koch served as president of Old Dominion from 1990–2001. Prior to that, he was president of the University of Montana, 1986–1990. An Exxon Foundation study of U.S. college presidents selected him as one of the 100 most effective college presidents in the United States. Dr. Koch is an economist, who has published nine books and 90 refereed journal articles in the field. His *Industrial*

Organization and Prices was the leading text in this specialty for several years. Dr. Koch earned his Ph.D. in economics from Northwestern University and has received four honorary doctoral degrees from universities in Japan, Korea and the U.S. He is the co-author of *Born, Not Made: The Entrepreneurial Personality.*